CRIME FICTION IN GERMA

DER KRIMI

Also in Series

Claire Gorrara (ed.)
French Crime Fiction

Andrew Nestingen and Paula Arvas (eds)
Scandinavian Crime Fiction

Nancy Vosburg (ed.)
Iberian Crime Fiction

Guiliana Pieri (ed.)
Italian Crime Fiction

Lucy Andrew and Catherine Phelps (eds)
Crime Fiction in the City: Capital Crimes

EUROPEAN CRIME FICTIONS

CRIME FICTION IN GERMAN

DER KRIMI

Edited by

Katharina Hall

CARDIFF
2016

www.uwp.co.uk

British Library Cataloguing-in-Publication Data
A catalogue record for this book is available from the British Library.

ISBN 978-1-78316-816-3 (hb)
978-1-78316-817-0 (pb)
e-ISBN 978-1-78316-818-7

DOI 10.16922/1783168163-01

Typeset in Wales by Eira Fenn Gaunt, Cardiff
Printed in Great Britain by CPI Antony Rowe, Chippenham, Wiltshire

Contents

Acknowledgements

My warmest thanks to the contributors for their expertise, hard work and patience throughout the production of this volume. Thank you also to the Research Institute for Arts and Humanities at Swansea University for granting me research leave in 2014, and to my colleagues and friends in the Department of Languages, Translation and Communication – particularly Brigid Haines, Kathryn Jones, Tom Cheesman and Julian Preece.

Special thanks to Sarah Lewis, commissioning editor at the University of Wales Press, for her unstinting support and invaluable advice, to our peer reviewer, whose observations and suggestions were extremely helpful, and to the series editors, especially Claire Gorrara, for the opportunity to edit this volume.

I would also like to thank the readers of the 'Mrs Peabody Investigates' crime fiction blog for their enthusiasm and helpfulness in relation to this project, and the following members of the global crime community for their support (and numerous curries): Barry Forshaw, Karen Meek, Sarah Ward, Quentin Bates, Jacky Collins, Ewa Sherman, Andy Lawrence, William Ryan, Anya Lipska, Karen Sullivan, Jochen Vogt, Anthea Bell, Margot Kinberg, Marina Sofia, Raven; and 'Swansea Sleuths' Maura Robinson and Karen Small.

As ever, I am hugely grateful to my English-German-Norwegian-Welsh family for providing me with just the right measure of distraction and support down the years. Inge, Kevin and Jack – the ice-creams at Verdi's are on me.

This volume is dedicated to the memory of Jane Dunnett, a much respected scholar of Italian studies, whose enthusiasm for crime fiction is greatly missed.

Swansea
February 2016

Extract from *The Dead Man of St. Anne's Chapel*, written by Otto Ludwig Emil Freiherr von Puttkammer, translated by Mary W. Tannert and Henry Kratz. © Mary W. Tannert 1999. Translation © Mary W. Tannert.

Extract from *The Sweetness of Life*, written by Paulus Hochgatterer, translated by Jamie Bulloch. © MacLehose 2008. Translation © Jamie Bulloch.

Extract from *In Matto's Realm*, written by Friedrich Glauser, translated by Mike Mitchell. © Bitter Lemon Press 2005. Reprinted with permission of Bitter Lemon Press. Translation © Mike Mitchell.

Extract from *Steinland*, written by Bernhard Jaumann, translated for this volume by Katharina Hall. © Kindler 2012.

Extract from *How Many Miles to Babylon*, written by Doris Gercke, translated by Anna Hamilton. © Women in Translation 1991. Translation © Anna Hamilton.

Extract from *Alone in Berlin*, written by Hans Fallada, translated by Michael Hofmann. Reproduced by permission of Penguin Books Ltd. © Penguin Classics 2009 and © Aufbau Verlagsgruppe 1994. Translation © Michael Hofmann 2009.

Map of Central Europe © Shutterstock Inc. Used under the terms of the Single User Standard License, held by the editor.

Notes on Contributors

Julia Augart is Senior Lecturer in German at the University of Namibia. She received her PhD in German literature in 2004 from the University of Freiburg, Germany, on Clemens Brentano and Sophie Mereau. She has held various teaching positions at Yale University, Trinity College (USA), Freiburg University and as a DAAD-Lecturer at Kenyatta University (Kenya) and Stellenbosch University (South Africa). She has published widely on German literature, Africa in German literature and also on German crime fiction set in Africa. She is currently working on a book on Africa in German crime fiction.

Katharina Hall is Associate Professor of German at Swansea University, Wales. She has published widely on representations of the history and memory of National Socialism in the works of Günter Grass, Esther Dischereit and Bernhard Schlink. Her current project, 'Detecting the Past', explores transnational, Nazi-themed crime fiction from 1945 to the present day, with recent articles on representations of German wartime suffering and the 'Nazi detective'. A member of Swansea's Centre for Contemporary German Culture, she also runs the international crime fiction blog 'Mrs Peabody Investigates' (*http://mrspeabodyinvestigates.wordpress.com/*).

Marieke Krajenbrink is Lecturer in German and Course Director of the MA in Comparative Literature and Cultural Studies at the University of Limerick. She has published on German and Austrian crime fiction, intertextuality and intermediality, and representations of cultural identity in literature. She is the author of *Intertextualität als Konstruktionsprinzip. Transformationen des Kriminalromans und des romantischen Romans bei Peter Handke und Botho Strauß* (Amsterdam and Atlanta, GA: Rodopi, 1996), and co-editor, with Kate Quinn, of *Investigating Identities: Questions of Identity in Contemporary International Crime Fiction* (Amsterdam and New York: Rodopi, 2009). A founding member of the International Crime Genre Research Network, Ireland, she is currently working on a project on 'Consuming Crime'.

Martin Rosenstock is Assistant Professor of German at Gulf University for Science and Technology in Kuwait. He received his PhD in German literature in 2008 from the University of California, Santa Barbara. Prior to his appointment at GUST in 2011, he held visiting positions at Iowa State University and the University of Connecticut. He has published on the depiction of crime and detective work in German, English and American culture. He is currently working on a book project that investigates the portrayal of failed detectives in German-language literature. Recently, he published a co-edited volume of essays on German-East Asian encounters.

Faye Stewart is Associate Professor of German at Georgia State University, where she is also affiliated with the Institute for Women's, Gender and Sexuality Studies and the Center for Human Rights and Democracy. Her teaching and research interests are twentieth- and twenty-first-century German literature and film, gender and sexuality studies, and transnationalism, justice and human rights. Publications include the book *German Feminist Queer Crime Fiction: Politics, Justice and Desire* (Jefferson, NC: McFarland, 2014) and several articles on mystery fiction. She is currently working on projects on Antje Rávic Strubel, Islam in contemporary Germany and depictions of the death penalty.

Mary Tannert's interest in the history of German-language crime fiction dates to her doctoral work in the early 1990s and her dissertation on Auguste Groner. Her publications include the anthology *Early German and Austrian Detective Fiction*, which she translated and edited with Henry Kratz (Jefferson: McFarland & Company, Inc., 1999), several articles on early German-language crime fiction for *Lexikon der Kriminalliteratur* and more than twenty-five translated short crime stories for *Ellery Queen's Mystery Magazine*. She works as a freelance translator of marketing, legal and financial texts as well as contemporary German-language crime fiction.

German-speaking Areas in Europe

German is an official language in Germany, Austria, Switzerland, Liechtenstein, Belgium, Luxembourg and the South Tyrol (Italy). In addition, there are pockets of German speakers in other countries, especially bordering those listed above. German is also a national language of Namibia.

Chronology of Crime Fiction in German

This chronology lists historical, political, criminal and publishing milestones in the German-speaking world, together with key primary texts. Where the English title in brackets is italicized, this indicates that the text has appeared in translation.

Country abbreviations: AUS – Austria, CZE – Czechoslovakia, FRA – France, FRG – West Germany, GDR – East Germany, GER – Germany, SWE – Sweden, SWI – Switzerland, TUR – Turkey, UK – United Kingdom, USA – United States of America.

Date	Key historical, political, criminal events	Key publishing milestones, primary texts, trends
800–1806	In 800, Charlemagne is appointed Emperor by Pope Leo III. By the thirteenth century, the *Heiliges Römisches Reich Deutscher Nation* (Holy Roman Empire of the German Nation) is well established, with a patchwork of kingdoms and states making up the areas we know as Austria and Germany today. *Die Schweizerische Eidgenossenschaft* (Old Swiss Confederacy) was established in 1291, with formal separation from the Holy Roman Empire in 1648. During the 18th century, the *Aufklärung* (Enlightenment) flourishes in Europe and the American colonies. At its core is an ethos of critical questioning and a belief in science and rationality. Its ideas have a profound impact on the law and on notions of crime and punishment.	From around 1450, Gutenberg's printing press revolutionizes access to the written word in Europe. Wittenberg theologian Martin Luther, a key figure in the Protestant Reformation, publishes his influential German translation of the Bible in 1534.
1734–43		François Gayot de Pitaval, *Causes célèbres et intéressantes* (Famous and Interesting Cases, FRA; twenty volumes). These encyclopedic works on real criminal cases were known as *Pitaval* and were highly popular in Europe.
1786		Friedrich Schiller, *Der Verbrecher aus verlorener Ehre* (*The Criminal of Lost Honour*, GER)
1806–14	Napoleon defeats Prussia and occupies Germanic territory, effectively dissolving the Holy Roman Empire of the German Nation. The Napoleonic Code (1804) is influential in reconciling differences in civil law between German regions.	

Date	Key historical, political, criminal events	Key publishing milestones, primary texts, trends
1810–		The publication of tales and novellas that feature elements of detective fiction, such as: Heinrich von Kleist, *Der Zweikampf* (*The Duel*, 1811, GER) E. T. A. Hoffmann, *Das Fräulein von Scudéri* (*Mademoiselle de Scudéri*, 1819, GER)
1815	*Der Deutsche Bund* (German Confederation) is created.	
1828		The first German detective story is published: Adolph Müllner, *Der Kaliber* (*The Caliber*, GER)
1830	The first criminal investigation department in a state police force is created in Berlin.	
1831	Torture is abolished in all German states.	
1840		Otto Ludwig, *Der Tote von St.-Annas Kapelle* (*The Dead Man of St. Anne's Chapel*, GER)
1841		Edgar Allan Poe, *The Murders in the Rue Morgue* (USA)
1842–90		Julius Eduard Hitzig and Willibald Alexis, *Der neue Pitaval* (The New Pitaval, GER). In total, sixty volumes of the German-language *Pitaval* are published by Brockhaus in Leipzig. Works of Poetic Realism are published that draw on crime conventions:

Date	Key historical, political, criminal events	Key publishing milestones, primary texts, trends
1842–90 *(cont.)*		Annette von Droste-Hülshoff, *Die Judenbuche* (*The Jew's Beech*, 1842, GER) Theodor Fontane, *Unterm Birnbaum* (*Under the Pear Tree*, 1885, GER) Wilhelm Raabe, *Stopfkuchen* (*Stopfkuchen*, 1890, GER)
1848	The *Märzrevolution* (March Revolution) by liberal reformers advocating democracy ends in failure. The Swiss *Bundesstaat* (federal Swiss state) is established.	
1853–		*Die Gartenlaube* (The Garden House), a popular literary newspaper in which many crime stories appear, is established in Leipzig and runs until 1944.
1867	The establishment of the Austro-Hungarian empire under Habsburg Emperor Franz Josef I.	
1870		Adolf Streckfuss, *Der Sternkrug* (*The Star Tavern*, GER)
1871	German unification. *Das Deutsche Reich* (German Empire) is established under Prussian chancellor Otto von Bismarck and Wilhelm I.	
1872		J. D. H. Temme, *Der Studentenmord in Zurich* (The Murder of a Student in Zurich, SWI)
1873		J. D. H. Temme, *Wer war der Mörder?* (Who was the Murderer? SWI)

Date	Key historical, political, criminal events	Key publishing milestones, primary texts, trends
1892		The first police detective series in German-language crime fiction appears: Auguste Groner, *Die goldene Kugel* (*The Golden Bullet*, AUS). 'Joseph Müller' series. Arthur Conan Doyle, *The Adventures of Sherlock Holmes* (UK)
1900		Sigmund Freud, the Jewish-Austrian founding father of psychoanalysis, publishes *Traumdeutung* (*On the Interpretation of Dreams*, AUS).
1907		Auguste Groner, *Warenhaus Groß und Komp.* (*Department Store Groß and Co.*, AUS)
1909		Balduin Groller, *Detektiv Dagobert* (*Detective Dagobert*) novellas (AUS)
1912		Luise Westkirch, *Der Todfeind* (Deadly Foe, GER)
1913	The Redl spying affair takes place in Austria.	
1914	Archduke Franz Ferdinand of Austria is assassinated by a Bosnian Serb nationalist in Sarajevo. Start of the First World War.	Franz Kafka, *Der Prozess* (*The Trial*, CZE/GER). Written in 1914–15, but published posthumously in 1925.
1918	End of the First World War. Abdication of German Emperor Wilhelm II. German and Austrian women gain the right to vote.	

Date	Key historical, political, criminal events	Key publishing milestones, primary texts, trends
1919	The Treaty of Versailles is signed. *Die Weimarer Republik* (German Weimar Republic) is founded. *Die Republik Österreich* (Republic of Austria) is established.	
1920		The modernist movement, which strongly influences art, literature and architecture, is at its height. The *Großstadtkrimi* (urban crime novel) flourishes in this decade.
1923	The *Hitler-Ludendorff-Putsch* (Munich Beer Hall Putsch).	
1924	The Hitler-Ludendorff trial takes place. Adolf Hitler is imprisoned, but is released after serving nine months of a five-year sentence.	Hitler writes *Mein Kampf* (*My Struggle*) while in prison.
1924–5		Berlin's Verlag Die Schmiede publishes the series 'Außenseiter der Gesellschaft: Die Verbrechen der Gegenwart' (Outsiders of Society: The Crimes of Today): Theodor Lessing, *Haarmann: Die Geschichte eines Werwolfs* (Haarmann: The Story of a Werewolf, GER) Leo Lania, *Der Hitler-Ludendorff Prozeß* (The Hitler-Ludendorff Trial, GER) Thomas Schramek, *Freiherr von Egloffstein* (Baron von Egloffstein, GER)

Date	Key historical, political, criminal events	Key publishing milestones, primary texts, trends
1924–5 *(cont.)*		Franz Kafka, *Der Prozess* (*The Trial*, CZE/GER), written in 1914–15, is published posthumously by Verlag Die Schmiede in 1925.
1926		Rahel Sanzara, *Das verlorene Kind* (The Lost Child, GER)
1927	The acquittal of right-wing radicals in the *Schattendorfer Prozess* (Schattendorf trial) in Austria leads to the *Julirevolte* (July revolt).	
1928		Jakob Wassermann, *Der Fall Maurizius* (*The Maurizius Case*, GER)
1929	The American Wall Street Crash leads to global depression and mass unemployment.	Alfred Döblin, *Berlin Alexanderplatz* (*Berlin Alexanderplatz*, GER) Erich Kästner, *Emil und die Detektive* (*Emil and the Detectives*, GER) Carl Albert Loosli, *Die Schattmattbauern* (The Farmers of Schattmatt, SWI)
1931		*M – Eine Stadt sucht einen Mörder* (*M – A City Searches for a Murderer*, dir. Fritz Lang, GER)
1933	The Berlin Reichstag Fire; Communist Marinus van der Lubbe is executed for this crime in 1934. Hitler becomes chancellor of Germany; the National Socialists take power and establish a dictatorship. The *Geheime Staatspolizei* (*Gestapo*; Nazi secret state police) is created.	The book burnings of works by Jewish and left-wing writers take place, including those of Erich Kästner and Rahel Sanzara. Alexander Lernet-Holenia, *Ich war Jack Mortimer* (*I was Jack Mortimer*, AUS)

Date	Key historical, political, criminal events	Key publishing milestones, primary texts, trends
1934	The Nazi *Juliputsch* fails in Austria.	Agatha Christie, *Murder on the Orient Express* (UK)
1935	The 'Nürnberger Rassengesetze' (Nuremberg race laws) are passed, depriving Jewish-Germans of a number of fundamental rights, including German citizenship.	
1936	The Berlin Olympics take place.	Friedrich Glauser, *Matto regiert* (*In Matto's Realm*, SWI)
1938	The Nazi annexation (*Anschluss*) of Austria and the Sudetenland takes place. The *Reichskristallnacht* pogrom (Night of Broken Glass) takes place in Germany: there are nationwide attacks on Jewish synagogues and property, which result in a number of deaths.	
1939	Germany invades Poland. Start of the Second World War. The Nazi 'T4' euthanasia programme begins (200,000 victims).	Pieter Coll, *Der Fall Nagotkin* (The Nagotkin Case, GER). 'Nagotkin' series.
1941–4	The number of German citizens executed annually rises from 900 (1940) to 5,000 (1943).	The Nazi Propaganda Ministry and Reich's Principal Criminal Department produce the 'Neuzeitliche Kriminalromane' (Modern Crime Novels) series with publisher Hermann Hillger.
1940–1	German bombing raids take place on London and Coventry.	
1941		Adam Kuckhoff and Peter Tarin, *Strogany und die Vermissten* (Strogany and the Missing Ones, GER)

Date	Key historical, political, criminal events	Key publishing milestones, primary texts, trends
1942	The Wannsee Conference is held in Berlin, after which the 'Final Solution' is implemented; six million Jews are murdered in the course of the Holocaust. Heavy Allied bombing of German cities begins (Berlin, Cologne, Dresden, Hamburg, Lübeck).	
1943	Several members of the 'Weisse Rose' (White Rose) resistance group are executed by the state.	Hans Rudolf Berndorff, *Shiva und die Galgenblume* (Shiva and the Gallows Flower, GER)
1944	The Stauffenberg plot, which attempts the assassination of Hitler, is unsuccessful. The conspirators are executed.	Axel Alt (Wilhelm Idhe), *Der Tod fuhr im Zug* (Death Travelled by Train, GER) J. Bernitt, *Briefe in grauen Umschlägen* (Letters in Grey Envelopes, GER)
1945	End of the Second World War. Liberation of the Auschwitz extermination camp, where over one million Jews were murdered. Millions of German civilians flee or are expelled from eastern European territories as the Soviets advance westward.	
1945–6	The International Military Tribunal presides over the Nuremberg war crimes trial of high-ranking National Socialists.	*Die Mörder sind unter uns* (*The Murderers are Among Us*, dir. Wolfgang Staudte, 1946, GER)
1945–9	Allied Occupation of Germany and Austria by America, Britain, France and the Soviet Union.	Hans Fallada, *Jeder stirbt für sich allein* (*Alone in Berlin*, 1947, GER)

Date	Key historical, political, criminal events	Key publishing milestones, primary texts, trends
1945–9 *(cont.)*		Robert Stemmle, *Affäre Blum* (1948); *Affaire Blum* (The Blum Affair, dir. Erich Engel, 1948, GER)
1949	Beginning of the Cold War; division of Germany into East Germany (*Die Deutsche Demokratische Republik*/German Democratic Republic, GDR) and West Germany (*Die Bundesrepublik Deutschland*/Federal Republic of Germany, FRG) until 1990. Konrad Adenauer (Christian Democratic Union/CDU) becomes West German chancellor. Walter Ulbricht (Socialist Unity Party of Germany/SED) becomes East German leader. Introduction of the West German *Grundgesetz* (Basic Law) and the East German *Verfassung* (constitution).	
1950	The East German *Ministerium für Staatssicherheit* (MfS; Ministry for State Security) is established. Its secret police are known as the *Stasi*.	Friedrich Dürrenmatt, *Der Richter und sein Henker* (*The Judge and his Hangman*, SWI). 'Bärlach' series.
1951	Adenauer announces that compensation will be paid to the Jewish victims of Nazism.	The *Amt für Literatur und Verlagswesen* (Office for Literature and Publishing Houses) is founded in the GDR to coordinate and grant licences for literary production. Friedrich Dürrenmatt, *Der Verdacht* (*Suspicion*, SWI). 'Bärlach' series. The first East German crime novel is published: Hannes Elmens, *Was geschah im D 121?* (What happened in D 121?).

Date	Key historical, political, criminal events	Key publishing milestones, primary texts, trends
1952	West Germany becomes a founder member of the European Coal and Steel Community (forerunner of European Union).	
1953	Death of Stalin. The East German workers' uprising is quashed by the government with Soviet backing.	Tightening up of East German cultural and literary policy.
1954	West Germany wins the Football World Cup in Bern, Switzerland.	Bastei-Verlag begins to publish the 'Jerry Cotton' FBI series (FRG). The publisher claims it is the most successful crime series in the world, with over 930 million copies sold to date.
1956		The *Amt für Literatur und Verlagswesen* is incorporated into the East German Ministry of Culture.
1957	West Germany becomes a founder member of the EEC (European Economic Community).	Egon Eis, *Duell im Dunkel* (Duel in the Dark, AUS)
1958	Elvis Presley is stationed in West Germany as part of his US army service.	Friedrich Dürrenmatt, *Das Versprechen: Requiem auf den Kriminalroman* (*The Pledge: Requiem for the Crime Novel*, 1958). The first West German television crime series airs: *Stahlnetz* (Steel Net). The East German 'Blaulicht' (Blue Light) crime series is established: over 280 dime novels appear from 1958 to 1990, published first by the Ministry of the Interior and then by Verlag Das Neue Berlin.

Date	Key historical, political, criminal events	Key publishing milestones, primary texts, trends
1959		West German crime films based on the work of British crime author Edgar Wallace begin to appear (–1972). The first East German television crime series airs: *Blaulicht – Aus der Arbeit unserer Kriminalpolizei* (Blue Light – The Work of our Criminal Police) Will Berthold, *Nachts, wenn der Teufel kam: Roman nach Tatsachen* (At Night, When the Devil Visited: A Documentary Novel, FRG)
1960		Hans Lebert, *Die Wolfshaut* (Wolf's Skin, AUS)
1961	The trial of Adolf Eichmann in Israel (executed 1962). The West German-Turkish labour recruitment agreement is signed, bringing Turkish migrant workers to the FRG. The Berlin Wall is erected by East Germany to stop the exodus of skilled workers to the west.	
1962	Peter Fechter is killed by West German border guards as he attempts to escape East Germany by climbing over the Berlin Wall.	Richard K. Flesch becomes editor at the West German Rowohlt publishing house. *Der Neue Deutsche Kriminalroman* (new German crime novel) is promoted via the 'rororo thriller' imprint, which produces 1,353 titles and over 30 million copes by 2000. The imprint showcases home-grown authors and international crime fiction by writers such as Sjöwall and Wahlöö (SWE).

Date	Key historical, political, criminal events	Key publishing milestones, primary texts, trends
1962 *(cont.)*		Gerhard Harkenthal, *Rendezvous mit dem Tod* (A Date with Death, GDR) Hans Hellmut Kirst, *Die Nacht der Generale* (*The Night of the Generals*, FRG)
1963	Konrad Adenauer resigns; Ludwig Erhard (CDU) becomes West German chancellor.	The *Hauptverwaltung Verlage und Buchhandel* (Central Administration for Publishers and the Book Trade) is established in the GDR's Ministry of Culture. Its remit is to censor/approve manuscripts and to scrutinize publisher lists (–1990).
1963–5	The Auschwitz war crimes trials take place in Frankfurt.	Peter Weiss, *Die Ermittlung* (*The Investigation*, 1965, FRG): a play based on the transcripts of the Auschwitz trials.
1965	The West German Statute of Limitations on murder (including war crimes) is extended for four years.	
1966	Kurt Georg Kiesinger (CDU) becomes chancellor of West Germany. His prior involvement with National Socialism causes controversy. The Grand Coalition is formed between the CDU and the Social Democratic Party/SPD (led by Willy Brandt).	
1967	Student Benno Ohnesorg is shot and killed by the police during a demonstration in West Berlin.	Peter Handke, *Der Hausierer* (*The Peddler*, AUS) Irene Rodrian, *Tod in St. Pauli* (Death in St. Pauli, FRG). Rodrian becomes the first woman to win the Edgar Wallace Prize.

Date	Key historical, political, criminal events	Key publishing milestones, primary texts, trends
1967 *(cont.)*		Tom Wittgen (pseudonym of Ingeburg Siebenstädt, the 'Agatha Christie of the GDR'), *Der Überfall* (The Assault, GDR)
1968	The student protest movement reaches its height. Student leader Rudi Dutschke is shot by a right-wing extremist but survives. The 'Dreher Law' is passed in West Germany. It allows a statute of limitations on certain crimes committed under National Socialism, such as accessory to murder.	The first of Maj Sjöwall and Per Wahlöö's 'Martin Beck' series is published in West Germany by Rowohlt (SWE).
1969	The West German Statute of Limitations for murder is extended to thirty years, enabling further prosecution of Nazi crimes. Willy Brandt (SPD) becomes chancellor of West Germany and seeks improved relations with the GDR and USSR via his *Ostpolitik* (eastern policy).	Adolf Muschg, *Mitgespielt* (*Played Along*, SWI)
1970	The *Rote Armee Fraktion* (Red Army Faction), a left-wing terrorist group, is founded in West Germany. It is initially known as the 'Baader-Meinhof gang' after two of its members.	The *Soziokrimi* flourishes in West Germany in this decade. The East German crime novel series 'DIE' is established and publishes 224 titles by 2001. The title is an acronym of *Delikte–Indizien–Ermittlungen* (crimes–clues–investigations). The West German television crime series *Tatort* (Crime Scene) begins; it is still running today. Peter Handke, *Die Angst des Tormanns beim Elfmeter* (*The Goalie's Anxiety at the Penalty Kick*, AUS)

Date	Key historical, political, criminal events	Key publishing milestones, primary texts, trends
1971	Erich Honecker (SED) becomes leader of East Germany. At the fourth convention of the SED Central Committee, he declares that art and literature, as long as they are rooted in socialism, should have no taboos. Swiss women gain the right to vote.	The East German TV crime series *Polizeiruf 110* (Police: Dial 110) begins; it is still running today. Albert Drach, *Untersuchung an Mädeln. Kriminalprotokoll* (Investigating the Girls. Criminal Report, AUS) Edgar Hilsenrath, *Der Nazi und der Friseur* (*The Nazi and the Barber*, FRG) is published in English. It is only published in German in 1977.
1972	The *Rote Armee Fraktion* carries out bomb attacks against US air bases. Massacre of Israeli athletes at the Munich Olympics by the Palestinian terrorist group Black September. The West German government passes the 'Radikalenerlass' (radical decree), which allows the state to bar individuals from public employment if they are suspected of undemocratic activities. The 'Grundlagenvertrag' (Basic Treaty) is signed by East and West Germany; both officially recognize one another as states for the first time.	Horst Bosetzky (writing as -ky), *Einer von uns beiden* (One of Us Two, FRG) Peter Handke, *Der kurze Brief zum langen Abschied* (*Short Letter, Long Farewell*, AUS) Gerhard Roth, *How to be a detective* (AUS)
1973		The first *Kommissarin* (female police inspector), Katharina Ledermacher, appears in German-language crime fiction: Richard Hey, *Ein Mord am Lietzensee* (Murder at Lake Lietzen, FRG). 'Ledermacher' series.

Date	Key historical, political, criminal events	Key publishing milestones, primary texts, trends
1974	Helmut Schmidt (SPD) becomes West German chancellor.	Heinrich Böll, *Die verlorene Ehre der Katharina Blum oder: Wie Gewalt entstehen und wohin sie führen kann* (*The Lost Honour of Katharina Blum or: How Violence Comes About and Where it Can Lead*, FRG) Irene Rodrian, *Küsschen für den Totengräber* (Kiss for the Gravedigger, FRG) Gerhard Roth, *Der große Horizont* (The Big Horizon, AUS)
1975		Peter Handke, *Die Stunde der wahren Empfindung* (*A Moment of True Feeling*, AUS)
1976	Helmut Schmidt (SPD) is re-elected as West German chancellor. Dissident singer-songwriter Wolf Biermann is expelled from East Germany.	Austrian television crime series *Kottan ermittelt* (Kottan Investigates) begins; it runs until 1984. Gert Prokop, *Einer muss die Leiche sein* (Someone has to be the Corpse, GDR) Gerhard Roth, *Ein neuer Morgen* (A New Morning, AUS)
1977	*Der Deutsche Herbst* (the German autumn): a series of terrorist actions – kidnappings, a plane hijacking and murders – instigated by the *Rote Armee Fraktion*, which elicits extensive responses from the West German state.	Publication of the first German-language *Afrika-Krimi*: Henry Kolarz, *Kalahari* (FRG).
1978		The first female police inspector appears on television in the *Tatort* episode 'Der Mann auf dem Hochsitz' (The Man in the Hide, FRG).

Date	Key historical, political, criminal events	Key publishing milestones, primary texts, trends
1979	The American mini-series *Holocaust* airs in West Germany, prompting extensive discussion about the Nazi past.	
1980	Bomb attack by right-wing terrorist/s at the Munich *Oktoberfest* in West Germany.	The *Frauenkrimi* and Turkish-German crime fiction blossom in this decade.
1981		Aras Ören, *Bitte nix Polizei: Kriminalerzählung* (*Please No Police: Crime Story*, TUR/FRG)
1982	Helmut Kohl (CDU) becomes West German chancellor.	
1983		Helga Riedel, *Einer muss tot* (Someone Must Die, FRG). Winner of the 1985 *Deutscher Krimi Preis*.
1984		The *Bochumer Krimi Archiv* (BKA) is established by author and journalist Reinhard Jahn. Claudia Wessel, *Es wird Zeit* (It's About Time, FRG)
1985	40th anniversary of the end of the Second World War. A state visit to West Germany by US President Ronald Reagan results in the 'Bitburg Affair'. The president of West Germany, Richard von Weizsäcker, emphasizes the need to remember the Nazi past and its crimes in a speech to the *Bundestag* (parliament) in Bonn.	The *Deutsche Krimi Preis* (German Crime Fiction Prize) is founded by the *Bochumer Krimi Archiv*. The first Turkish-German lead investigator appears in German crime fiction: Jakob Arjouni, *Happy Birthday, Türke!* (*Happy Birthday, Turk!*, FRG). 'Kayankaya' series. Patrick Süskind, *Das Parfum – Die Geschichte eines Mörders* (*Perfume – The Story of a Murderer*, FRG)

Date	Key historical, political, criminal events	Key publishing milestones, primary texts, trends
1986	The *Historikerstreit* (historians' dispute) takes place. This public debate on the uniqueness of the Holocaust sees some historians accused of revisionism. The Waldheim Affair: Kurt Waldheim is elected Austrian president in the midst of controversy about his role in the Second World War.	'Das Syndikat – Autorengruppe deutschsprachige Kriminalliteratur' (The Syndicate – German-language Crime Fiction Authors' Association) is founded. It actively promotes the genre through the annual *Criminale* convention and the *Friedrich-Glauser-Preis* (Friedrich Glauser Prize). *Lexikon der deutschen Krimi-Autoren*, an extensive database of German crime authors affiliated to the *Bochumer Krimi Archiv*, is established. Jurek Becker, *Bronsteins Kinder* (*Bronstein's Children*, FRG/GDR) Corinna Kawaters, *Zora Zobel zieht um* (Zora Zobel Moves In, FRG) Christine Grän, *Weiße sterben selten in Samyana* (Whites Seldom Die in Samyana, AUS)
1987		Establishment of the *Friedrich-Glauser-Preis* (Friedrich Glauser Prize for crime fiction). Pieke Biermann, *Potsdamer Abeleben* (Potsdam Demise, FRG). 'Karin Lietze' series. Bernhard Schlink and Walter Popp, *Selbs Justiz* (*Self's Punishment*, FRG). 'Selb' series.
1988	The president of the *Bundestag*, Philipp Jenninger, resigns after a controversial speech commemorating the 50th anniversary of the 1938 *Reichskristallnacht*.	Publisher Argument establishes the 'Ariadne' series dedicated to crime novels by female authors. Doris Gercke, *Weinschröter, du mußt hängen* (*How Many Miles to Babylon*, FRG). 'Bella Block' series.

Date	Key historical, political, criminal events	Key publishing milestones, primary texts, trends
1988 *(cont.)*		Sabine Deitmer, *Bye-bye, Bruno. Wie Frauen morden* (Bye-bye Bruno. How Women Murder, FRG)
1989	The Fall of the Berlin Wall and collapse of the East German state.	Akif Pirinçci, *Felidae* (FRG) Jacques Berndorf, *Eifel-Blues* (Eifel Blues, FRG). 'Siggi Baumeister/Eifel Krimi' series.
1990	The reunification of Germany. Helmut Kohl (CDU) is elected chancellor.	Historical crime fiction and regional crime fiction boom in this decade. The *Afrika-Krimi* begins its rise. Pieke Biermann, *Violetta* (GER). 'Karin Lietze' series. Winner of the 1991 *Deutscher Krimi Preis*. Peter Höner, *Rafiki Beach Hotel* (SWI). 'Mettler' series.
1991	The seat of German national government is moved from Bonn back to Berlin.	Elfriede Czurda, *Die Giftmörderinnen* (The Poison Murderesses, AUS) Ingrid Noll, *Der Hahn ist tot* (*Hell Hath No Fury*, GER)
1992	The Maastricht Treaty results in the establishment of the EU (European Union). A right-wing arson attack in Mölln, Germany, results in the death of three Turkish migrants. There are a number of similar attacks in this year.	Establishment of the literary magazine *Ariadne Forum* by Argument (GER). Pieke Biermann (ed.), *Mit Zorn, Charme und Methode: oder: Die Aufklärung ist weiblich!* (With Wrath, Charm and Method: or: Enlightenment Is Feminine!), short story collection with authors from Austria, Switzerland and Germany.

Date	Key historical, political, criminal events	Key publishing milestones, primary texts, trends
1992 *(cont.)*		Edith Kneifl becomes the first Austrian and the first female author to win the Glauser prize with her debut novel *Zwischen zwei Nächten* (Between Two Nights, 1991, AUS). Bernhard Schlink, *Selbs Betrug* (*Self's Deception*, GER). 'Selb' series. Winner of the 1993 *Deutscher Krimi Preis*.
1993	A right-wing arson attack in Solingen, Germany, results in the death of five members of a Turkish family. Harsher sentences start to be given by the courts for right-wing extremist crimes.	Gabriele Gelien, *Eine Lesbe macht noch keinen Sommer* (One Lesbian Does Not Make a Summer, GER) Dagmar Scharsich, *Die gefrorene Charlotte* (The Frozen Charlotte Doll, GER, former GDR) Hansjörg Schneider, *Silberkiesel* (*Silver Pebbles*, SWI). 'Hunkeler' series.
1994	The former leader of the GDR, Erich Honecker, dies in exile in Chile.	Ingrid Noll, *Die Apothekerin* (*The Pharmacist*, GER) Three television crime series featuring leading female investigators begin to air: *Bella Block* *Die Kommissarin* *Rosa Roth*
1995	Austria joins the EU.	Josef Haslinger, *Opernball* (Opera Ball, AUS) Gerhard Roth, *Der See* (*The Lake*, AUS)

Date	Key historical, political, criminal events	Key publishing milestones, primary texts, trends
1996		A German chapter of the American 'Sisters in Crime' organization is established. It becomes the *Mörderische Schwestern* (Murderous Sisters) organization in 2007. Wolf Haas, *Auferstehung der Toten* (*Resurrection*, AUS). 'Brenner' series.
1997		Doron Rabinovici, *Suche nach M.* (*The Search for M*, AUS)
1998	The *Rote Armee Fraktion* is officially dissolved.	Maria Gronau, *Weibersommer* (Women's Summer, GER) Alfred Komarek, *Polt muss weinen* (Polt has to Cry, AUS). 'Polt' series.
1999	*Jüdisches Museum Berlin* (Jewish Museum Berlin) opens in a new building designed by Daniel Libeskind.	Wolf Haas, *Silentium!* (Silence!, AUS). 'Brenner' series. Petra Hammesfahr, *Die Sünderin* (*The Sinner*, GER)
2000	The amended 'German Nationality Act' allows children of foreigners born in Germany to take German citizenship (they must opt for one nationality by the age of twenty-three). The EU threatens to suspend relations with the Austrian government due to the far-right policies of the Austrian Freedom Party (FPÖ) led by Jörg Haider.	Elfriede Jelinek, *Gier* (*Greed*, AUS) Heinrich Steinfest, *Cheng. Sein erster Fall* (Cheng. His First Case, AUS). 'Cheng' series.
2001	W. G. Sebald's *Luftkrieg und Literatur* (*On the Natural History of Destruction*) sparks debates about German wartime suffering and victimhood.	Katrin Kremmler, *Blaubarts Handy* (Bluebeard's Cell Phone, GER) Eva Rossmann, *Freudsche Verbrechen* (Freudian Crimes, AUS). 'Mira Valensky' series.

Date	Key historical, political, criminal events	Key publishing milestones, primary texts, trends
2002	Germany suffers severe flooding due to heavy rainfall. Euro banknotes and coins are introduced to Germany.	Establishment of the *Wiener Kriminacht* (Viennese Crime Night). Richard Birkefeld and Göran Hachmeister, *Wer übrig bleibt, hat recht* (To the Victor the Spoils, GER). Winner of the 2003 *Friedrich-Glauser-Preis* for best debut. Christian von Ditfurth, *Mann ohne Makel* (*A Paragon of Virtue*, GER). 'Stachelmann' series. Lisa Kuppler (ed.), *Queer Crime: Lesbisch-schwule Krimigeschichten* (Queer Crime: Lesbian-Gay Crime Stories, GER)
2003	The German Hartz labour market reforms begin to be implemented.	Establishment of the annual *Krimifestival München* (Munich Crime Festival). Pierre Frei, *Onkel Toms Hütte, Berlin* (*Berlin*, GER) Volker Klüpfel and Michael Kobr, *Milchgeld* (Milk Money, GER). 'Kluftinger' series. Urs Schaub, *Tanner* (SWI). 'Tanner' series. Wolfgang Schorlau, *Die blaue Liste* (The Blue List, GER). 'Dengler' series. Jan Costin Wagner, *Eismond* (*Ice Moon*, GER). 'Joentaa' series.
2004		The *Filmmuseum Berlin* exhibition 'Die Kommissarinnen' (The Female Police Inspectors) is held.

Date	Key historical, political, criminal events	Key publishing milestones, primary texts, trends
2004 *(cont.)*		Esmahan Aykol, *Hotel Bosporus* (*Hotel Bosphorus*, GER/TUR). 'Kati Hirschel' series. Heinrich Steinfest, *Nervöse Fische* (Nervous Fish, AUS)
2005	The Berlin Holocaust Memorial (Memorial to the Murdered Jews of Europe) opens to the public. Angela Merkel (CDU) becomes the first female chancellor of Germany.	Christine Lehmann, *Harte Schule* (School of Hard Knocks, GER). 'Lisa Nerz' series. Wolfgang Schorlau, *Das dunkle Schweigen* (Dark Silence, GER). 'Dengler' series.
2006	The Football World Cup takes place in Germany.	Christa Bernuth, *Innere Sicherheit* (Internal Security, GER) Sebastian Fitzek, *Die Therapie* (*Therapy*, GER) Paulus Hochgatterer, *Die Süße des Lebens* (*The Sweetness of Life*, AUS). 'Kovacs and Horn' series. Andrea Maria Schenkel, *Tannöd* (*The Murder Farm*, GER). Winner of the 2007 *Deutscher Krimi Preis*.
2007	Germany hosts the G8 Leaders' Summit.	*Mörderische Schwestern – Vereinigung deutschsprachiger KrimiAutorinnen* (Murderous Sisters – Association of German-language Women Crime Authors) becomes an independent organization. Jan Costin Wagner, *Das Schweigen* (*Silence*, GER). 'Joentaa' series. Rainer Gross, *Grafeneck* (GER). 'Mauser' series. Volker Kutscher, *Der nasse Fisch* (The Wet Fish, GER). 'Rath' series.

Date	Key historical, political, criminal events	Key publishing milestones, primary texts, trends
2008		Alina Bronsky, *Scherbenpark* (*Broken Glass Park*, GER) Iris Leister, *Novembertod* (November Death, GER). 'Kappe' series. Andreas Pittler, *Tacheles* (Plain Talking, AUS). 'Bronstein' series. Heinrich Steinfest, *Mariaschwarz* (Black Maria, AUS)
2009	Trial of Austrian Josef Fritzl for rape, incest, wrongful imprisonment, coercion and murder by negligence. Sentenced to life imprisonment.	Horst Bosetzky, *Der Teufel von Köpenick* (The Devil of Köpenick, GER) Zoran Drvenkar, *Sorry* (GER). Winner of the 2010 *Friedrich-Glauser-Preis*. Wolf Haas, *Der Brenner und der liebe Gott* (*Brenner and God*, AUS). 'Brenner' series. Nele Neuhaus, *Tiefe Wunden* (*The Ice Queen*, GER). 'Bodenstein and Kirchhoff' series. J. Monika Walther, *Goldbroiler oder die Beschreibung einer Schlacht: Kriminalgeschichte* (Roast Chicken or the Chronicle of a Slaughter: Crime Story, GER)
2010–11	The war crimes trial of former Sobibór camp guard John Demjanjuk takes place in Munich.	Ferdinand von Schirach, *Der Fall Collini* (*The Collini Case*, 2010, GER) Bernhard Jaumann, *Die Stunde des Schakals* (*The Hour of the Jackal*, GER 2010). 'Clemencia Garises' series. Winner of the 2011 *Deutscher Krimi Preis*.

Date	Key historical, political, criminal events	Key publishing milestones, primary texts, trends
2011	The exhibition 'Ordnung und Vernichtung: Die Polizei im NS-Staat' (Order and Annihilation: the Police and the Nazi Regime) takes place at the *Deutsches Historisches Museum*, Berlin. Commemoration of fifty years of Turkish immigration to Germany.	Horst Bosetzky, *Mit Feuereifer* (With Zeal, GER). 'Kappe' series. Simon Urban, *Plan D* (*Plan D*, GER)
2012	Minister of Justice Sabine Leutheusser-Schnarrenberger announces an independent commission will examine the Federal Ministry of Justice's engagement with the Nazi past (citing von Schirach's *Der Fall Collini*, 2010).	Katharina Höftmann, *Die letzte Sünde* (The Final Sin, GER). 'Rosenthal' series. Bernhard Jaumann, *Steinland* (Stoneland, GER). 'Clemencia Garises' series.
2013–	Trial in Munich of Beate Zschäpe, surviving member of the NSU neo-Nazi cell alleged to have killed nine Turkish (-German) men and a policewoman. Germany suffers extensive flooding.	Harald Gilbers, *Germania* (Germania, GER). Winner of the 2014 *Friedrich-Glauser-Preis* for best debut. Su Turhan, *Kommissar Pascha* (Inspector Pasha, TUR/GER). 'Demirbilek' series.
2014	Emergence of the German 'Pegida' movement (*Patriotische Europäer Gegen die Islamisierung des Abendlandes*/ Patriotic Europeans against the Islamization of the West). Mass demonstrations in Dresden and other cities are met with counter-demonstrations and political debate.	Bernhard Aichner, *Totenfrau* (*Woman of the Dead*, AUS) Sascha Arango, *Die Wahrheit und andere Lügen* (*The Truth and Other Lies*, GER) Franz Dobler, *Ein Bulle im Zug* (Cop on the Train, GER). Winner of the 2015 *Deutscher Krimi Preis*. Petra Gabriel, *Kaltfront* (Cold Front, GER). 'Kappe' series.

Date	Key historical, political, criminal events	Key publishing milestones, primary texts, trends
2015	70th anniversary of the liberation of Auschwitz. 25th anniversary of German reunification. Germany prepares to accept 800,000 refugees and asylum seekers, mainly from Syria.	Bernhard Jaumann, *Der lange Schatten* (The Long Shadow, GER)

1

Crime Fiction in German: Concepts, Developments and Trends

KATHARINA HALL

> Undoubtedly, the crime novel displays all the characteristics of a flourishing branch of literature.[1]

This volume, which forms part of the University of Wales Press 'European Crime Fictions' series, is the first in English to offer a comprehensive overview of German-language crime fiction from its origins in the early nineteenth century to the post-reunification Germany of the new millennium. Its primary aim is to introduce readers to key areas of crime fiction from the German-speaking world through this and subsequent chapters on early German-language crime, Austrian crime, Swiss crime, the *Afrika-Krimi* (German-language crime novels set in Africa or with African characters and themes), the *Frauenkrimi* (crime written by, about and for women) and twentieth-century historical crime. An additional aim is to highlight the richness of German-language crime fiction and to provide readers with a springboard for further reading, viewing and research. To this end, our understanding of the crime genre is purposefully broad, allowing hybrid crime narratives by literary authors to be considered, and relevant links to be made to films and the highly popular *Fernsehkrimi* (television crime drama), which is explored in chapter 8. A significant percentage of the crime narratives under discussion are already published in English, thus providing the non-German speaker with opportunities to access works (where a novel's English title is italicized, this indicates that the text has appeared in translation).[2] Chapters conclude with an English-language extract to showcase a primary text, as well as providing bibliographies of core primary and secondary materials. A substantial annotated bibliography at the end of the volume directs readers towards further German- and English-language resources.

More broadly, the volume aims to expand the notion of a German-language crime-writing tradition, drawing inspiration from publishers such as Edition Köln, which is reprinting forgotten early works, and from academic studies by contemporary scholars in the German- and English-speaking worlds, which are successfully illuminating neglected areas of research. Until remarkably recently, it was argued either that Germany had no proper tradition of crime fiction or that German crime fiction only came into being in the 1960s, when authors supposedly started to write crime narratives set in Germany that engaged with specifically German concerns.[3] These claims gained purchase due to a complex set of factors: a deeply entrenched distinction between *U- und E-Literatur* (entertaining literature and serious literature),[4] whose codified notions of quality discouraged research on so-called *Trivialliteratur* (trivial literature);[5] German academia's disinclination, even once crime fiction became a more legitimate area of study in the 1970s,[6] to explore its own crime fiction heritage, focusing instead on Edgar Allan Poe, Arthur Conan Doyle and British Golden Age writers;[7] and a self-perpetuating acceptance of the critical status quo until a post-reunification generation of researchers began to reassess the field in the 1990s. As a result, important examples of German crime fiction were often ignored, such as Hans Fallada's *Jeder stirbt für sich allein* (*Alone in Berlin*, 1947), as indeed were entire phases of crime fiction production, such as under National Socialism (1933–45).[8] As recently as 2008, Edition Köln's publicity slogans for two series reissuing neglected primary works were as follows: 'German-language crime fiction has no tradition? True. But it could have one' and 'Edition Köln – the publisher that's writing (crime) history'.[9]

In addition, a narrow critical focus on German crime fiction as 'crime fiction from Germany' rather than 'crime fiction in German' has tended to minimize the contribution of Swiss, Austrian and East German crime narratives to a German-language crime writing tradition.[10] The scholarly separation of Germany's crime fiction from that of other German-speaking countries may reflect certain value judgements (that they are 'minor' crime corpora due to the small size of the countries concerned and/or the negative assessment of their literary worth),[11] or an overzealous attitude to scholarly categorization (wishing to keep the outputs of different nations separate). However, a Germany-centred approach is limiting, because it excludes seminal crime novels and misses the opportunity to trace the similarities, differences and dialogues between the crime fiction of the four countries.[12] Obvious examples are the Swiss crime novels of Friedrich Glauser and Friedrich Dürrenmatt, which portray the Switzerland of the 1930s and 1950s, but also address the country's uneasy relationship with Germany before, during and after National Socialism. Both authors have also undoubtedly had a lasting influence in and beyond the German-speaking world. Accordingly, this volume includes chapters on crime fiction in specific national contexts, exploring the distinctive features of German, Austrian and Swiss crime, but also offers an integrated overview of German-language crime fiction in the 'Chronology of Crime Fiction in German' and in the chapter that follows.

This chapter will examine key terminology relating to crime fiction in German and provide a diachronic overview of its development. Spatial constraints prohibit an exhaustive survey: Jockers and Jahn's 2005 *Lexikon der deutschsprachigen Krimi-Autoren* (Encyclopedia of German-language Crime Authors) contains 600 contemporary writer entries alone, most of whom have authored multiple works. The aim is rather to highlight important texts and trends, alongside industry and publishing milestones. Particular attention is paid to areas that are touched on, but not covered in detail in other chapters, such as National Socialist and East

German crime fiction, the 1970s *Soziokrimi* (social crime novel) and Turkish-German crime fiction. In common with the volume's other chapters, the overview draws on a wide range of German- and English-language criticism, and places its discussion in the larger contexts of social, political and historical events.

Der Krimi

The crime novel is affectionately known as *der Krimi* in the German-speaking world – an abbreviation of the noun *der Kriminalroman* (the crime novel) – and is used as shorthand to describe all varieties of crime novel from the psychological thriller to the police procedural. However, it is worth noting a long-standing distinction between the *Kriminalroman* and the *Detektivroman* (the detective novel) in the reception of German-language crime fiction, which allows an appreciation of different narrative approaches taken by crime authors. Definitions vary from critic to critic, but Richard Alewyn provides the following summation: 'the *Kriminalroman* tells the story of a crime; the *Detektivroman* tells the story of the solving of a crime'.[13] As Heinrich Henel usefully elaborates,

> the crime narrative first acquaints the reader with the perpetrator, then with the crime, and lastly with the consequences of the crime; it is interested in the psychological developments that led to the crime . . . The detective narrative is the opposite. It begins with the discovery of the body, reconstructs the crime using clues and tracks down the criminal at the end; it is interested in the intellectual work of the detective, so that the perpetrator's motives only function as clues or as a means of securing the legal aspects of the case.[14]

An example of the *Kriminalroman* in its purest form is Ingrid Noll's satirical crime novel *Die Apothekerin* (*The Pharmacist*, 1994), in which a perpetrator relates the story of a series of murders, with the police playing a minor role. The first quarter of the narrative focuses on the events leading up to the first murder and explores the murderer's motivation, thereby contrasting with a *Detektivroman* such as Jakob Arjouni's *Happy Birthday, Türke!* (*Happy Birthday, Turk!*, 1987), which shows the crime at the beginning of the narrative, and only reveals the perpetrator and motive through the rational deductions of the detective at its end. The *Detektivroman* is often explored by German critics through reference to classic detective narratives and iconic detectives (Poe's Dupin, Conan Doyle's Holmes, Georges Simenon's Maigret and Agatha Christie's Poirot),[15] but applies equally to later police-led investigations (such as Nele Neuhaus's 'Bodenstein and Kirchhoff' series, 2006–), or *noir* detective fiction featuring private investigators (such as Arjouni's 'Kayankaya' series, 1987–2012). Predominantly, the distinction between the two types of narrative rests on the perspective from which it is told – that of the perpetrator or the investigator. However, it is entirely possible for crime narratives to carry elements of both approaches through the adoption of a dual perspective, thereby creating hybrid forms, as seen in Jan Costin Wagner's 'Kimmo Joentaa' series (2003–), which alternates between the perpetrator's and the policeman's point of view, and pays detailed attention to the psychology of both.

A number of subgenres are referenced in discussions of German-language crime fiction, many of which draw on other national crime-writing traditions. Examples include the *Rätselkrimi* (puzzle crime novel), influenced by British Golden Age writers such as Christie;[16] the *Soziokrimi* (social crime novel), shaped by Swedish authors Maj Sjöwall and Per Wahlöö;[17] the *Polizeikrimi* (police novel/ police procedural), which draws on Simenon's Belgian 'Maigret' series, the French *roman policier* and the works of Sjöwall and Wahlöö;[18] the *Frauenkrimi*, which grew from the work of Anglo-American authors such as Sara Paretsky and Val McDermid;[19] *der psychologische Krimi* or *Psychothriller* (psychological crime novel/ thriller), influenced by American author Patricia Highsmith,[20] and the *Privatermittler* (private investigator) crime narrative, which emerged belatedly from the hard-boiled tradition of Hammett and Chandler.[21] Unsurprisingly, given the rich and turbulent history of German-speaking countries, *der historische Krimi* (historical crime novel)[22] also plays a prominent role, particularly in post-1945 crime fiction. These subgenres frequently overlap with one another, making rigid categorization impossible and undesirable: for example, a historical crime novel such as Richard Birkefeld and Göran Hachmeister's *Wer übrig bleibt, hat recht* (To the Victor the Spoils, 2002) also contains elements of the police novel and psychological crime. Hybrid crime novels by 'literary' authors must also be acknowledged, as they constitute some of the most powerful and innovative works in the field: examples include Patrick Süskind's *Das Parfum – Die Geschichte eines Mörders* (*Perfume – The Story of a Murderer*, 1985), East German author Jurek Becker's *Bronsteins Kinder* (*Bronstein's Children*, 1986) and Austrian Nobel Prize-winning novelist Elfriede Jelinek's *Gier* (*Greed*, 2000; see Marieke Krajenbrink's analysis in chapter 3 on Austrian crime).

At first glance there may be few contemporary subgenres – such as the *Regionalkrimi* (regional crime novel) or the *Öko-Krimi* (ecological crime novel highlighting environmental concerns) – that appear to be home-grown, but as this volume will show, German-language crime writers have taken narrative forms from British, American and European arenas and made them their own, refining and extending them in the context of their individual cultures and national concerns. For example, many German-language crime narratives draw on long-standing traditions of political satire in magazines, cabaret and literature, resulting in blackly humorous critiques of past and present society (see chapters 3, 6 and 7 on Austrian, women's and historical crime). This is a process of acculturation in its complex, modern sense. As Eva Kushner and Milan Dimic argue,

> [i]n the past, acculturation has often manifested itself through the dominance of an invading or invasive culture over another . . . Yet, it can be shown that the receptor culture, far from being passive, has the ability to appropriate and transform the

> invader culture which in turn undergoes acculturation, a dynamic of great complexity, never at a standstill.[23]

Here, then, acculturation is figured as a vibrant cross-fertilization that leads to innovation on the part of the receptor culture rather than simply reproducing existing cultural forms. However, it should be emphasized that German-language crime fiction has also been shaped by its own crime-writing heritage, for in the case of the early detective story, it was German-speaking crime writers who led the way.

The pioneers (1828–1933)

Scholars begin the history of German-language crime fiction in different places. Some, like Winfried Freund, view early works by major writers as origin texts: Friedrich Schiller's *Kriminalbericht* (crime report) *Der Verbrecher aus verlorener Ehre* (*The Criminal of Lost Honour*, 1786), which is based on a genuine case, Heinrich von Kleist's *Der Zweikampf* (*The Duel*, 1811) and E. T. A. Hoffmann's *Das Fräulein von Scudéri* (*Mademoiselle de Scudéri*, 1819), set in France during the reign of Louis XIV.[24] However, as Ailsa Wallace argues, 'concentrating on the canonical "greats" of German literature', perhaps in order 'to invoke respectability for the German tradition of crime writing', can result in overlooking the works of less famous authors who are the true innovators in the field.[25] By contrast, Hans-Otto Hügel's groundbreaking 1978 study of nineteenth-century German detective stories excavates an arguably more detailed and precise history of popular German crime, and it is this developmental arc that Mary Tannert foregrounds in chapter 2 of the volume.[26]

Tannert explores the emergence of German-language crime fiction in the context of its relatively early maturity: Adolph Müllner's *Der Kaliber* (*The Caliber*, 1828), the first German-language detective story, was published a full thirteen years before the text usually regarded as the model for the genre, Edgar Allan Poe's *The Murders in the Rue Morgue* (1841). She shows how Müllner, Otto Ludwig and other nineteenth-century authors from German-speaking Europe were crime-writing pioneers: influenced by Romanticism, the Enlightenment and manifold legal advances in the German-speaking world, they developed the detective story ahead of both America and Britain. A complementary exploration of another key text, Annette von Droste-Hülshoff's Poetic Realist novella *Die Judenbuche* (*The Jew's Beech*, 1842), is provided by Faye Stewart in chapter 6 on the *Frauenkrimi*.

Tannert goes on to analyse 1870s crime narratives by J. D. H. Temme and Adolf Streckfuss, which feature public servants as investigators, as well as the influence of Conan Doyle's Holmes on Balduin Groller's Austrian Dagobert novellas (1910–1912), and the prolific work of pioneering female crime authors such as Auguste Groner (also Austrian), Luise Westkirch and Eufemia von Adlersfeld-Ballestrem between 1890 and 1936. In addition, Martin Rosenstock's discussion of early

Swiss crime fiction in chapter 4 shows how the French eighteenth-century *Pitaval* (encyclopedic volumes about notorious criminal cases, 1734–43) stimulated the interest of the bourgeois European reading public in criminality, and analyses two important texts: Temme's *Der Studentenmord in Zurich* (The Murder of a Zurich Student, 1872) and Carl Albert Loosli's *Die Schattmattbauern* (The Farmers of Schattmatt, 1929), which depicts Switzerland on the brink of modernity.

While Conan Doyle's 'Sherlock Holmes' stories (1887–1927) were extremely popular in 1920s and 1930s Germany, along with whodunits by English-language writers such as Christie, S. S. Van Dine, Dorothy L. Sayers and Edgar Wallace, there is also evidence of considerable German-language crime production in this period, shaped by contemporary events and by the modernist movement. The demise of the German empire at the end of the First World War, along with the impact of industrialization and a global economic recession, led to urban life, political unrest and criminality becoming major preoccupations in the Weimar Republic (1919–33) – as illustrated by Alfred Döblin's modernist masterpiece *Berlin Alexanderplatz* (1929), which relates the experiences of Franz Biberkopf following his release from prison. In addition, the stories of German serial killers such as Carl Grossmann (Berlin), Fritz Haarmann (Hannover) and Peter Kürten (Düsseldorf) exerted a fascination over writers, the media and the public, which, as we will see, has endured to the present day.

An eclectic crime series published by Berlin's Verlag Die Schmiede, entitled 'Außenseiter der Gesellschaft: Die Verbrechen der Gegenwart' (Outsiders of Society: Crimes of the Present Day, 1924–5), reflected contemporary concerns through book-length studies on the serial killer Haarmann (by Theodor Lessing), the 1924 Hitler-Ludendorff trial (by Leo Lania) and the case of confidence trickster 'Freiherr von Egloffstein' (by Thomas Schramek). While similar to the *Pitaval* volumes in their focus on genuine criminal cases, Todd Herzog argues that these texts constitute 'an odd genre that falls between nonfiction (trial reports, criminological treatises) and literary fiction'.[27] As he shows, their 'dossier-like multi-perspectival narrative[s]' are notable for countering the dominant, 'single connected [crime] narrative' of Conan Doyle's Holmes stories, thereby refusing easy closure to questions of criminality and calling Enlightenment certainties into question.[28] Verlag Die Schmiede also posthumously published Franz Kafka's landmark work *Der Prozess* (*The Trial*, 1925), which confronts readers with the nightmarish tale of Josef K.'s arrest, trial and punishment for an unspecified crime by a sinister state authority.

A focus on the city, the urban serial killer and the rise of fascism is also visible in Fritz Lang's film *M – Eine Stadt sucht einen Mörder* (*M – A City Searches for a Murderer*, 1931), which features Peter Lorre as the child murderer 'M', loosely based on Peter Kürten.[29] A psychological thriller heavily influenced by expressionism, the film is innovative in its use of sound, parallel editing and the realistic depiction of modern police techniques such as fingerprinting. Its final section shows Berlin's criminals, who have apprehended murderer Hans Beckert ('M'), deciding that he should be executed at a makeshift trial. Horst Lange argues that the film, released shortly before the Nazis came to power in 1933, can be read as a warning allegory: crime boss Schränker, presiding as judge in a *Gestapo*-like leather coat, declares that child murderers should forfeit their legal rights and, using language foreshadowing the Nazis, be 'ausgerottet' (exterminated).[30] The argument of the lone 'defence lawyer' – that Beckert cannot control his actions due to a psychiatric disorder and should be treated by doctors – is rejected by Schränker and the criminals watching the trial, who are only prevented from lynching Beckert by the arrival of the police. The scene thus illustrates the criminal nature of a future fascist state (murderers visiting arbitrary judgement on the accused) and the ease with which the masses can be manipulated into holding fascist views. However, like the 'Outsiders of Society' series, the film refuses narrative closure. The question of how society should deal with Beckert is left open: the sentence handed down by the state is not disclosed and the film ends with a shot of the grieving mothers exhorting society to take better care of its children.[31]

The key factors that make children vulnerable in *M* are the size of the city and its criminal elements. A *Großstadtkrimi* (urban crime novel) examining similar themes to different ends is Erich Kästner's *Emil und die Detektive* (*Emil and the Detectives*, 1929). This highly popular children's novel tells the story of Emil Tischbein, who is tasked with delivering 120 Mark to his grandmother in Berlin. Falling victim to a criminal on the train, who gives him drugged chocolate and steals his money, he eventually captures the thief with the help of some Berlin youngsters – his 'detectives'. The criminal threat to children is thus still present (as in *M* they have a dangerous weakness for sweets), but is overcome by youthful resilience, resourcefulness and teamwork. Unlike the mothers in *M*, Emil's mother need not reproach herself or society at the end of the narrative: her son has proven he can negotiate the dangers of the big city without adult help.

This section closes with two other notable texts. *Ich war Jack Mortimer* (*I was Jack Mortimer*, 1933) by Alexander Lernet-Holenia is an Austrian *Großstadtkrimi* that imports its criminals from the gangster culture of America – albeit with a twist. The crime novel is told from the perspective of Viennese taxi driver Ferdinand Sponer, who picks up American gangster Jack Mortimer only to find that he has been shot dead when they reach their destination. Sponer panics, disposes of the body in the Danube and starts to investigate the crime, while the police, on finding blood in his taxi, make him their prime suspect. The situation is resolved when an American woman confesses to murdering her husband in revenge for his killing of her lover, a certain Jack Mortimer. A relatively sophisticated crime novel for the period with a strong sense of place, the work provides nuanced psychological portraits of the victim and murderers, as well as the hapless Sponer.[32]

Finally, Rahel Sanzara's *Das verlorene Kind* (The Lost Child, 1926) was a publishing sensation that was critically acclaimed by writers Carl Zuckmayer and Gottfried Benn, translated into eleven languages and awarded the 1926 Kleist Prize.[33] Possibly based on a nineteenth-century case chronicled in *Der neue Pitaval*, but tapping into contemporary anxieties about child killers and *Lustmord* (sex murders), it tells the story of a murderer, his four-year-old victim and her father's eventual forgiveness of his crime. Along with Erich Kästner, Sanzara became one of the authors blacklisted by the National Socialists, whose works were destroyed in the Nazi book-burnings of 10 May 1933.[34] The authorship of crime fiction was not the decisive factor in their ostracism, but rather their political stance or perceived Jewish origin. Ironically, Rahel Sanzara was a stage name: Johanna Bleschke, who selected the pseudonym when embarking on her first career as a dancer and actress, was not actually Jewish at all.

Crime fiction under National Socialism (1933–45)

As Carsten Würmann shows, crime fiction was published for a mass readership under National Socialism, with 3,000 novels with print runs of over one million appearing between 1933 and 1945.[35] However, it was only following 1939 that Nazi propaganda officials such as Erich Langenbucher actively sought to shape crime fiction, exhorting crime authors to set their novels in Germany; to present crime realistically, drawing on the model of newspaper reports; to depict the criminal without excusing his behaviour; and, perhaps most importantly, to present German policemen as heroic representatives of the state.[36] More broadly, crime writers were encouraged to depict Nazi Germany as a modern industrial society with an efficient police force operating in accordance with the rule of law.[37] Thus, novels like Fred Andreas's *Das vollkommene Verbrechen* (The Perfect Crime, 1944) emphasize that the Nazi police will always catch the perpetrator, no matter how clever his crime.[38]

Support for the regime was therefore given in a discreet manner by crime fiction, as part of a supposedly apolitical entertainment culture.[39] Hardly any crime novels made specific reference to National Socialism: their narratives were generic, with pronounced similarities to those of the 1920s and 1950s.[40] Nor were many overtly anti-Semitic. Exceptions include Pieter Coll's three *Nagotkin* novels (1939), featuring a global Jewish crime organization, and J. Bernitt's *Briefe in grauen Umschlägen* (Letters in Grey Envelopes, 1944), which depicts a decadent Viennese society of aristocrats, foreigners and rich Jews as a thinly disguised justification for the Nazi annexation of Austria.[41]

However, between 1941 and 1944 the *Reichsministerium für Volksaufklärung und Propaganda* (Reich Ministry of Public Enlightenment and Propaganda) and the *Reichskriminalhauptamt* (Reich Principal Criminal Office) worked together with publisher Hermann Hillger to create the 'Neuzeitliche Kriminalromane' (Modern Crime Novels) series, whose works promoted the ideology of the state and can therefore be regarded as National Socialist crime novels.[42] Hans Rudolf Berndorff's *Shiva und die Galgenblume* (Shiva and the Gallows Flower, 1943), shows police official Shiva using *Sippentafeln* (genetic family trees) as an investigative tool to deduce the criminal disposition of an individual. We see Shiva warn Herr van der Haardt against employing a thief due to his family background: he is the son of an alcoholic barkeeper and the grandchild of a prostitute. When van der Haardt employs the man, because he thinks social disadvantage drove him to steal, the novel refutes this theory by showing him steal again. The narrative thereby promotes a biological theory of crime that enables Shiva, in his role as an official of the state, to deliver a racial lesson to readers: 'It's the blood. It's the ancestry. The bad blood of the clan.'[43] These sentiments are echoed in the anti-Semitic historical drama *Jud Süss* (*The Jew Süss*, dir. Veit Harlan, 1940), which details the crimes of Joseph Süss Oppenheimer in eighteenth-century Württemberg. Süss is tried and executed for financial corruption and having sexual intercourse with a Christian woman, after which a decree is passed banning Jews from the state. The film's final words express the hope that German citizens will adhere to this ban to safeguard their children's bloodline.[44]

Würmann argues that the policeman in the 'Neuzeitliche Kriminalromane' series acts 'as a doctor on the body of the people'.[45] The aim is the excision of deviant or un-German elements from Nazi society, often symbolized, as in *Jud Süss*, by the execution of the criminal. This type of denouement reflected the reality of the Nazi state: from 1940–3, the number of citizens executed annually rose from 900 to 5,000, with the infamous *Volksgerichtshöfe* (People's Courts) sentencing 45 per cent of defendants to death between 1934 and 1945.[46] The function of the death penalty is illustrated in *Der Tod fuhr im Zug: Den Akten der Kriminalpolizei nacherzählt* (Death Travelled by Train: Told According to the Files of the Criminal Police, 1944), by Axel Alt, the pseudonym of Wilhelm Idhe, a Ministry of Propaganda official. The novel depicts the case of the Berlin *S-Bahn* strangler, railway worker Paul Ogorzow, a Nazi Party member arrested by the Berlin police in 1941 and executed following a fast-track trial. As Irmtraud Götz von Olenhusen asserts, 'the novel was designed to show not only how effective the powers of law and order were, but also to propagate the ideological line that "degenerate" people must be swiftly exterminated without further consideration'[47] – even if, as in this case, they form part of the Nazi body politic.

A fascinating contrast is provided by Will Berthold's post-war, West German novel *Nachts, wenn der Teufel kam: Roman nach Tatsachen* (At Night, When the Devil Visited: A Documentary Novel, 1959) on the Bruno Lüdke case.[48] Lüdke allegedly killed eighty people between 1924 and 1943, and the text shows him being apprehended by Berlin *Kriminalkommissar* Heinrich Franz in the face of ideologically motivated incompetence: the Nazi authorities deny a serial killer is at work, categorizing the deaths as suicides to keep murder statistics down, and restrict public information about the case, placing citizens at risk.[49] The Nazi state's criminality is also highlighted when Lüdke targets a Jewish woman, only to find she has been deported: 'This time the murderer . . . arrives too late. Other murderers, paid for by the state, have got there before him.'[50] Later research has cast doubt on Lüdke's guilt, suggesting that he was bullied into giving a false confession by Franz.[51] Berthold's depiction of Franz as a 'good' Nazi-era policeman is further undermined by Horst Bosetzky's *Der Teufel von Köpenick* (The Devil of Köpenick, 2009), which depicts Franz using Lüdke to advance his police career.

The Nazi state's control over literary production via the Ministry of Propaganda, together with an understandable self-censorship on the part of authors, resulted in an almost totally conformist body of crime fiction during the Nazi era. Given its direct engagement with the law, policing and justice, using the crime genre for oppositional purposes carried a high level of risk. Würmann found only one example critical of the system: Adam Kuckhoff and Peter Tarin's *Strogany und die Vermissten* (Strogany and the Missing Ones, 1941).[52] This novel adopts a strategy similar to works by other possibly dissenting writers, such as Ernst Junger's *Auf den Marmorklippen* (*On the Marble Cliffs*, 1939), encoding its critique in a narrative set in another place and historical moment – in this case, a tsarist Russia populated with corrupt politicians and secret police. In a tragic coda, Kuckhoff was executed in 1943 for his communist opposition to the regime. The only other overt criticism of National Socialism appears to come from outside Germany, in the work of Friedrich Glauser, whose 'Sergeant Studer' series (1936–41) critiques Swiss society, but also shows an acute awareness of larger political developments. As Martin Rosenstock's analysis in chapter 4 shows, Glauser's *Matto regiert* (*In Matto's Realm*, 1936) vividly signals the dangers of the Nazi regime.

The vast majority of crime novels written during the Nazi era are thus striking for what they cannot or do not show, namely the criminal actions of the state: the systematic persecution, deportation and murder of Jewish-German citizens and other political, religious, ethnic and sexual minority groups; the appropriation of Jewish businesses and property; and the ideologically determined, extra-judicial actions of the police. As chapter 3 on Austrian crime fiction, chapter 4 on Swiss crime fiction and chapter 7 on historical crime fiction show, it has been left to post-war authors to harness the genre's focus on criminality, guilt and justice to explore National Socialist crimes and to reflect on the legacy of the Nazi past.

Early post-war crime narratives (1945–60) and East German crime fiction (1949–71)

The earliest post-war *Kriminalroman* to critique Nazi Socialism is Hans Fallada's *Jeder stirbt für sich allein* (*Alone in Berlin*, 1947), which explores the case of Elise and Otto Hampel, executed for treason in 1943 for distributing postcards critical of the regime (see chapter 7). It is one of a group of crime narratives around the time of the Nuremberg War Crime Tribunals (1945–6) that was funded by the Soviet occupiers and sought to lay bare the criminality of the Nazi regime. They include Wolfgang Staudte's film *Die Mörder sind unter uns* (*The Murderers are Among Us*, 1946), which was initially entitled *Der Mann, den ich töten werde* (The Man I will Kill) and showed traumatized ex-soldier Mertens shooting former Nazi commander Brückner, now a successful businessman in spite of his war crimes. This ending was changed by the Soviet authorities to reflect and reinforce the judicial activities at Nuremberg: Mertens is persuaded by Susanne Wallner, a concentration camp survivor, to hand Brückner over to the police so that he can be properly tried by the state. Another film, *Affaire Blum* (The Blum Affair, 1948), an adaptation of Robert Stemmle's 1948 novel, examines the 1926 case of a Jewish-German businessman who was falsely accused of murder by the victim's right-wing German murderer. One of the first texts to explore the origins of National Socialism, it highlights how institutional anti-Semitism predisposed police investigators to believe the murderer's accusations and to prosecute an innocent man.

While some 1950s crime novels engage with the Nazi past, such as Berthold's *Nachts, wenn der Teufel kam*, others gloss over it. For example, Austrian writer Egon Eis's *Duell im Dunkel* (Duel in the Dark, 1957) tells of two former soldiers who meet in post-war Hamburg as a policeman and criminal, but studiously avoids mentioning National Socialism. The year 1956 saw the emergence of a West German crime fiction phenomenon representing pure escapism – the 'Jerry Cotton' series, published by the publisher Bastei, which followed the eponymous FBI agent's crime-fighting activities in New York. Served by a collective of over one hundred German-language crime writers, these *Heftromane* (novels published in booklet form) have been translated into nineteen languages and have a circulation of around 930 million to date.[53] It is tempting to see the initial success of this series in the 1950s as a reflection of readers' desires for entertainment far removed from West Germany's own social circumstances or its difficult historical past. However, the success of the first West German television crime series, *Stahlnetz* (1958–68) and its East German counterpart *Blaulicht* (1959–68), shows that audiences were receptive to crime narratives set on German soil that engaged with local and national concerns (see chapter 8 on the *Fernsehkrimi*).

The crime-writing luminary of the 1950s was Swiss dramatist and author Friedrich Dürrenmatt, who wrote three novels during this decade: *Der Richter und sein Henker* (*The Judge and His Hangman*, 1950), *Der Verdacht* (*Suspicion*, 1951) and *Das Versprechen: Requiem auf den Kriminalroman* (*The Pledge: Requiem for the Crime Novel*, 1958). Martin Rosenstock analyses these groundbreaking novels in chapter 4, focusing on the way that metaphysical and philosophical thought influence the characterization of the 'dying detective' in the two Bärlach novels and the 'failed detective' of *Das Versprechen* – figures who ultimately embody a critique of the Enlightenment tradition. As Kutch and Herzog argue, such 'anti-detective' novels were ahead of their time and illustrate the capacity of German-language crime fiction for innovation.[54] Dürrenmatt's texts have had a lasting impact within but also beyond the German-speaking world, as Sean Penn's well-received film adaptation, *The Pledge* (2001), starring Jack Nicholson, Sam Shepherd and Robin Wright, attests.

Crime fiction in the newly formed German Democratic Republic (GDR/East Germany, 1949–90) was shaped by ideological considerations that reflected a rise in Cold War tensions: East German popular fiction was to have a socialist, anti-fascist, political-pedagogical function, and to act as a 'dam' against the tide of popular literature produced by West Germany.[55] The *Amt für Literatur und Verlagswesen* (Office for Literature and Publishing Houses), which was established in 1951 and subsumed into the *Ministerium für Kultur* (Ministry of Culture) in 1956, approved publishing licenses and publishers' lists in line with state guidelines, which became increasingly restrictive following the June 1953 workers' uprising and remained stringent until 1961.[56] Throughout the forty-year lifetime of the GDR, crime fiction, along with all forms of literature, was subject to pendulum swings in state cultural policy, which were tightened or relaxed depending on changes in leadership or larger political events.

Dorothea Germer argues that the first GDR crime novel, Hannes Elmens's *Was geschah im D 121?* (What happened in D 121?, 1951) is representative of 1950s East German crime fiction in its thematization of class conflict, and its use of a plotline that shows crimes being committed by West German agents or saboteurs and solved by East German citizens or the *Volkspolizei* (people's police).[57] This model, which also frequently elides West Germany and fascism, is still visible in the 1960s: the murderer in Gerhard Harkenthal's *Rendevous mit dem Tod* (A Date with Death, 1962) is a West German former Nazi, who masquerades as an East German citizen while plotting the overthrow of the state. However, the building of the Berlin Wall under East German leader Walter Ulbricht in 1961, which halted significant movement between East and West Germany and reduced Cold War tensions, made this agent/saboteur model increasingly redundant.

In the more culturally relaxed period between 1961 and 1965, East German crime fiction was thought of as a form of high quality popular fiction that could bridge the divide between *U-* and *E-Literatur*, leading readers to more serious literary texts.[58] However, a key problem remained for authors. How to write crime fiction about a communist, classless East Germany in which major crime has been officially eliminated, without also being critical of the state? In 1963, the *Hauptverwaltung Verlage und Buchhandel* (Central Administration for Publishers and the Book Trade) was established in the GDR's Ministry of Culture and tasked with approving manuscripts and scrutinizing publisher lists. During the politically constrained period that followed between 1965 and 1971, GDR writers such as Gert Prokop and Erich Loest responded to ideological pressures by setting their crime novels outside the GDR, attacking capitalism and linking it to a fascistic West Germany, in what was essentially a reimagining of the old saboteur model.[59] Thus, Loest's *Das Waffenkarussell* (The Weapons Carousel, 1968) is set in Nigeria and critiques colonialism, the capitalist trade in illegal weapons and fascism through the depiction of former Nazis fermenting political unrest (see also chapter 5 on the *Afrika-Krimi*).

The West German Soziokrimi (1960–) and later East German crime fiction (1971–89)

The 1960s and 1970s saw the emergence of the West German *Soziokriminalroman* or *Soziokrimi* (social crime novel), also known as the *Neue Deutsche Kriminalroman* (new German crime novel), whose aim was to explore and critique society.[60] Two sets of influences contributed to this turn in West German crime fiction. The first was political: Chancellor Adenauer's departure from office in 1963 heralded an era in which the 'second generation' – those born after the end of the Second World War – came of age and began to reflect on the actions of their parents under National Socialism. The Eichmann (1961) and Frankfurt Auschwitz trials (1963–5) were extensively reported, with the latter forming the basis for Peter Weiss's play *Die Ermittlung* (*The Investigation*, 1965), which used court transcripts to confront audiences with the crimes of the Holocaust and the reluctance of perpetrators to admit guilt or responsibility.[61] In 1966, the appointment of former Nazi propaganda official Kurt Georg Kiesinger as chancellor was seen as evidence of a flawed West German democracy and politicized many young West Germans. The *Ausserparlamentarische Opposition* (extra-parliamentary opposition movement) and 1968 student movement campaigned against what they saw as the excessive powers of the CDU/SPD Grand Coalition (1966–9), and for the regulation of the right-wing Springer press. More broadly, influenced by the left-wing analyses of the Frankfurt School, they condemned capitalism and protested against America's involvement in the Vietnam War. The fatal police shooting of student Benno Ohnesorg at a 1967 demonstration was viewed as confirmation of the state's brutal and essentially fascist character. These elements also fed into the emergence of radical left-wing terrorism – the Baader-Meinhof gang or *Rote-Armee Frakion* (Red Army Faction) in West Germany in the 1970s.

The second factor that encouraged the emergence of the *Soziokrimi* was literary. In 1962, Richard K. Flesch became editor of Rowohlt's 'rororo thriller' imprint and commissioned the translation of Maj Sjöwall and Per Wahlöö's Swedish ten-part 'Martin Beck' series (1965–75).[62] In his study on the *Soziokrimi*, Jürg Brönnimann shows how Sjöwall and Wahlöö turned the crime novel into a vehicle for social criticism, using it to illustrate the negative effects of capitalism on Swedish society. Ending with the near-collapse of Swedish social structures, the series points to the need for an anti-capitalist alternative via the tenth novel's final word – 'Marx',[63] and proved to be enormously influential on West German crime authors.[64]

Brönnimann argues that *Soziokrimi* authors such as -ky (Horst Bosetzky), Felix Huby, Hansjörg Martin, Michael Molsner, Irene Rodrian and Fred Werremeier, many of whom were also championed by Rowohlt, were key in transforming ideas about the social function of literature in West Germany. In their view, literary texts were only truly effective when made accessible to a mass audience.[65] They therefore harnessed the popularity of the crime genre when critiquing West German society, taking care to show a recognizable world that allowed readers to identify with characters, and by extension with certain socio-political positions.[66] *Soziokrimi* authors also sought to redefine the notion of crime: 'crime was not to be regarded as an individual act, but rather as a direct, negative consequence of social circumstances'.[67] While the ideas of Frankfurt School thinkers such as Adorno, Habermas and Marcuse were widely discussed at the time, the influence of sociologists such as Emile Durkheim and Robert Merton, who argued that criminal behaviour was the product of societal structures and pressures, appears to have been more pronounced on *Soziokrimi* authors.[68] Notably, this theorization of crime contrasted sharply with National Socialist ideas of a biologically determined and hereditary criminality.

The writer known as '-ky' was revealed to be sociology professor Horst Bosetzky in 1981. His first crime novel, *Einer von uns beiden* (One of the Us Two, 1972) is the darkly humorous tale of Berlin sociology professor Dr Rüdiger Kolczyk, who is blackmailed by student Berndt Ziegenhals following his discovery that Kolczyk's doctoral thesis was plagiarized. Neither is a likeable character. Kolczyk is a pompous academic who lectures on working-class history, but is keen to protect his status and affluent lifestyle. Ziegenhals is lazy, with a history of criminal activity, including a spell as a pimp. However, Bosetzky shows how both are at least partially formed by their social backgrounds: the professor falsified his thesis because he needed money for his wife's medical treatment just after the Second World War; the student was orphaned as a result of wartime bombing and placed in a home. Post-war materialism has subsequently shaped their outlooks, and in Ziegenhals's case, led him to take up the role of blackmailer. These insights do not make readers like the characters more, but encourage an understanding of their actions. The text is also careful to refuse judgement: at the end of the narrative, neither character emerges victorious from the duel. Bosetzky went on to write numerous social crime novels set in Berlin and in Bramme, a fictional lower Saxony town with a representative function. As is shown below, the technique of figuring an individual or setting as representative of social types or political/class attitudes is characteristic of the *Soziokrimi*.

Irene Rodrian was one of the first West German woman crime authors to achieve publishing success and recognition (for further analysis, see chapter 6). Her social crime novel *Küsschen für den Totengräber* (Kiss for the Gravedigger, 1974), which can also be regarded as an early *Frauenkrimi*, opens with the attempted murder of unmarried young mother Margot Grimm after giving birth in hospital. Her assailant is the baby's father, Ernst Lorenz, who needs to present the boy as his legitimate offspring in order to secure the family inheritance, a pharmaceutical company. Lorenz uses his wealth as a weapon when trying to gain custody of the baby, paying a porter, senior nurse and Grimm's landlady for information about her movements. Rejected by her bourgeois parents and friends, Grimm is befriended by the Ghanaian Kofi Ocran and finds sanctuary in his student collective. When Lorenz attempts to murder Grimm again, but accidentally kills another person, he is finally caught by the police.

While depicted as rounded individuals, Grimm and Lorenz also represent social types – the disempowered single mother and the amoral capitalist playboy. Lorenz's murderous impulses have their roots in his late father's will, which sets him against his sister in a race to produce a male heir. His descent into madness and eventual suicide figures patriarchal capitalism as an entity that destroys even its own. The narrative ends on a more hopeful note for Grimm: she realizes that her passivity, particularly her silence following the attempt on her life, placed herself and others in danger, and develops a more assertive female agency. She applies for a job and moves out of the collective rather than entering into a relationship with Ocran; her professional abilities and a good childcare system will enable her to make an independent life. This ending is radical for the time: being an unmarried mother and choosing to remain so were still largely a social taboo.

Richard Hey's 'Katharina Ledermacher' police procedural series (1973–80) features the first *Kommissarin* (female police inspector) of German-language crime fiction. The opening novel, *Ein Mord am Lietzensee* (Murder at Lake Lietzen, 1973), shows the highly capable Ledermacher investigating the murder of an old man. A gang of youths called 'Lucifer's Darlings' is suspected, but Ledermacher establishes that Brückner was actually killed by fellow residents in his old people's home. The novel explores different philosophies of policing, with Ledermacher's boss asserting the guilt of 'Lucifer's Darlings' and advocating the use of force: the novel shows gang members being beaten up by police in a display of state violence. By contrast, Ledermacher's own youth in a children's home helps her to understand how the gang's criminality arises from a combination of social deprivation and a disengagement from society. Her own more risky approach involves engaging gang members in dialogue, which helps her to close the case. The perpetrators turn out to be outwardly respectable older members of society, who have formed what amounts to a geriatric gang. Its leader, Dr Erwin Bockelmann, is a former Nazi judge who uses his legal knowledge to evade justice at the end of the narrative. However, Ledermacher's progressive role within the police force lends *Ein Mord am Lietzensee* a redemptive quality, and her depiction helps to inspire a new generation of female crime writers. Pieke Biermann may have named her police investigator Karin Lietze in homage to the novel (see also chapter 6).[69]

In Austria during the 1970s, as Marieke Krajenbrink shows in chapter 3, two second-generation writers, Peter Handke and Gerhard Roth, were experimenting with crime fiction in a different way to *Soziokrimi* authors, by simultaneously employing and subverting genre conventions to problematize the idea of an objective truth in the context of Austrian history and politics. Three first-generation authors should also be mentioned, whose work strongly reflects concerns of the time. The first is the Austrian writer Hans Lebert, whose novel *Die Wolfshaut* (Wolf's Skin, 1960) draws heavily on the crime genre to expose historical amnesia in relation to the National Socialist past (see chapter 3 for further analysis). The second is Hans Hellmut Kirst, whose satirical crime novels, such as *Die Nacht der Generale* (*The Night of the Generals*, 1962), are often set in the Nazi era and figure their murderers as embodiments of a psychopathic, criminal regime (see chapter 7).[70] Lastly, Nobel Prize winner Heinrich Böll caused significant controversy with his novel *Die verlorene Ehre der Katharina Blum oder: Wie Gewalt entstehen und wohin sie führen kann* (*The Lost Honour of Katharina Blum or: How Violence Comes About and Where It Can Lead*, 1974). Adopting *Kriminalroman* conventions, it tells the story of a woman whose reputation is destroyed by the press following contact with a suspected left-wing terrorist, and subsequently feels driven to murder a journalist. Misinterpreted by some as a legitimization of violence,[71] the text sought to dissect the conditions that make violence possible by critiquing the West German tabloids' commercial exploitation of fears about terrorism, the unconstitutional legal steps to combat extremism (such as the 1972 'Radikalenerlass', a decree prohibiting 'radicals' from taking up public employment) and the criminalization of innocent citizens. Adapted for film in 1975 by directors Volker Schlöndorff and Margarethe von Trotta, with Angela Winkler in the leading role, this powerful novel is viewed as an origin text for later crime novels and thrillers that have engaged with the legacy of Baader-Meinhof terrorism.[72]

On the other side of the Berlin Wall, crime fiction benefitted from a comparatively relaxed cultural policy following Erich Honecker's appointment as East German head of state in 1971 and his pronouncement at the Fourth Conference of the SED Central Committee that socialist literature should not be subject to taboos.[73] Germer notes that some East German crime fiction now began to engage with criminality within the GDR,[74] a development that dovetailed with the creation of the television crime drama *Polizeiruf 110* (Police: Dial 110, 1971–), set in cities such as East Berlin, Rostock and Dresden (see also chapter 8). Crime fiction published in this period can appear surprisingly critical of the regime. Gert Prokop's *Einer muss die Leiche sein* (Someone has to be the Corpse, 1976) features an SED Party loyalist who murders his mistress after she threatens to derail his political career. Fielitz's confession at the end of the narrative not only reveals the extreme levels of party loyalty needed to rise through the ranks, but also the advantages of being engaged to the daughter of an important party functionary. It is the fear that the engagement will be broken off, thereby terminating opportunities for travel outside the GDR, that leads Fielitz to kill. The novel was published in the wittily named 'DIE' series, established in 1970 by the Verlag Das Neue Berlin. This acronym, which stands for *Delikte–Indizien–Ermittlungen* (crimes–clues–investigations), indicates a shift in attitude: crime novels are viewed less as political-pedagogical tools and more as an accepted form of entertainment – perhaps one reason why the denouement of *Einer muss die Leiche sein* passed through the publication system uncensored.

The expulsion from the GDR of dissident singer-songwriter Wolf Biermann in 1976 signalled the beginning of a more restrictive cultural era. Crime fiction resumed its status as an uncritical literary form and state-sanctioned refuge for writers who were politically out of favour,[75] as already seen in Erich Loest's case in 1964.[76] However, it was not possible for the state to completely reverse the advances made during more culturally open times. While ideological restrictions were in place in the 1980s, crime fiction developed a number of diverse functions: as a form of reportage at a time when news coverage told citizens little about the realities of their state, as a means of documenting the problems of everyday life and by extension of GDR society, and as an assertion of the shift from a collective 'ermittelnde Gesellschaft' (investigating society) to a more individual mindset.[77] Investigators, typically depicted as confident representatives of the state apparatus, might now be shown as uncertain about their methods or the purpose of their work, and perpetrators, previously figured as outsiders or enemies of the state, were increasingly depicted as normal GDR citizens who commit murder due to complex social and psychological factors.[78] Thus, as Germer argues, crime fiction becomes 'an indirect chronicler of the collapse of the GDR' in the final decade of the state's existence.[79] After the fall of the Berlin Wall in 1989, well-known East German authors such as Jan Eik, Hartmut Mechtel and Ingeburg Siebenstädt (writing as Tom Wittgen; see chapter 6) continued to publish successfully. More recently, the best texts from the 'DIE' series have been republished by Komet, evidencing reader interest in a rebranded, 'cult' East German crime, while contemporary crime authors, such as Simon Urban, have sought to address the legacy of the GDR in their work (see chapter 7 on historical crime fiction).

Turkish-German crime fiction and the Frauenkrimi (1980–)

The 1980s and 1990s were notable for a number of crime fiction industry developments. In 1984, the *Bochumer Krimi Archiv* (BKA) was established by West German author and journalist Reinhard Jahn, which in turn set up the annual *Deutscher Krimipreis* (German Crime Prize) in 1985, judged by a jury of critics, booksellers and academics. 'Das Syndikat – Die Autorengruppe deutschsprachige Kriminalliteratur' (The Syndicate – German-language Crime Fiction Authors' Association), which currently has over 800 members from Austria, Germany and Switzerland, was formed in 1986. It organizes an annual crime convention (*Criminale*, 1986–) and created the *Friedrich-Glauser-Preis* (Friedrich Glauser Prize, 1987–), judged by a jury of crime authors. In 1996, the German chapter of the American 'Sisters in Crime' network was established, which became the *Mörderische Schwestern – Vereinigung deutschsprachiger KrimiAutorinnen* (Murderous Sisters – Association of German-language Women Crime Authors) in 2007. Each of these organizations aims to promote German-language crime fiction and the interests of German-language crime authors in rapidly evolving publishing contexts.

The 1980s saw the emergence of a number of Turkish-German crime narratives in West Germany. An important early example is by Aras Ören, a Turkish author who migrated to Germany in 1969: his novel *Bitte nix Polizei: Kriminalerzählung* (Please No Police: Crime Story) was translated into German and published in 1981. Set in 1973, when *Gastarbeiter* (foreign guest workers) represented nearly 10 per cent of West Germany's workforce,[80] its multi-layered narrative can be read as 'a tale of post-war reconstruction on the anvil of Turkish migration'.[81] However, as the novel's subtitle indicates, it is also a story about crime, and is used by the author to highlight the fraught relationship between migrants, West German citizens and the authorities. Its central protagonist, Ali Itir, is unjustly accused of two crimes in the course of the narrative – a sexual assault and an attack on an old man, who subsequently dies. Ali had actually tried to help the man following a winter fall, but fled when the police were called; racist witnesses then misinterpreted his actions as criminal. It is in fact a neighbour, Frau Gramke, who is responsible for the old man's death: she saw him fall, but left him lying in the snow as punishment for another crime, a rape he committed thirty years before. The novel ends with the discovery of a body in a canal, which may or may not be Ali. As Tom Cheesman argues, here 'realism gives way to an unobtrusively postmodernist refusal of closure': the reader is left pondering the cause of death (murder/suicide/drowning) and the identity of the corpse.[82] Ali thus 'becomes an icon not only of the migrant worker as quintessential victim, but also of the migrant worker as quintessentially unknowable subject'.[83]

Four years later, a crime novel appeared that revolutionized depictions of Turkish-Germans in West German culture. Written by Jakob Arjouni, a 20-year-old German of non-Turkish heritage, *Happy Birthday, Türke!* (*Happy Birthday, Turk!*, 1985) employed a subgenre that had rarely been seen in German-language crime fiction – the hard-boiled, private detective novel – as a vehicle for introducing the first Turkish-German lead investigator, Kemal Kayankaya.[84] Kayankaya is the opposite of Ali Itir: he holds German citizenship, speaks German as his first language, has a state-approved private detective's licence, and asserts himself with wise-cracking confidence when dealing with fellow West Germans and their racist stereotypes. It is difficult to overestimate how groundbreaking this figure was in the 1980s, when public attitudes towards migrants were deteriorating; right-wing arson attacks in the 1990s would claim a number of Turkish lives. Asking German readers to identify with the likeable, football-and-herring-loving Kayankaya directly challenged the dominant image of the Turk as a poorly integrated kebab-shop owner, rubbish collector or criminal, and confronted essentialist notions of German national identity. Drawing on the model of the *Soziokrimi, Happy Birthday, Türke!* also exposes the corruption of the state and the racism at the heart of West German society. The focus is on German criminality, with the crimes of Turks and other minorities shown in the larger context of unequal social power-relations: a Turkish 'criminal' is shown to have been blackmailed into dealing drugs by corrupt police officers who threatened him with deportation should he not comply.[85]

Crime writer Akif Pirinçci, who migrated to West Germany as a child in 1968, has arguably positioned himself as a writer of popular fiction rather than as a migrant author.[86] However, as Jim Jordan shows, his eight internationally best-selling *Felidae* crime novels (1989–2014) featuring Francis the cat detective can be read as allegories of the migrant experience.[87] The first in the series, *Felidae* (1989), depicts Francis as a marginalized outsider following his arrival in a new neighbourhood, who gains social acceptance by solving a series of cat murders. The third, *Cave canem* (*Cave canem*, 1993), explores intergenerational relations, contrasting the migrant and post-migrant attitudes of Francis and his son towards questions of integration and identity.[88] However, the texts also invite wider, multiple readings: the 'mad scientist' plot in *Felidae*, which involves the kidnapping of neighbourhood strays for a gruesome programme of experiments, calls the ethics of animal experimentation into question, but in a specifically German context also evokes memories of Nazi medical experimentation in concentration camps. One of the scientist's victims later attempts to create a pure race of undomesticated cats to subjugate the human race, but is stopped by Francis, who 'rejects the replacement of one form of tyranny with another, accepts the desirability of interbreeding, and argues for a future vision of a society in which all animals (including humans) are equal'.[89]

New millennium Turkish-German works include Feridun Zaigmoglu's *Leinwand* (Canvas, 2003), a parody of a hard-boiled police detective novel. *Leinwand* is Zaigmoglu's only foray into crime fiction, and shows Kiel police detective Seyfeddin Karasu investigating the torching of a homeless man and the drowning of a woman from eastern Germany. However, Zaigmoglu subverts the genre by showing one of the cases being solved without Karasu and by killing him in a car-bomb explosion before he can solve the second. The first Turkish-German police inspector in German-language history thus has a regrettably short career.

More recently, Su Turhan's 'Kommissar Pascha' series (2013–) shows Turkish-German police inspector Zeki Demirbilek investigating migrant/racist crimes as the head of Munich's *Sonderdezernat Migra* (Special Migration Unit). Demirbilek is a highly integrated Turkish migrant, who moved to Germany aged twelve and has enjoyed a successful career in the German police. His identity is an almost perfect blend of German and Turkish: he views Munich and Istanbul as his home cities, speaks German and Turkish fluently, supports Bayern and Fenerbahçe football clubs, and observes Ramadan, but drinks alcohol and eats pork. He holds a German passport, but would have preferred dual Turkish-German citizenship (not allowed under German law at that point). Demirbilek thus differs substantially from Arjouni's Kayankaya, an insider-outsider figure operating beyond police structures who speaks no Turkish, and from *Tatort*'s Cenk Batu, a Hamburg policeman who works in an undercover capacity and speaks little Turkish (see chapter 8 on the *Fernsehkrimi* for analysis of this figure).

Demirbilek can be regarded as an overly idealized Turkish-German character, whose attachment to traditional Turkish barbers and delicacies makes him interesting to German readers without being threatening: he is the 'civilized' Turkish German who allows the vision of an integrated society to seem achievable. However, his depiction can also be applauded for normalizing the idea of a senior Turkish-German police officer respected for his experience, integrity and expertise. In addition, his integration into German society – rather than complete assimilation – asserts the right of Turkish Germans to retain a strong sense of Turkish identity, rather than having to face the 'entweder-oder' (either-or) of German citizenship law. Demirbilek has successfully become German but has also remained Turkish, and this dual identity is shown to enrich both German policing and society.

As this survey chapter has already illustrated, women writers such as Annette von Droste-Hülshoff, Auguste Groner, Luise Westkirch, Eufemia von Adlersfeld-Ballestrem, Rahel Sanzara and Irene Rodrian contributed significantly to German-language crime fiction between the 1840s and 1970s with a number of rich and complex texts. Scholars like Ailsa Wallace continue to rediscover women crime writers, such as Hermynia Zur Mühlen, who, while best known for her anti-fascist exile literature, also wrote six crime novels in the 1920s under the name of Lawrence H. Desberry, featuring socialist reporter-detective Brian O'Keefe.[90] Like Groner and Sanzara, Zur Mühlen was extremely successful in her lifetime. The O'Keefe novels were serialized in newspapers, published in multiple editions and translated, but then, like Groner's and Sanzara's works, they largely disappeared from literary histories that privileged high culture and the output of male authors.[91]

In chapter 6, Faye Stewart places the work of women crime writers centre stage, exploring how the *Frauenkrimi* (women's crime novel) flourished in the 1980s, partly due to the legacy of the 1968 student movement and partly due to the influence of Anglo-American feminist crime writers such as Sara Paretsky, Val McDermid and Sue Grafton. Written by, about and for women, the *Frauenkrimi* contested inequality through the agency of its female sleuths, celebrated new constructions of sexuality and queerness, and cast a critical eye on patriarchal society. As Brigitte Frizzoni argues, gender hierarchies of the 1980s and 1990s were thoroughly subverted by the increased presence in crime narratives of the 'Kommissarin, Forensikerin, Privatermittlern, Amateurin, Täterin oder Rächerin' (female police inspector, female forensics expert, female private investigator, female amateur detective, female perpetrator or female avenger).[92] Stewart's wide-ranging chapter explores the work of pioneering female crime writers in the 1950s and 1960s such as Irene Rodrian and Ingeburg Siebenstädt (the 'Agatha Christie of the GDR'), and the literary, publishing and critical contexts in which the *Frauenkrimi* emerged. She goes on to examine the socio-political issues addressed by seminal German and Austrian feminist authors such as Pieke Biermann, Doris Gercke, Christine Grän and Ingrid Noll – from women's rights and gay rights to the expansion of the European Union. Chapter 3 by Marieke Krajenbrink provides additional discussion of Austrian women crime writers such as Elfriede Jelinek, as does chapter 8 on the depiction of female investigators in the *Fernsehkrimi*.

This section ends with a genre outlier: Patrick Süskind's extraordinary literary-historical crime narrative *Das Parfum – Die Geschichte eines Mörders* (*Perfume – The Story of a Murderer*, 1985), which enjoyed enormous international success and was adapted for film by German director Tom Tykwer in 2006. Set in eighteenth-century France, the narrative is told in the first person by perfumer Jean-Baptiste Grenouille, whose astonishing sense of smell leads him to kill young virgins in an obsessive quest to distil the perfect scent. A novel about the relationship of the senses, desire and morality, it has sold over 15 million copies, been translated into numerous languages and remains an outstanding example of twentieth-century German literature.

Historical crime fiction, regional crime fiction and the rise of the Afrika-Krimi (1989–)

A diverse range of German-language crime fiction has been produced since the fall of the Berlin Wall in 1989. As Katharina Hall shows in chapter 7, the intensive re-examination of Germany's twentieth-century history following German reunification has led to a boom in historical crime fiction. Key examples include Christian von Ditfurth's 'Stachelmann' series (2002–), which uses a historian-detective to examine the Nazi past, Andreas Pittler's 'Bronstein' series (2008–), which explores Austrian history between 1913 and 1955, Ferdinand von Schirach's *Der Fall Collini* (*The Collini Case*, 2010), which examines the failure of post-war justice in relation to Nazi crimes, and Simon Urban's *Plan D* (*Plan D*, 2011), an alternative history of the GDR that implicitly critiques post-reunification Germany. In chapter 3, Marieke Krajenbrink also provides analysis of a number of Austrian crime novels that engage with the fascist past and its legacies, such as Wolf Haas's *Auferstehung der Toten* (*Resurrection*, 1996) and Paulus Hochgatterer's *Die Süße des Lebens* (*The Sweetness of Life*, 2006), which probe the disjunction between idyllic tourist images and the more complex reality beneath, thereby subverting the *Heimatroman* (homeland novel) tradition and its problematic associations.

The 1990s saw the *Regionalkrimi*, *Regiokrimi* or *Heimatkrimi* (regional crime novel) become increasingly popular. As Sascha Gerhards argues, this subgenre complements the emphasis of historical crime novels on the 'vertical' axis of the past through a 'geographical, horizontal mapping' of provincial and rural spaces, dialects and cultures.[93] Its origins are to be found in the strongly regional character of the *Heiliges Römisches Reich* (Holy Roman Empire of the German Nation; 800–1806), whose echo persists in the federal *Länder* (states) of modern Germany, and in the German fascination with landscape, evidenced in the work of Romantic artists such as Caspar David Friedrich (1774–1840), which depicts nature for allegorical ends, but also celebrates specific regional spaces, such as Greifswald or the island of Rügen. Droste-Hülshoff's *Die Judenbuche* (1842), set in the Westphalian mountains, could well be viewed as a regional crime narrative, as could the television crime series *Tatort* (1970–), which features investigative teams in different cities and regions (see also chapter 8). Ralf Koss argues that while *Tatort* and crime novels such as Jürgen Lodemann's *Anita Drögemöller und die Ruhe an der Ruhr* (Anita Drögemöller and the Peaceful Ruhr, 1975) were targeted at an 'überregionales Publikum' (an audience beyond the region in question), the 'new regional crime novel' of the 1990s was hyperlocal, placing such emphasis on topographical detail and dialect that 'crime novels from Cologne [held] barely any attraction for crime fans from Munich'.[94] Christine Lehmann notes in 2008 that the popularity of *Regionalkrimis* has led publishers to specialize in the subgenre and specific regions, such as Grafit Verlag (Dortmund), Emons Verlag (Cologne) and Gmeiner Verlag (Meßkirch).[95] She concedes that local detail can take precedence over quality, with the *Regionalkrimi* often reviewed as a local event rather than as a literary text.[96] Too cosy to be 'gesellschaftskritisch' (critical of society),[97] the *Regionalkrimi* 'becomes, in a best case scenario, part of a native folklore, and in the worst, relapses into provincialism'.[98]

However, many crime authors have challenged negative perceptions of regional crime fiction by combining local settings – arguably no different to that of small-town Ystad in Henning Mankell's best-selling Swedish 'Wallander' series – with crime narratives that examine larger issues, such as Rainer Gross's Baden-

Württemburg *Krimis*, which engage with the legacy of Nazi euthanasia.[99] Other examples include Jacques Berndorf's 'Siggi Baumeister/Eifel Krimi' series (1989–), set in the Eifel region in western Germany; Wolf Haas's 'Simon Brenner' private detective series (1996–2009), located in Salzburg (see chapter 3); and Nele Neuhaus's 'Bodenstein and Kirchhoff' police procedural series (2006–), set in the Taunus region of western Germany. Volker Klüpfel and Michael Kobr's highly successful *Allgäukrimis*, which feature Inspector Kluftinger and are located in the southern German region of Allgäu in Swabia, have sold 750,000 novels since 2003 and resulted in a television adaptation. They demonstrate how a regional crime series can become a national success and disprove Koss's view that regional crime authors target a narrow audience.[100] Rather, as Kutch and Herzog argue, their 'hyperlocal customs, locations and speech patterns combine with global concerns to form a potent mix that locates these novels both specifically and globally'.[101]

As Julia Augart shows in chapter 5, the subgenre of the *Afrika-Krimi* – German-language crime novels set in Africa or with African characters and themes – also grew significantly in the 1990s, due to rising interest in literary representations of Africa and increased discussion of postcolonial issues. While crime novels set in Africa have existed since the golden age of crime, the first German *Afrika-Krimi* was Henry Kolarz's *Kalahari* (1977), set in Zimbabwe, Botswana and South Africa. Nearly one hundred other examples have been published since then, especially since the beginning of the new millennium. Augart discusses the *Afrika-Krimi* in the context of the contemporary German Africa novel and African crime fiction, but also in relation to historical and regional crime fiction from the German-speaking world. Through comparative analysis, she explores how German, Austrian and Swiss authors deploy African settings, address a range of topics and themes, and critique the West's past and present relations with Africa. The chapter also includes analysis of Bernhard Jaumann's Namibia crime novels, with a particular focus on *Steinland* (Stoneland, 2012), the second in the 'Clemencia Garises' series, which explores the complex legacy of Germany's colonial past in *Deutsch-Südwest-Afrika* (German South West Africa), as Namibia was termed between 1884 and 1915.

Crime fiction of the new millennium and the lacuna of Jewish-German crime fiction

Present-day German-language crime fiction is vibrant and diverse. In the past, it has occupied the position of poor relation to English-language crime fiction in the German book market: as late as 2008, only one-third of crime novels published in Germany were by home-grown authors (180–200 compared to around 600 translated foreign works).[102] However, today bookshops showcase a mixture of German-language and international crime fiction, and best-sellers are often German, suggesting that a more equal balance is evolving. These texts may celebrate a German-speaking or specifically regional culture, such as Klüpfel and Kobr's *Allgäukrimis*; shine a spotlight on the police treatment of ethnic minorities, like Franz Dobler's *Ein Bulle im Zug* (Cop on the Train, 2014); address issues such as globalization and the power of the pharmaceutical industry, like Wolfgang Schorlau's *Der letzte Flucht* (The Last Escape, 2011); explore cross-border criminality in the context of European expansion, like Maria Gronau's *Weiberschläue* (Women's Shrewdness, 2003), or fruitfully exploit Anglo-American commercial models, like Frank Schätzing's apocalyptic thriller, *Der Schwarm* (*The Swarm*, 2004). As Martin Rosenstock shows in chapter 4, Swiss crime fiction has also found worthy successors to Glauser and Dürrenmatt in recent years, with Hansjörg Schneider's 'Hunkeler' series and Urs Schaub's 'Tanner' series drawing adeptly on their crime fiction heritage, while reinvigorating modern Swiss crime writing through their social critique and international outlook.

German-language crime fiction is now also increasingly seen in English translation, thanks in part to the promotional activities of the *Goethe-Institut* and *New Books in German*.[103] Long-translated authors include Jakob Arjouni, Pieke Biermann, Friedrich Dürrenmatt, Friedrich Glauser, Petra Hammesfahr, Ingrid Noll and Patrick Süskind. More recently a new wave of contemporary German-language crime fiction has been translated into English by Anthea Bell, Jamie Bulloch and Katy Derbyshire, and published by MacLehose, Orion, Pan, Penguin, Simon & Schuster, Weidenfeld & Nicolson, Quercus, Vintage and Serpent's Tail. These texts draw on diverse subgenres and national crime-writing traditions, and include Bernhard Aichner's revenge thriller *Totenfrau* (*Woman of the Dead*, 2014; see chapter 3), Sascha Arango's Patricia Highsmith homage *Die Wahrheit und andere Lügen* (*The Truth and Other Lies*, 2014), Jan Costin Wagner's Finnish 'Joentaa' police procedural series, which draws on Scandinavian *noir*, Sebastian Fitzek's disturbing psychological thrillers, Hochgatterer's *Die Süße des Lebens* (see chapter 3), Bernhard Jaumann's *Die Stunde des Schakals* (*The Hour of the Jackal*, 2010; see chapter 5), Elfriede Jelinek's *Gier* (see chapter 3), Neuhaus's 'Bodenstein and Kirchhoff' police procedural series, von Schirach's courtroom drama *Der Fall Collini* (see chapter 7), Andrea Maria Schenkel's *Tannöd* (*The Murder Farm*, 2006; see chapter 7) and Urban's *Plan D* (see chapter 7). Young German writers with Eastern European heritage, such as Alina Bronsky, whose novel *Scherbenpark* (*Broken Glass Park*, 2008) explores a teenage Russian migrant's experiences following the murder of her mother, and Croatian-born Zoran Drvenkar, whose hard-hitting thriller *Sorry* (*Sorry*, 2009) won the 2010 Friedrich Glauser Prize, have also attracted international interest and praise.

The traditional distinctions between high and low culture noted at the beginning of this chapter have also become less rigid over time. Journalist and critic Tobias Gohlis has contributed significantly to the increased cultural appreciation of crime fiction in Germany through his establishment in 2001 of a crime-writing column in the broadsheet *Die Zeit*, along with the online *KrimiZEIT-Bestenliste* (monthly crime fiction highlights). In common with English-language authors, German-language crime writers are also consciously creating and promoting hybrid texts that fuse 'literary' and 'popular' fiction, extracting what they regard to be the best of both genres. As Simon Urban, interviewed about the influence of Michael Chabon's work on his own, comments:

> what fascinated me was precisely this unbelievably rare mixture: an aesthetic concept, which logically suggests *E-Literatur* [serious literature], combined with an original crime fiction concept, the best of *U-Literatur* [popular fiction]. When this kind of combination succeeds, then in principle we are talking about a new genre, *EU-Literatur* [serious popular fiction].[104]

Such hybridity has of course long been visible in works by Austrian, German and Swiss writers such as Jelinek, Fallada and Dürrenmatt, but the confidence with which younger writers are embracing and challenging the conventions of crime fiction promises the continued emergence of high-quality German-language texts that address complex political, social and historical questions, while successfully reaching mass audiences through this enduringly popular literary form.

This chapter closes with an acknowledgement of an absence. When surveying German-language crime fiction of the twentieth century, there is a lack of readily identifiable texts by Jewish-German, Jewish-Austrian or Jewish-Swiss authors, particularly in contrast to the numerous works by Jewish crime writers in the English-speaking world, such as Harry Kemelman's 'Rabbi Small' series (1964–96), Faye Kellerman's 'Decker and Lazarus' series (1986–), Michael Chabon's *The Yiddish Policeman's Union* (2007) and many more.[105] The reasons for this absence could be numerous. Most obviously, the mass migration and mass murder of Jewish citizens under National Socialism had a devastating, long-term effect on Jewish culture in Europe. However, the question of whether there has ever been a tradition of crime writing by Jewish authors in the German-speaking world remains largely unexplored. It may be that there are only a small number of such texts; alternatively, Jewish German-language crime novels may exist, but have yet to be properly unearthed or researched. A recent German encyclopedia that surveys *Juden und Judentum im Detektivroman* (Jews and Jewishness in the Detective Novel), but contains neither entries for Jewish German-language crime novels nor a recognition of this absence in its introduction, suggests that a further academic focus on this area is required.[106]

Research for this volume has not identified any contemporary Jewish German-language crime authors who have produced significant numbers of texts, although the possibility that some exist but do not identify themselves publicly as Jewish cannot be excluded. However, a number of post-war Jewish German-language texts draw on the conventions of crime fiction, especially when writing about National Socialist crimes. One example is Edgar Hilsenrath's controversial novel *Der Nazi und der Friseur* (*The Nazi and the Barber*), which was first published in translation by Doubleday in 1971 and by German publisher Helmut Braun in 1977. This highly satirical *Kriminalroman* is narrated by Max Schulz, a Nazi SS-perpetrator, who steals the identity of Jewish concentration camp victim Itzig

Finkelstein to escape persecution for his war crimes. Schulz's post-war story becomes increasingly grotesque: not only does he emigrate to Israel as a Holocaust survivor, complete with circumcision and fake Auschwitz prisoner number, he also confesses his crimes to a retired West German magistrate in 1967, who refuses to take him seriously. Thus, even when Nazi war criminals freely admit their crimes, the West German legal system is shown turning a blind eye.

In Austrian contexts, Albert Drach's *Untersuchung an Mädeln. Kriminalprotokoll* (Investigating the Girls. Criminal Report, 1971) critiques sexism and social prejudice through the depiction of a court case in which two young women are accused of murdering a man who raped them while they were hitchhiking, even though his body has never been found. Doron Rabinovici's *Suche nach M.* (*The Search for M*, 1997), makes use of crime genre elements in its depiction of two second-generation children of Holocaust survivors who are psychologically scarred by their parents' experiences: Dani Morgenthau has a compulsive desire to claim guilt for crimes he did not commit, while Arieh Scheinowitz works for the Israel Secret Service, identifying 'enemy targets' for the assassin's bullet. Notable, too, is the novel *Bronsteins Kinder* (*Bronstein's Children*, 1986), by East/West German author Jurek Becker, set in a 1973 GDR, which shows teenager Hans Bronstein discovering that his Holocaust-survivor father has kidnapped a former concentration camp guard. Hans is presented with a moral quandary – whether to let the man go or to allow his father to exact extra-judicial justice for past crimes.

The most mainstream recent crime novel by a Jewish-German author is J. Monika Walther's *Goldbroiler oder die Beschreibung einer Schlacht: Kriminalgeschichte* (Roast Chicken or the Chronicle of a Slaughter: Crime Story, 2009). Set shortly after the fall of the Berlin Wall in Warnemünde, it shows former East German citizens floundering economically in the new order. The villains are former Nazis from the west, who co-opt eastern neo-Nazis, former *Stasi* members and disgruntled former GDR citizens into activities such as extortion, smuggling and importing women as sex workers from Eastern Europe. While overloaded, the narrative provides an interesting depiction of how essentially good people, such as private eye Ida Waschinski, can be corrupted due to financial pressures. Although some villains are shown receiving Old Testament-style justice (they are shot with a gun from Buchenwald concentration camp), the novel's ending is bleak: the law is shown to be fundamentally corrupt, and the most powerful villains maintain their power.

Two other interlinked crime fiction developments are worth noting. The first is the use of Jewish-German figures in crime fiction by Turkish-German writers. Hilal Sezgin's *Der Tod des Maßschneiders* (Death of a Tailor, 1999), set in Frankfurt in 1885, follows a young Jewish-German woman investigating an apparently anti-Semitic murder and has been called 'an important debut that implicitly and sensitively poses in a new way the question about a Turkish and Jewish "shared fate" in Germany'.[107] More recently, Esmahan Aykol's *Hotel Bosporus* (*Hotel Bosphorus*, 2004) introduces readers to Kati Hirschel, a German with Jewish heritage, who owns a crime bookshop in Istanbul and investigates cases with

Turkish police inspector Batuhan Önal. Secondly, the Jewish voice in German-language crime fiction is increasingly represented by non-Jewish writers, a proxy that may be viewed as problematic in certain contexts. For example, the main protagonist of Harald Gilbers's recent crime novel *Germania* (2013), which is set in 1944 Nazi Germany, is Jewish former police inspector Richard Oppenheimer, who is ordered to help the SS to solve a serial killer case. Neither the historical (im)plausibility of such a scenario nor the issue of a third-generation German author writing from the perspective of a Jewish person living under Nazism has been addressed by German reviewers. Lastly, Katharina Höftmann, a young German writer living in Israel, has broken new ground in her 'Assaf Rosenthal' series (2012–). The opening novel, *Die letzte Sünde* (The Final Sin, 2012), introduces readers to Tel Aviv police detective Rosenthal, a former army officer who worked in the occupied territories. He is depicted as a committed Zionist who, in spite of discussions with a more liberal colleague, holds hard-line views on the Palestinian conflict. It will be interesting to see if Rosenthal's attitudes are challenged in future investigations of the series. A far more welcome development, however, would be to see the history, society and culture of the German-speaking world refracted through the gaze of a new wave of Jewish crime writers from Austria, Germany and Switzerland.

Notes

[1] 'Ohne Zweifel trägt der Kriminalroman alle Merkmale eines blühenden Literaturzweiges zur Schau.' Bertolt Brecht, 'Über die Popularität des Kriminalromans (1939–40)', in Jochen Vogt (ed.), *Der Kriminalroman: Poetik – Theorie – Geschichte* (2nd edn; Munich: Fink Verlag, 1998), pp. 33–7 (p. 33). My translation.

[2] For example, Jan Costin Wagner's *Das Schweigen* (*Silence*) is available in translation, but Richard Hey's *Ein Mord am Lietzensee* (Murder at Lake Lietzen), is not as yet.

[3] This lack of academic engagement is explored in Volker Neuhaus, '"Zu alt, um nur zu spielen": Die Schwierigkeiten der Deutschen mit dem Kriminalroman', in Sandro M. Moraldo (ed.), *Mord als kreativer Prozess: Zum Kriminalroman der Gegenwart in Deutschland, Österreich und der Schweiz* (Heidelberg: Universitätsverlag Winter, 2005), pp. 9–19.

[4] 'Unterhaltungsliteratur' and 'Ernstliteratur'.

[5] See Nicola Barfoot, *Frauenkrimi/polar féminin: Generic Expectations and the Reception of Recent French and German Crime Novels by Women* (Frankfurt a. M.: Peter Lang, 2007), pp. 61–2.

[6] See Jochen Vogt's seminal 1971 edition of *Der Kriminalroman*, which also contains essays on crime fiction by Walter Benjamin, Bertolt Brecht and Siegfried Kracauer. Jochen Vogt (ed.), *Der Kriminalroman – Zur Theorie und Geschichte einer Gattung* (Munich: Wilhelm Fink Verlag, 1971), 2 vols.

[7] Studies often only analyse German-language authors in sections on post-1960s crime fiction. Neuhaus singles out Hans-Otto Hügel's study *Untersuchungsrichter, Diebsfänger, Detektive: Theorie und Geschichte der deutschen Detektiverzählung im 19. Jahrhundert* (Stuttgart: J. B. Metzler, 1978) as an exception to this rule. Neuhaus, '"Zu alt, um nur zu spielen"', p. 11.

[8] As late as 1997, Alf Meyer-Ebeling claimed that crime novels were banned in Nazi Germany. See Carsten Würmann, 'Zum Kriminalroman im Nationalsozialismus', in Bruno Franceschini and Carsten Würmann (eds), *Verbrechen als Passion. Neue Untersuchungen zum Kriminalgenre* (Berlin: Weidler, 2004), pp. 143–86 (p. 180).

[9] 'Die deutschsprachige Kriminalliteratur hat keine Tradition? Stimmt, aber sie könnte eine haben.' Advert for *Criminalbibliothek* (crime library) *1850–1933* in Michael Molsner, *Rote Messe* (Cologne: Edition Köln, 2008), p. 238. 'Edition Köln – der Verlag der (Krimi–) Geschichte schreibt.' Advert for *Kriminelle Sittengeschichte Deutschlands* (German History of Criminal Vices) *1957–1993*, in Emilie Heinrichs, *Leibrenten* (Cologne: Edition Köln, 2008), p. 412.

[10] Ulrike Götting is one of the first to explore 'crime fiction in German' in her study *Der deutsche Kriminalroman zwischen 1945 und 1970: Formen und Tendenzen* (Wetzlar: Kletsmeier, 1998), which examines West German, East German, Austrian and Swiss crime.

[11] Current population statistics are as follows: Germany, 80 million; Austria, 8.5 million; Switzerland, 8 million. The population of East Germany was 16 million in 1989. According to Almuth Heuner, Austria contributes 5 per cent and German-speaking Switzerland 3 per cent of all authors, books, publishers and readers to the German-language book market. Cited in Barry Forshaw, *Euro Noir: The Pocket Essential Guide to European Crime Fiction, Film and TV* (Harpenden: Pocket Essentials, 2014), p. 85.

[12] This volume views the German-speaking world as Germany, Austria, Switzerland and the former East Germany, and discusses former German colonies in Africa, such as Namibia. However, other countries where German is an official language, such as Liechtenstein, Belgium, Luxembourg and the province of South Tyrol (Italy), could equally be included.

[13] 'Der Kriminalroman erzählt die Geschichte eines Verbrechens, der Detektivroman die Geschichte der Aufklärung eines Verbrechens.' Richard Alewyn, 'Anatomie des Detektivromans', in Vogt (ed.), *Der Kriminalroman*, pp. 52–72 (p. 53).

[14] 'Die Kriminalgeschichte macht den Leser zuerst mit dem Täter, dann mit der Tat, zuletzt mit den Folgen der Tat bekannt; sie interessiert sich für die seelischen Vorgänge, die zu der Tat geführt haben . . . Umgekehrt die Detektivgeschichte. Sie beginnt mit dem Auffinden der Leiche, rekonstruiert die Tat aus Indizien und kommt am Ende dem Verbrecher auf die Spur; ihr Interesse gilt der geistigen Arbeit des Detektivs, so daß die Motive des Täters nur als Indizien oder zur Sicherung des juristischen Tatbestands in Betracht kommen.' Heinrich Henel, 'Der Indizienstil und die Haltung des Lesers', in Annette von Droste-Hülshoff, *Die Judenbuche. Mit Materialien*, ed. Helmuth Widhammer (Stuttgart: Klett, 1979), pp. 82–8 (p. 86).

[15] See, for example, Peter Nusser, *Der Kriminalroman* (3rd edn; Stuttgart: J. B. Metzler, 2003 [1980]), pp. 80–106.

[16] Nusser, *Der Kriminalroman*, pp. 93–8.

[17] Jürg Brönnimann, *Der Soziokriminalroman: ein neues Genre oder ein soziologisches Experiment? Eine Untersuchung des Soziokriminalromans anhand der Werke des schwedischen Autoren Sjöwall and Wahlöö und des deutschen Autors -ky* (Wupperthal: NordPark, 2004).

[18] Tom Zwaenepoel, *Dem guten Wahrheitsfinder auf dem Spur: Das populäre Krimigenre in der Literatur und im ZDF-Fernsehen* (Würzburg: Könighausen und Neumann, 2004), p. 35.

[19] Barfoot, *Frauenkrimi/polar féminin*, pp. 9–13.

[20] Zwaenepoel, *Dem guten Wahrheitsfinder auf dem Spur*, p. 114.

[21] Arlene Teraoka, 'Detecting Ethnicity: Jakob Arjouni and the Case of the Missing German Detective Novel', *The German Quarterly*, 72/3 (1999), 265–89.

[22] Barbara Korte and Sylvia Paletschek, 'Geschichte und Kriminalgeschichte(n): Texte, Kontexte, Zugänge', in Barbara Korte and Sylvia Paletschek (eds), *Geschichte im Krimi: Beitrage aus den Kulturwissenschaften* (Cologne/Weimar/Vienna: Böhlau, 2009), pp. 7–28.

[23] Eva Kushner and Milan V. Dimic, 'Introduction', in Eva Kushner and Milan V. Dimic (eds), *Acculturation* (Berlin: Peter Lang, 1994), pp. 1–3 (p. 3).

[24] Winfried Freund, *Die deutsche Kriminalnovelle von Schiller bis Hauptmann. Einzelanalysen unter sozialgeschichtlichen und didaktischen Aspekten* (Paderborn: Schöningh, 1975).

[25] Ailsa Wallace, 'Murder in the Weimar Republic: Prejudice, Politics and the Popular in the Socialist Crime Fiction of Hermynia Zur Mühlen', in Bruce B. Campbell, Alison Guenther-Pal and Vibeke Rützou Petersen (eds), *Detectives, Dystopias and Poplit: Studies in Modern Genre Fiction* (New York: Camden House, 2014), pp. 91–116 (p. 92).

[26] Hügel, *Untersuchungsrichter, Diebsfänger, Detektive.*

[27] Todd Herzog, 'Crime Stories: Criminal, Society, and the Modernist Case Study', *Representations*, 80 (2002), 34–61 (42).

[28] Herzog, 'Crime Stories', 56.

[29] Lang also directed the influential Dr Mabuse films, which trace the activities of a criminal mastermind: *Dr. Mabuse, der Spieler* (1922), *Das Testament des Dr. Mabuse* (1933) and *Die 1000 Augen des Dr. Mabuse* (1960).

[30] Horst Lange, 'Nazis vs. the Rule of Law: Allegory and Narrative Structure in Fritz Lang's *M*', *Monatshefte*, 101/2 (2009), 170–85 (174).

[31] Lang, 'Nazis vs. the Rule of Law', 180–5.

[32] See Götting, *Der deutsche Kriminalroman zwischen 1945 und 1970*, pp. 84–94.

[33] Anon., 'Erkaltete Herzen', *Der Spiegel*, 52 (1983), 115–17.

[34] Volker Weidermann, *Das Buch der verbrannten Bücher* (Cologne: Kiepenheuer & Witsch, 2008), pp. 96–8.

[35] Carsten Würmann, 'Volksgemeinschaft mit Verbrechen – zum Krimi im Dritten Reich', *Krimijahrbuch 2008* (Wupperthal: Nordpark Verlag, 2008), pp. 162–75 (p. 162).

[36] Würmann, 'Zum Kriminalroman im Nationalsozialismus', pp. 152 and 160–2.

[37] Carsten Würmann, 'Sternstunden für Mörder: Zur Auseinandersetzung mit der nationalsozialistischen Vergangenheit im Kriminalroman', *literaturkritik.de*, 9 (2005), *http://www.literaturkritik.de/public/rezension.php?rez_id=8525&ausgabe=200509* (accessed 31 July 2015).

[38] Würmann, 'Zum Kriminalroman im Nationalsozialismus', pp. 163–4.

[39] Würmann, 'Sternstunden für Mörder'.

[40] Würmann, 'Zum Kriminalroman im Nationalsozialismus', p. 173.

[41] Würmann, 'Zum Kriminalroman im Nationalsozialismus', p. 170.

[42] Würmann, 'Sternstunden für Mörder' and Irmtraud Götz von Olenhusen, 'Mord Verjährt nicht. Krimis als historische Quelle (1900–1945)', in Korte and Paletschek (eds), *Geschichte im Krimi*, pp. 105–26 (p. 125).

[43] 'Es ist das Blut. Das ist die Herkunft. Das schlechte Blut der Sippe.' Cited in Thosaeng Chaochuti, 'What Evil Looked Like: The Practice of Reading the Criminal Body in 19th and 20th Century Europe' (doctoral thesis, University of California, 2008), 123.

[44] See also Susan Tegel, *Jew Süss: Life, Legend, Fiction, Film* (London: Continuum, 2011).
[45] 'als Arzt am Volkskörper.' Würmann, 'Sternstunden für Mörder'.
[46] James Taylor and Warren Shaw, *Dictionary of the Third Reich* (London: Penguin, 1997), pp. 155–6.
[47] 'Der Roman soll nicht nur zeigen, wie effectiv die Ordungsmächte waren, sondern auch die ideologische Linie propagieren, dass "entartete" Menschen schnell und ohne jede Rücksicht ausgerottet werden müssten.' Götz von Olenhusen, 'Mord Verjährt nicht. Krimis als historische Quelle (1900–1945)', p. 126.
[48] The novel was based on articles Berthold wrote for the *Münchner Illustrierte* in 1957, which were also adapted for film (*Nachts, wenn der Teufel kam*, dir. Robert Siodmak, 1957).
[49] Götting, *Der deutsche Kriminalroman zwischen 1945 und 1970*, pp. 106–18.
[50] 'Diesmal ist der . . . Mörder zu spät dran. Andere, vom Staat bezahlte Mörder, sind ihm zuvorgekommen.' Cited in Götting, *Der deutsche Kriminalroman zwischen 1945 und 1970*, p. 116.
[51] Peter Kirschey, 'Das NS-Opfer von Köpenick', *neues deutschland*, 12 April 2014, *http://www.neues-deutschland.de/artikel/929909.das-ns-opfer-von-koepenick.html?sstr=Bruno%7CL%FCdke* (accessed 31 July 2015).
[52] Würmann, 'Zum Kriminalroman im Nationalsozialismus', p. 143.
[53] Barfoot, *Frauenkrimi/polar féminin*, p. 61 and the Bastei Luebbe website, *https://www.luebbe.de/bastei-entertainment/autoren/jerry-cotton/id_2667267* (accessed 31 July 2015).
[54] Lynn M. Kutch and Todd Herzog, 'Introduction', in Lynn M. Kutch and Todd Herzog (eds), *Tatort Germany: The Curious Case of German-language Crime Fiction* (New York: Camden House, 2014), pp. 1–19 (p. 5).
[55] Reinhard Hillich cited in Dorothea Germer, *Von Genossen und Gangstern: Zum Gesellschaftsbild in der Kriminaliteratur der DDR und Ostdeutschlands von 1974 bis 1994* (Essen: Verlag Die Blaue Eule, 1998), p. 39.
[56] Carol Anne Costabile-Heming, '"Der Fall Loest": A Case Study of Crime Stories and the Public Sphere in the GDR', in Kutch and Herzog (eds), *Tatort Germany*, pp. 139–54 (p. 140).
[57] Germer, *Von Genossen und Gangstern*, p. 39.
[58] Reinhard Hillich (ed.), *Tatbestand. Ansichten zur Kriminalliteratur der DDR 1947–1986* (Berlin: Akademie Verlag, 1989), p. 21.
[59] Germer, *Von Genossen und Gangstern*, p. 44.
[60] Brönnimann, *Der Soziokriminalroman*, p. 50.
[61] See Olaf Berwald, *An Introduction to the Works of Peter Weiss* (New York: Camden House, 2003), pp. 22–32.
[62] The imprint published 1,353 titles from 1962 to 2000, producing over 30 million copies. See *http://www.rowohlt.de* (accessed 31 July 2015).
[63] Brönnimann, *Der Soziokriminalroman*, p. 18. The Beck series was also published in the GDR, as its critique of capitalism dovetailed with East German views.
[64] Brönnimann, *Der Soziokriminalroman*, p. 50.
[65] Brönnimann, *Der Soziokriminalroman*, pp. 54–5.
[66] Brönnimann, *Der Soziokriminalroman*, pp. 55 and 50.
[67] 'Das Verbrechen sollte nicht als individuelle Tat betrachtet werden, sondern als direkte, negative Folge gesellschaftlicher Umstände', Brönnimann, *Der Soziokriminalroman* p. 50.
[68] Brönnimann, *Der Soziokriminalroman*, pp. 60–9.

[69] Barfoot, *Frauenkrimi/polar féminin*, pp. 70–1.
[70] See Achim Saupe, 'Der NS-Täter als Psychopath', in Achim Saupe, *Der Historiker als Detektiv – der Detektiv als Historiker. Historik, Kriminalistik und der Nationalsozialismus als Kriminalroman* (Bielefeld: Transcript, 2009), pp. 395–400.
[71] Robert C. Conard, *Understanding Heinrich Böll* (Columbia: University of South Carolina Press, 1992), p. 120.
[72] Julian Preece, *Baader-Meinhof and the Novel: Narratives of the Nation/Fantasies of the Revolution 1970–2010* (New York: Palgrave MacMillan, 2012), pp. 99–100.
[73] Germer, *Von Genossen und Gangstern*, p. 47.
[74] Germer, *Von Genossen und Gangstern*, p. 48.
[75] Germer, *Von Genossen und Gangstern*, p. 49.
[76] See Costabile-Heming, '"Der Fall Loest"'.
[77] Germer, *Von Genossen und Gangstern*, pp. 51–3.
[78] Germer, *Von Genossen und Gangstern*, p. 52.
[79] 'Kriminalliteratur wird . . . indirekt zur Chronistin des Niedergangs der DDR.' Ibid., p. 53.
[80] Mary Fulbrook, *History of Germany 1918–2000: The Divided Nation* (2nd edn; Oxford: Blackwell, 2002), p. 162.
[81] Leslie A. Adelson, *The Turkish Turn in Contemporary German Literature* (annotated edn; London: Palgrave Macmillan: 2005), p. 140.
[82] Tom Cheesman, *Novels of Turkish-German Settlement: Cosmopolite Fictions* (New York: Camden House, 2007), p. 84.
[83] Cheesman, *Novels of Turkish-German Settlement*, p. 157.
[84] See Teraoka, 'Detecting Ethnicity: Jakob Arjouni and the Case of the Missing German Detective Novel'.
[85] A film adaptation of *Happy Birthday, Türke!* was released in 1992 (dir. Doris Dörrie, EuroVideo, 2005).
[86] Cheesman, *Novels of Turkish-German Settlement*, pp. 88–9.
[87] Jim Jordan, 'Of Fables and Multiculturalism: The Felidae novels of Akif Pirinçci', in Arthur Williams, Stuart Parkes and Julian Preece (eds), *German-language Literature Today: International and Popular?* (Bern and Oxford: Peter Lang, 2000), pp. 255–68.
[88] Jordan, 'Of Fables and Multiculturalism', p. 226.
[89] Jordan, 'Of Fables and Multiculturalism', p. 263. An animated version of *Felidae* is available in German and English (dir. Michael Schaak, UFA, 2004).
[90] Wallace, 'Murder in the Weimar Republic: Prejudice, Politics and the Popular in the Socialist Crime Fiction of Hermynia Zur Mühlen', p. 93.
[91] Wallace, 'Murder in the Weimar Republic', p. 93.
[92] Brigitte Frizzoni, *Verhandlungen mit Mordsfrauen. Geschlechterpositionierungen im "Frauenkrimi"* (Zurich: Chronos Verlag, 2009), p. 10.
[93] Sascha Gerhards, 'Krimi Quo Vadis: Literary and Televised Trends in the German Crime Genre', in Kutch and Herzog (eds), *Tatort Germany*, pp. 41–60 (p. 56).
[94] 'dass Kölner Krimis für Münchener Krimi-Fans kaum noch attraktiv sind.' Ralf Koss, 'Spielart der Freiheit. Kurze Geschichte des neuen deutschen Kriminalromans', *Der Spiegel*, 10 (1995), *http://www.spiegel.de/spiegel/spiegelspecial/d-9259296.html* (accessed 31 July 2015).
[95] Christine Lehmann, 'Doch die Idylle trügt: Über Regionalkrimis', *Das Argument*, 278 (2008), 517–31 (517).
[96] Lehmann, 'Doch die Idylle trügt', 517 and 518.
[97] Lehmann, 'Doch die Idylle trügt', 526.

[98] 'wird im besseren Fall Teil einer Heimatfolklore, im schlechteren fällt er zurück in den Provizialismus.' Koss, 'Spielart der Freiheit. Kurze Geschichte des neuen deutschen Kriminalromans'.

[99] See Susanne C. Knittel, 'Case Histories: The Legacy of Nazi Euthanasia in Recent German *Heimatkrimis*', in Kutch and Herzog (eds), *Tatort Germany*, pp. 120–38.

[100] Their author website illustrates how local dialect and imagery can be exploited for publishing ends, while promoting tourism in the region: see *http://klufti.de/* (accessed 31 July 2015).

[101] Lynn M. Kutch and Todd Herzog, 'Introduction', in Kutch and Herzog (eds), *Tatort Germany*, p. 10.

[102] Tobias Gohlis, 'Murder and Manslaughter in Germany', *http://www.goethe.de/kue/lit/thm/en26884* (accessed 31 July 2015).

[103] See *http://www.new-books-in-german.com/english/home/-/273,273,129002,liste9.html* (accessed 31 July 2015). *New Books in German* promotes German-language literature to publishers and readers in the English-speaking world and frequently showcases crime fiction from Austria, Germany and Switzerland.

[104] 'Was mich fasziniert hat, war genau diese unglaublich seltene Mischung: ein ästhetisches Konzept, das konsequent E-Literatur bedeutet, kombiniert mit einem originellen Krimi-Konzept, das beste U-Literatur ist. Wenn so eine Kombination gelingt, haben wir es im Grunde mit einer eigenen Gattung zu tun: EU-Literatur.' Joachim Feldmann, 'Interview mit Simon Urban', *CULTurMAG*, 27 August 2011, *http://culturmag.de/rubriken/buecher/ein-gesprach-mit-dem-schriftsteller-simon-urban/32414* (accessed 31 July 2015).

[105] See Laurence Roth, *Inspecting Jews: American Jewish Detective Stories* (New Brunswick: Rutgers University Press, 2004).

[106] Anna-Dorothea Ludewig (ed.), *Im Anfang war der Mord: Juden und Judentum im Detektivroman* (Berlin: be.bra Verlag, 2012).

[107] Cheesman, *Novels of Turkish-German Settlement*, p. 92.

Select bibliography

Arjouni, Jakob, *Happy Birthday, Türke!* (Zurich: Diogenes, 1987 [1985]). *Happy Birthday, Turk!* (Harpenden: No Exit Press, 2005).

Berndorff, Hans Rudolf, *Shiva und die Galgenblume* (Berlin: Hillger, 1943).

Berthold, Will, *Nachts, wenn der Teufel kam: Roman nach Tatsachen* (Bad Wörishofen: Aktueller Buchverlag, 1959).

Bosetzky, Horst, *Einer von uns beiden* (Berlin: Rowohlt, 1972).

Costin Wagner, Jan, *Das Schweigen* (Frankfurt a. M.: Eichborn, 2007). *Silence*, trans. Anthea Bell (London: Vintage, 2011).

Hey, Richard, *Ein Mord am Lietzensee* (Munich: Piper, 1998 [1973]).

Hilsenrath, Edgar, *Der Nazi und der Friseur* (Munich: dtv, 2006 [1977]). *The Nazi and the Barber*, trans. Andrew White (Berlin: Barber Press, 2013).

Kästner, Erich, *Emil und die Detektive* (Hamburg: Dressler, 2010 [1929]). *Emil and the Detectives*, trans. Eileen Hall (London: Vintage Classics, 2012).

Lang, Fritz (dir.), *M – eine Stadt sucht einen Mörder* (StudioCanal, 2009 [1931]).

Lernet-Holenia, Alexander, *Ich war Jack Mortimer* (Munich: Droemer Knaur, 1985 [1933]).

Noll, Ingrid, *Die Apothekerin* (Zurich: Diogenes, 1996 [1994]). *The Pharmacist* (London: HarperCollins, 1995).

Ören, Aras, *Bitte nix Polizei: Kriminalerzählung* (Düsseldorf: Claassen, 1994 [1981]).
Pirinçci, Akif, *Felidae* (Munich: Goldmann, 1989). *Felidae. A Novel of Cats and Murder* (New York: Sage, 1993).
Rodrian, Irene, *Küsschen für den Totengräber* (Hamburg: Rowohlt, 1974).
Sanzara, Rahel, *Das verlorene Kind – Ein Krimi-Klassiker von Johanna Bleschke* (e-artnow, 2014 [1926]).
Süskind, Patrick, *Das Parfum – Die Geschichte eines Mörders* (Zurich: Diogenes, 1994 [1985]). *Perfume – The Story of a Murderer*, trans. John E. Woods (London: Penguin, 2010).
Turhan, Su, *Kommissar Pascha. Ein Fall für Zeki Demirbilek* (Munich: Knaur, 2013).
Walther, J. Monika, *Goldbroiler oder die Beschreibung einer Schlacht: Kriminalgeschichte* (Klagenfurt: Verlag Orange Cursor, 2013 [2009]).

Further secondary reading

See the annotated bibliography at the end of this volume.

2

The Emergence of Crime Fiction in German: an Early Maturity

MARY TANNERT

Two elements are necessary to the development of any crime fiction tradition: a narrative form that lends itself to the description and unravelling of a mystery, and social structures that support a search for causality and the exercise of inquiry and ratiocination. This chapter will concern itself with these two factors – narrative form and social developments – in the German-speaking countries of Europe from the late eighteenth century onward, and discuss how in combination they produced a unique crime fiction tradition. In particular, early German-language crime fiction authors distinguish themselves more through their understanding of class (as transferred to characters) and their narrative intent (the communication of particular social or political messages to the reader) than through sociocultural or national identity.[1]

Until recently, scholarship located the origins of German-language crime fiction primarily in the belles-lettres of Romanticism, in tales and novellas such as Heinrich von Kleist's *Der Zweikampf* (*The Duel*, 1811) or E. T. A. Hoffmann's *Das Fräulein von Scudéri* (*Mademoiselle de Scudéri*, 1819).[2] Although these works were never intended as detective stories according to the classic definition – a story in which the focus of the narration is the use of human ratiocination to solve a puzzle on the basis of physical evidence – the reader will nonetheless find incipient detective functions exercised in the aftermath of a mysterious event: questions are asked, witnesses are sought, theories are formed. What keeps these novellas from being fully fledged detective fiction is a preference for suprarational conclusions: the outcome of the story is not the result of these detective functions, but of what the characters understand to be fate, divine intervention or the triumph of virtue over evil.[3] For example, in Kleist's *Der Zweikampf*, the duel for which the novella is named is chosen as the preferred method of establishing the guilt or innocence of a key figure in a murder investigation. The assumption is that the winner of the duel has God on his side, and God's will matters more than physical evidence in determining guilt.

Also limited for our modern understanding of detective fiction are the early sensationalistic crime tales, such as the *Pitaval* stories of the eighteenth century, which conform most closely to what we now call the 'true crime' narrative: they describe a closed case in which all the 'facts' are known, assume that the person punished was truly guilty and concentrate on the relationship between criminal and crime.[4] Detection is irrelevant. These early works thus only offer waypoints for the development of the German-language detective story rather than being pure examples of ratiocinative literature. However, many western European detective fictions emerged from literary traditions that also produced Romantic or Gothic literature, and detective fiction from Poe to Gaboriau, Conan Doyle and all the way to P. D. James continues to make use of Romantic, Gothic and Poetic-Realistic elements of suspense, horror, criminal psychology, fate and the tradition of the tragic hero.

Yet a discussion of detective fiction's Romantic roots represents a purely literary-historical view of the genre's beginnings in German-speaking Europe. Just as important are the social conditions necessary for its development: ratiocinative stories require a social context in which the reasons for a course of action or an event are regarded as an acceptable object of human inquiry, and in which the physical evidence of what happens has meaning and value for our understanding of the action or event and for the outcome of its investigation. To our twentieth-century, western sensibility, this may seem self-evident, but in centuries or traditions in which events are understood to represent the will of God or the hand of fate, in which the interpretation of events and the definition of truth are the prerogative of absolutist rulers (religious or secular) rather than science or reason, questions about why things happen and a search for 'objective' evidence imply an undesirable dissatisfaction with the prescribed order of things and may be discouraged, if not actively opposed. In such a culture, generally the only public actions in the aftermath of a crime were the announcement and execution of the sentence on the person deemed guilty by the prevailing powers.

To make this exercise more palatable in capital cases such as murder, the condemned person's confession was often presented at the gallows to satisfy the crowd that justice had been served. As with the logic by which the suspect's guilt was established, it did not matter whether this confession was coerced, or involved no proof, or that the entire process of acquiring it ruled out anything that cast doubt on its conclusions. Thus for centuries in Europe, confession was the single most significant piece of judicial evidence, obtainable through torture where it was not offered freely. Any physical evidence was used primarily to confirm the guilt of the prime suspect and to prompt a confession sooner rather than later. In such a social context, there is little call for stories that describe a search for the truth of an event on objective grounds alone.

By the late eighteenth century, largely due to the influence of the Enlightenment, torture to obtain a confession had been reduced in western Europe to the most egregious cases, generally capital crimes.[5] By 1831 torture had been formally eradicated in all the German states.[6] Yet while this marked a turning point in judicial procedure, people's sensibilities did not change overnight: only gradually did physical evidence gain credibility over confession. As Hans-Otto Hügel notes, 'for the judge of the reformed inquisitorial process that was not preceded by torture, the confession as evidence did not lose its dominant role', continuing to be regarded as the most satisfactory resolution of a criminal investigation and as what Hügel calls 'the poetic restoration of the just order of things'.[7] Thus detective functions in a criminal investigation are observable from the early nineteenth century onward, but years pass before they are prominent enough to become the focus of a narrative tradition.

The judicial procedures that replaced the old scheme (prime suspect + confession = justice done) included both jury trials and the practice of 'ruling on the record' – that is, of a written decision by one or more judges handed down upon the basis of a written defence presented by a defence lawyer. The latter was more common early in the nineteenth century, as was the crime-solving role of the investigating magistrate, who combined the functions of police detective and district attorney in one. Both the custom of ruling on the record and the investigating magistrate are features of the work that most merits the claim of being the first German-language detective story – the novella *Der Kaliber* (*The Caliber*, 1828), written by the lawyer, journalist, dramatist and writer Adolph Müllner (1774–1829).

Detective fiction's historians tend to regard Edgar Allan Poe as the 'father' of the detective story for his 'Auguste Dupin' tales, but Müllner's *Der Kaliber* was published some thirteen years prior to *The Murders in the Rue Morgue* (1841). Similarly, Otto Ludwig's *Der Todte von St. -Annas Kapelle* (*The Dead Man of St. Anne's Chapel*, 1839) preceded Poe's story, if only by two years. These are only two examples of the phenomenon noted by Hügel – the early maturation of the German-language genre compared with the English-language genre.[8] Indeed, it is possible that the very variety of political entities that made up the German-speaking countries of Europe during the nineteenth and early twentieth centuries, accompanied by a profusion of legal and investigative structures, contributed to this rich and early growth. It is clear at any rate that claims to the 'parentage' of this literary genre must be revisited to reflect the contributions of all cultures with detective story traditions, not just France, England and America.

Der Kaliber offers the first fictional instance of the use of bullet calibre to determine a suspect's guilt or innocence. Yet lest the reader conclude that, having embraced the doctrine of physical evidence, Müllner rejected anything but rationality, this novella presents us with an utterly Romantic prime suspect – a man who, in a fit of madness, believes himself guilty of fratricide despite the evidence to the contrary, and is convinced that his defence lawyer's efforts to prove him innocent are the work of the devil. The structural vehicle in *Der Kaliber* is thus the tension between reason and passion, the conflict between Romantic extremes of emotion and the methodical course of criminal investigation. It owes much to Friedrich Schiller, whose Romantic robber-heroes and fate tragedies clearly influenced Müllner and are echoed in the scenes involving the prime suspect. Yet it bears equal witness to Müllner's own legal training in the rational, scientific exercise of jurisprudence by the lawyer for the defence, Dr Rebhahn.

The plot is quickly told: Heinrich Albus, accompanied by his younger brother Ferdinand, is taking a large sum of cash through the woods to another town. The two men begin to argue: Ferdinand, high-spirited and charming, wants an advance on his inheritance in order to marry his beloved Mariane, daughter of the merchant who employs them both. Heinrich, frugal and unfeeling, refuses the advance and suggests he may try, as elder of the two, to claim Mariane for himself. In a jealous rage, Ferdinand draws his pocket pistol. A shot rings out, and Heinrich dies.

At first Ferdinand's version of events (a bandit shot Heinrich) seems to vindicate him, but in the weeks that follow he is tortured by the notion that he might have been responsible for Heinrich's death: during their argument, he struck at Heinrich's arm with the pistol to prevent Heinrich drawing his sword cane. He cannot remembering the pistol firing, yet Heinrich is dead, and his death will enable Ferdinand, as Heinrich's heir, to realize his dreams of independence and marry Mariane – of whom he now feels unworthy. To Ferdinand, it ultimately does not matter whether he killed Heinrich. He wanted to, in his jealous rage, and that makes him guilty; a very Romantic notion, and one that precipitates the madness in which he believes himself a murderer.

Enter Dr Rebhahn, who is asked to prepare Ferdinand's defence and whose judicially trained mind immediately spots the dilemma: 'Magnificent case! A borderline between intent and chance, deed and accident, like the blade of a razor!'[9] Rebhahn's investigation results in the recovery of Ferdinand's double-barrelled pocket pistol, which the latter had thrown away in horror, and the discovery that both of its bullets are still chambered. Ergo, the bullet in Heinrich's body must be from a different weapon than Ferdinand's. Yet in his madness, Ferdinand will not accept this conclusion. What to do? The reader may guess that the only figure who can reconcile science with sentiment is Mariane, whose role as Ferdinand's beloved recalls the 'schöne Amazone' (beautiful Amazon) of Goethe's *Wilhelm Meisters Lehrjahre* (*Wilhelm Meister's Apprenticeship*, 1795). Mariane's impassioned appeal to Ferdinand – handily strengthened by the gallows confession of the forest bandit Curly, who overheard the two men arguing about money and decided to test the range of his new 'popgun' on them – saves the day and Ferdinand too.

In this novella, therefore, as much space is given to Romantic themes (the forest, fratricide, the inevitability of fate, the redemptive power of love) as to the judicial investigation undertaken by the narrator (the investigating magistrate) and the defence lawyer Dr Rebhahn, even if the investigation is an accurate and convincing example of early nineteenth-century jurisprudence that could certainly stand on its own. In *Der Kaliber*, sentiment and science both weigh large; science triumphs because sentiment accepts its primacy.

In the years that follow, developments in the practice of criminal investigation rapidly find their way into popular literature, as is evident in Otto Ludwig Emil Freiherr von Puttkammer's novella *Der Todte von St. -Annas Kapelle*, which was published in Leipzig under the author's pen name Otto Ludwig in 1839. The few known facts about Puttkammer (1802–75) include studies in law and philosophy and a career that culminated in the position of privy counsellor in Potsdam, which doubtless informed the course of events in this novella, an early example of the courtroom drama.

The story opens with an unidentified corpse. The first two paragraphs, which are given at the end of this chapter, resemble a police report in their painstaking description of the discovery and appearance of the body, and highlight the importance of physical clues for the course of the novella. The narration continues with a description of the work and evidence required to identify the victim, a young nobleman, then moves to the investigation of his death. Every step is shared with the reader, including witness statements about the physical evidence and the movements of people at and around the crime scene. The result of this phase of the investigation is the discovery that the dead man's estranged wife was involved in his death. She, however, refuses to speak, and there remains no other course but to arrest her and put her on trial. The second half of the novella thus recounts the trial, and here again, the physical evidence takes centre stage.

Unlike the narrator of *Der Kaliber*, whose personal attachment to the other primary figures in the novella drives his narrative, Puttkammer's third-person narrator maintains a distance from the course of events that lends the novella the quality of a journalistic investigation. This is particularly true of the trial. After several days of witness testimony and discussion of the evidence, the prosecution and the defence make their closing remarks to the jury. Just as the jury is withdrawing, a surprise witness interrupts proceedings with new information that vindicates the defendant – a device instantly recognizable to any fan of the American crime drama *Perry Mason* (CBS, 1957–66). The trial ends with the disclosure that the dead man had taken his own life to punish his estranged wife for rejecting him.

As Jacques Barzun said of the detective story, '[i]t is not enough that one of the characters in the story should be called a detective – nor is it necessary. What is required is that the main interest of the story should consist in finding out, from circumstances largely physical, the true order and meaning of events that have been part disclosed and part concealed'.[10] This definition is illustrated admirably by *Der Todte von St.-Annas Kapelle*. The novella is notable not just for the amount and variety of physical evidence it presents, but for the sophisticated treatment of that evidence, including uncertain witnesses, scientific examination and conflicting interpretations of the meaning of an object. The reader will not find a strong central detective figure, but the functions that a detective would exercise are fulfilled by all the characters in the novella – largely lawyers and judges – whose task it is to question witnesses and analyse the physical evidence. The story still has a faint echo of romanticism (e.g. in the victim's death, which is a variant on a *crime passionnel*, its setting and treatment, and the oath that binds the defendant), but this serves largely to add colour and to set the stage. The clear focus of the story is the ratiocinative investigation into the victim's death.

Two historical events affected the development of German crime fiction as the nineteenth century approached its mid-point. First, on 16 May 1830, the first criminal investigation department in a German police force was created in Berlin as the result of a royal order.[11] Secondly, the revolution of 1848, which saw the middle classes challenge the establishment with relatively liberal and pro-democratic ideals, led to the introduction of concepts that had an influence on criminal investigation and trials, such as the right to a public jury trial with oral proceedings and the replacement of the 'legal' theory of proof with the free weighing of evidence.[12] The latter developments also strengthened the role of the police, who took on ever more responsibility for criminal investigation as the judiciary focused on assessing evidence and preparing for trials.

The result is the parallel development from mid-century onward of three primary types of German-language crime stories involving public servants as investigators. The first, the investigating magistrate story (or *Richtergeschichte*, as Hügel calls it) remains popular, because this group of public servants continued to play a significant role in criminal investigation in rural areas (police officers who specialized in criminal investigation were initially the privilege of large cities, such as Berlin and Vienna).[13] *Richtergeschichten* necessarily focus on the way a lawyer or judge investigates a crime – that is, by using the resources of the judicial structure (forensic medicine and legal procedure, for example) rather than the feet of a dozen constables.

The master of the mid-nineteenth-century investigating magistrate story was indisputably J. D. H. Temme (1798–1881), who produced several dozen pieces of crime fiction over an eventful career as judge, politician, writer and newspaper editor. Temme was a political liberal whose early career culminated in a charge of high treason in the aftermath of the revolution of 1848. The episode resulted in his summary dismissal from public service and the loss of his pension. Temme and his family went into exile in Switzerland in 1851, where he lived and wrote prolifically for most of the rest of his life: in addition to more than three dozen detective stories, Temme produced a seventeen-volume description of true criminal cases, entitled *Criminal-Bibliothek. Merkwürdige Criminal-Prozesse aller Nationen* (Crime Library. Curious Criminal Cases from Around the World, 1867–74).

In Temme's novellas, the investigating magistrate (or judge or director of police: their functions are interchangeable) appears as an unnamed first-person narrator. This authorial habit and the fact that we never learn anything personal about them makes these figures blend into a single series detective, but one whose persona is in some sense a reflection of the author's own views:

> Temme endows his heroes with the traits of an ideal German civil servant, . . . [who has] a great sense of duty that considers the laws of the country and the citizen in equal degrees . . . Temme's magistrate stories draw their critical effect from the liberal attitude of the protagonist, the realistic and enlightened presentation of the problems attendant on the investigative process and an openly anti-reactionary political position.[14]

This phenomenon can be seen in Temme's novella *Wer war der Mörder?* (Who was the Murderer?, 1873) in which the narrator describes himself as the director of a police department. He receives a letter from a farmer whose son has been shot dead by the local forester, Gottfried Wolf, in the course of an argument about a load of wood. The forester was completely within his rights to shoot, since during the argument the farmer's son had brandished an axe. He explains:

> I shot him. I shot him down calmly, in cold blood. He did not want to obey me. He defied me. . . Official authority in the forest would have been at an end forever if I had yielded. . . I asked God in my heart for forgiveness if I was committing a sin . . . Then I shot him down.[15]

The horrified narrator regards Wolf's statement as 'the conviction and the truth of . . . quiet, cold, hairsplitting fanaticism that was capable of the greatest extremes', but is helpless to take any action against him.[16]

Shortly thereafter, the narrator is called to the deathbed of a local poacher who was imprisoned six years ago for a murder of which he has always maintained he is innocent. Before dying, he offers new information on the murder, and the story of that crime takes up the next major section in the novella. It tells of an apprentice forester who was in love with the beautiful daughter of his master, Marianne, and of the man who was then the old forester's hunter, one Gottfried Wolf. When the apprentice forester is found dead in the woods one night, the signs point to the poacher as the murderer, who was cutting up a deer nearby and would, if caught, have faced a long sentence for having poached it. Suspicion against him outweighs the curious circumstances suggesting he was not the killer, and he receives a life sentence. Weakened by shock, the old forester retires, and Gottfried Wolf takes the post of forester and Marianne, too, now that the young apprentice is dead. By marrying him, Marianne ensures that her father does not lose his home, but she is never happy again.

The reader may guess that Gottfried Wolf, driven by jealousy, murdered the apprentice for having won Marianne's affections. He had discovered a shortcut through the moors that would help him reach the site of the crime very quickly on foot, and by disguising himself that night in the cloak and cap of the old forester he ensured that anyone who saw him in the dark would not recognize him. In retrospect, Temme appears, at the beginning of the story, to be hinting at the identity of the murderer by drawing attention to Wolf's true nature in the scene in which Wolf shoots the farmer's son.

Typical for this type of story, the narrator uncovers the truth more by talking to people than by searching for physical evidence. His skill in assessing character, choosing the right conversational approach and drawing out confidences ensures his success, not his sharp eye for a thread hanging on a bush or the size of a footprint. The story is laced with his commentary on situations and people, often designed to make us think either well or ill of a person aside from his or her actions. This emphasis on character-oriented detection rather than evidence-based detection may reflect the narrator's social status as a person more likely to strike up conversation than to crouch in the dirt examining a clue.

Two further qualities should be noted with regard to Temme's *Richtergeschichten*. First, they reveal a certain simplicity compared with other crime fiction of the second half of the nineteenth century. As Hügel notes, Temme's narrators encounter the crime when its basic elements are already clear – in particular the nature of the crime and the identity of any suspects. The stories also generally take place in rural areas or towns where the social structures are more transparent to both reader and narrator.[17] Secondly, these novellas are realistic in their often unhappy outcomes – what Hügel calls the 'disintegration motif' that represents the destructive power of crime.[18] This quality can, on the one hand, be seen as a consequence of Temme's political convictions and personal experiences. On the other, it is possible that the genre had achieved enough stability that a socially uplifting conclusion was no longer necessary in order to avoid alienating readers. In *Wer war der Mörder?* the story ends with the scene in which Marianne, having just discovered that Wolf murdered her beloved six years ago, informs the narrator that he has taken his own life rather than be arrested for that murder. In some ways, this is the best possible outcome: it spares her the scandal of a husband in prison. Yet in every other respect her happiness has been destroyed by his lies and betrayal. As Temme concludes: 'Crime can only bring about unhappiness. Why, then, mostly for the innocent?'[19]

While the judiciary and the scope and nature of their powers in criminal investigations were familiar to readers, police detectives in nineteenth-century Germany had to grow into their work. In crime fiction, this made itself noticeable in the second and third types of crime stories involving public investigators (both police stories), which Hügel calls *Indagationsgeschichte* or 'the detectives on the trail of the criminal', and *Entdeckungsgeschichte* or 'the detectives on the trail of the crime'.[20] The *Indagationsgeschichte* concerns itself less with a hunt for or an assessment of physical evidence than with the coordinated efforts of the police to catch someone whose guilt is regarded as established. In this respect, it bears witness to the *Pitaval* tradition, which also focused on the criminal rather than the crime.

The *Entdeckungsgeschichte* is a story in which we follow a police detective whose work starts with the discovery of a crime. Everything is still open to interpretation: the detective must decide what is important, where to look, what constitutes a clue, whom to question. This forces him to leave the routine of police work behind, to adapt his methods, to experiment in his efforts to uncover the truth of a particular crime. His professional success is much more dependent on the outcome of his investigations than that of a police officer who works as part of a team in an *Indagationsgeschichte*. As Hügel notes, this led police detectives in *Entdeckungsgeschichten* to a keener awareness of the social character and ramifications of their work, as is manifest in the detective's reflections on his investigative methods and their suitability.[21]

A new tension and complexity in German-language detective stories arose as stereotypes about society's role models and wrongdoers began to break down. An investigating magistrate was an educated man from a social class high enough to ensure opened doors. In contrast, even if the upper echelons of most police forces were peopled with the educated or noble, at the bottom of the ladder were men from socially modest backgrounds who saw in the profession opportunities for advancement. The image of the criminal changed, too. In Romantic novellas and their successors, a criminal of social standing was often portrayed as mad or tyrannical to explain his predilection – as witness Ferdinand in *Der Kaliber* (when he was initially believed guilty) or the deranged nobleman in *Der Todte von St.-Annas Kapelle*. Gross criminality was considered a function of low birth – e.g. Curly in *Der Kaliber*. But as the century wore on, the evildoer was increasingly likely to be a functional and socially prominent member of society. German-language crime fiction of the mid- and late nineteenth century was thus predestined to explore the shape of justice in a classed society, in particular whenever a detective had to investigate someone of a higher social standing.

The works examined thus far have all been novellas – a fact largely due to the scope of the stories themselves and the popularity of the novella form during the nineteenth century. Much crime fiction of the time also debuted in popular literary newspapers such as *Die Gartenlaube* (The Garden House, 1853–1944), which reached an estimated peak readership of two to five million people owing to subscriptions for lending libraries and cafés. For such newspapers, short stories and novellas had the advantages of being a manageable length and having a compact narrative focus.

The second half of the nineteenth century, however, saw the rise of longer works of crime fiction: with the technological and social development of detection as an activity, a criminal investigation was able to claim the foreground of an entire novel. A good example is the detective novel *Der Sternkrug* (*The Star Tavern*), an *Entdeckungsgeschichte* with an undercover police detective published by Adolf Streckfuss (1823–95) in 1870. Like Temme, Streckfuss's original plans for a career in public service fell victim to his support of the 1848 revolution. However, his new life in Berlin as a tobacco dealer helped him rise to prominence in the city and gain the financial independence he needed to pursue his literary and civic activities, including writing a history of Berlin and serving on its city council from 1872 to 1884, when Berlin's population numbered several million.

Der Sternkrug has a rural setting – a tavern at a seven-point crossroads, or star, near the train station of Weidenhagen. The station and all the neighbouring towns are connected by lonely dirt roads that offer perfect opportunities for crime; not for nothing is the road between The Star Tavern and the town of Beutlingen known as the Thieves' Heath. Police Inspector Werder of M***, working undercover as Cornelius Steinert, a travelling wholesaler, has been sent to investigate the robbery and murder of a young landholder that took place there two weeks earlier – the latest in a string of similar crimes to plague the area over many years.

An omniscient narrator makes sure we miss none of Steinert's attempts to discover the truth. First, he wins the confidence of key figures and tempts them into telling him all the local gossip (one of the first scenes in the novel is the recounting of all the area's grisly murders by the Weidenhagen station restaurant's proprietor after having been plied by Steinert with several bottles of wine – a modus operandi Steinert uses repeatedly in the novel). Then he travels to the Thieves' Heath himself after dark, noting where an attack would be likely. Returning to the spot the next day, he searches the area for clues: he discovers and measures the footprints of two men in addition to those of his own coachman, finds the scene of the last murder cleverly disguised by a layer of pine needles, recovers threads of various kinds that have caught on the bushes, and tracks the two sets of footprints to their origins. One set of footprints and the threads lead Steinert to Mr von Heiwald, regarded by the rest of the citizenry as the killer. They believe he has only avoided arrest because he is noble. By the time Steinert discovers the truth, he has fallen hopelessly in love with von Heiwald's daughter, Ida. His detecting skills lead him to question his overhasty conclusion and identify the true killer, but in a move that presages E. C. Bentley's 1913 novel *Trent's Last Case*, Steinert gives up detecting at the end of the story in his horror at having nearly arrested the wrong man.

An interesting feature of the novel is its depiction of common social views of the police. In conversation with Steinert, the station restaurateur vents his anger that von Heiwald has not yet been arrested for the murders:

> When [the police] are dealing with a gentleman from a noble aristocratic family, and on top of that a good Conservative . . . then they put on kid gloves! The commissioner interrogated [von Heiwald and his brother] as they did everybody else, but as witnesses. In the end he got to be good pals with them.[22]

Here, the police appear to be irresolute, craven and easily swayed by a title. Several pages later, Ida von Heiwald offers her own view of the 'boys in blue'. When Steinert suggests, 'I beg you to confide in me only as much as you would confide in any policeman', she answers, 'then you would certainly hear very little from me, for I abhor the police, and even more those people who lower themselves to be police spies'.[23] Her dismissal of Steinert's protestations of the importance of undercover detection is absolute:

> Can you approve of it when spies in disguise sneak into the midst of a family, when they deceptively obtain trust by hypocritical protestations of friendship, only later to use a careless or jesting word or a confidential communication to ruin these unsuspecting unfortunate people?[24]

Beyond the irony that Ida's rhetorical question underscores the impossibility of Steinert's position, these two views reflect the social status of the speakers involved. The working-class station restaurateur is angered by what he regards as a different standard of justice for the upper classes than for the common man, the nobleman's daughter by what she sees as the unjust treatment of a reputable family despite its possibly harbouring a criminal. Such class and role dilemmas provide rich material for crime fiction in many cultures; that they are explored so substantively here is an indication of the stability that the German genre had reached by the time the novel was written.

Der Sternkrug can compare, investigatively and ratiocinatively, with any modern detective novel – and could pass, were it not for its style, as a piece of historical crime fiction written today. Nor was it alone in this regard: by the third quarter of that century, German-language detective fiction had reached an early maturity that was not to be England's or America's for another fifteen to twenty years. As Hügel notes,

> as important as the developments were that the detective story made in Germany after 1890, . . . between 1860 and 1880 it had already won its independence and [completed] its formal development. The breakthrough success that was Conan Doyle's after 1890 encountered in Germany a genre already existent in a variety of forms.[25]

Although early and mid-nineteenth-century detective fiction was largely the province of men, the end of the century saw a number of women establish themselves in the genre. Their work suggests that they saw in the detective figure possibilities for vicarious enjoyment of the freedom and adventure that bourgeois life then denied respectable women in Europe. In their hands, the detective story gained new dimensions. For example, not only did women make use of male detectives and all the settings common to them, they created female protagonists who helped them exploit the criminal potential of domesticity – its settings, routines and figures. Because the professions of police detective and investigating magistrate were confined to men, the figure of the amateur sleuth also took a developmental step forward with the rise of these female protagonists.

Among the women who were most active in the genre, Auguste Groner (1850–1929), Luise Westkirch (1853–1941) and Eufemia von Adlersfeld-Ballestrem (1854–1941) should be mentioned. Groner and Westkirch were both from middle-class families – Groner's father was a civil servant and Westkirch's a merchant – and both women began their professional lives as teachers. Adlersfeld-Ballestrem came from old Silesian nobility and likewise married a nobleman, a career military man whom she followed around Europe. Common to all three women was a love of literature and art that manifested itself in a gift for storytelling, the fruits of which included crime fiction but also encompassed romance novels, plays and juvenile literature, among other genres. All three were prolific, and both Adlersfeld-Ballestrem and Groner developed series detectives whose cases they chronicled in several works: Adlersfeld-Ballestrem's Dr Franz Xaver Windmüller appeared in eleven novels and a volume of tales (1907–36), and Groner's Joseph Müller, the first police detective in German-language crime fiction, appeared in fifteen novels and novellas (1890–1922).

This gift for storytelling had an additional effect: compared with their male contemporaries, these three women were less afraid of enriching their detective stories with elements of style and plot that were not traditional to crime fiction – a quality that lends their works a particular freshness and energy. Westkirch, for example, had a cinematographic narrative style and was gifted at capturing the atmosphere of outdoor settings – woods, moors, swamps – to conjure up mood and tension. Auguste Groner's writing stands out for her command of a remarkable variety of social classes and urban landscapes. One of her liveliest novels – *Warenhaus Groß und Komp.* (*Department Store Groß and Co.*, 1907) – borrows a department store in Vienna's *Mariahilferstrasse* for its setting: her protagonist, a young lady from an impoverished noble family who is desperate for work, obtains a position there as a *Probiermamsell* (she models the store's clothing for customers) and becomes the victim of a hate campaign. Groner's descriptions of the activities in big-city department stores at the turn of the twentieth century are part of the novel's appeal.

Detective fiction's historians have been unkind to the devices women employ when they write mystery fiction – the most familiar being the criticism levelled at the 'had I but known' school of suspense writing made so popular by American crime writer Mary Roberts Rinehart (1876–1958). These criticisms stem from a wish to rule out overly subjective, circumlocutive and conversational (read: feminine) ways of telling stories, but the popularity of Groner, Westkirch and Adlersfeld-Ballestrem in the German-speaking world during the years they wrote demonstrated that the detective story did not suffer by their 'unmasculine' approach to writing it.

The close of the nineteenth century and the early twentieth century saw the German crime fiction landscape respond to the international popularity of the Sherlock Holmes model, in part through parodies and pastiches of the Sherlock Holmes figure and stories.[26] Surely the most remarkable homage to Conan Doyle's achievement are the twenty-two *Detektiv Dagobert* (*Detective Dagobert*) novellas published between 1910 and 1912 by Balduin Groller (1848–1916; pseudonym of Adalbert Goldscheider), a newspaper editor and feature writer. Groller's detective, Dagobert Trostler, is a quintessentially Viennese answer to Sherlock Holmes and the novellas are largely a glimpse of high-society Viennese problems – compromising letters, cheating at cards, jewel theft, embezzlement and the like – and the justice of the wealthy and noble. Whereas Conan Doyle's narrative style was focused and austere, Groller's writing is arch, ironic, gossipy and full of scenes that gently mock detective story conventions. For example, in *Der große Schmuckdiebstahl* (*The Great Jewel Theft*), Dagobert is asked to explain the theft of a jewel box belonging to Violet Grumbach, the wife of his best friend, the industrialist and banker Andreas Grumbach. He quickly deduces that Andreas has stolen the box as a practical joke. Nonetheless, he plays along: he goes up to Violet's boudoir with the announced intention of making a search, but instead takes a nap on the divan. Then he makes Andreas and Violet wait twenty-four hours for the 'results' of his 'investigation' so that he can wager a dinner on the outcome. In stark contrast to Conan Doyle, Groller's stories convey the sense that life with a detective is charmed.

The adoption of the Holmes model by German-language crime writers illustrates how important it is to consider the cultural constraints under which crime fiction is produced. Like its English and American counterparts, German-language detective fiction was shaped by literary tradition, scientific and judicial progress and diversity of narrative approach, yet detective stories from the German and

Austro-Hungarian empires also focused on the nature of justice in a classed society and its effects on criminal investigation. For German and Austrian writers of the nineteenth and early twentieth centuries, the detective's very survival depended on his awareness of the way others – in particular those of socially superior standing – viewed his work. In Groller's hands, the detective is an independently wealthy, socially prominent bachelor – not just a mirror of *fin de siècle* Vienna but a figure to whom any door is open and who is beholden to no one. In contrast, Auguste Groner's detective Joseph Müller is a policeman with Holmesian skills but a working-class background, whose investigations of his 'betters' reflect the tightrope walk between the interests of justice and those of social survival. Both authors are reacting to life in a rigid social hierarchy – Groller by writing from the vantage point of unquestioned social privilege, Groner by constructing moral and ethical situations that challenge the reader to examine class prejudice.[27]

The most conservative views of crime fiction (Dorothy Leigh Sayers and Howard Haycraft spring to mind) rely traditionally on a twentieth-century, Anglo-American view of the appropriate structure and content of a detective story, but in so doing they ignore the realities of answers to crime in other centuries and cultures.[28] Criminal investigation involves not merely ratiocination applied to the physical evidence, but also a society's values with regard to justice and punishment. As a consequence, there is much to be learned from discovering the differences between Anglo-American values and those of the principalities that made up the German Empire during most of the nineteenth century, of the Germany unified under Bismarck in 1871, of the Weimar Republic and of the Austro-Hungarian Empire and the Austria that emerged from the First World War – especially since their modern counterparts, thanks to two world wars, are fundamentally different societies. Fortunately, the study of the crime fictions of other cultures is increasing in sophistication and today's readers and scholars can look forward to a more nuanced and insightful treatment of their contributions to the genre.

* * *

Extract from Otto Ludwig Emil Freiherr von Puttkammer's *The Dead Man of St. Anne's Chapel*

This extract is taken from the opening of the story.

In the early hours of August 26, 1816, a farmer from one of the outlying villages of the valley walked the narrow footpath to the chapel. His little son ran ahead of him. A short distance before the chapel, the little boy turned to his father breathlessly and tried, with confused and frightened shouts, to pull him forward. The astonished father hurried after his son, and his first glance, as he reached the open space in front of the chapel, fell upon a corpse. The lifeless body of a well-featured young man lay upon the steps of the little church, smeared with blood, half undressed, wearing only a shirt, long, light-coloured Nanking trousers,.and boots with spurs. On the right hand of the dead man, which lay upon the upper torso, there gleamed a heavy gold signet ring . . .

The corpse was inspected. Resuscitation was unthinkable; traces of beginning decomposition were already visible on the exposed body parts. Soon the experts discovered the cause of death. Under the dead man's shirt was a wide, brightly coloured silk bandage, apparently a fragment of a woman's shawl, carefully knotted around the torso. Under it, on the left side of the chest, lay a second cloth, wadded into a ball and glued firmly to the body by dried blood. This cloth covered a deep, broad stab wound. It had penetrated directly into the heart, as the autopsy shortly revealed, and had brought the unfortunate man a death as unavoidable as it was instantaneous. The nature of the wound indicated a long, double-bladed tool, probably a knife. Moreover, the dead man's stomach and intestines betrayed that he had died immediately after the enjoyment of a considerable amount of strong wine, perhaps even while drunk.

Otto Ludwig Emil Freiherr von Puttkammer, *The Dead Man of St. Anne's Chapel* (1839), trans. Mary W. Tannert and Henry Kratz, in Mary W. Tannert and Henry Kratz (eds), *Early German and Austrian Detective Fiction: An Anthology* (Jefferson: McFarland & Company, Inc., 1999), pp. 55–6.

Notes

[1] The nineteenth century saw dramatic geopolitical changes take place in German-speaking Europe. Unlike France and Britain, which were centralized nation states by 1800, the areas we now know as Austria and Germany were made up of a patchwork of states under the Habsburg *Kaiser* (emperor) within the *Heiliges Römisches Reich Deutscher Nation* (Holy Roman Empire of the German Nation). After a period of flux, 1868 saw the establishment of the Austro-Hungarian empire, and in 1871 the politically unified *Deutsches Reich* (German Realm) by Prussian Chancellor Otto von Bismarck. *Die Republik Österreich* (the Republic of Austria) and *die Weimarer Republik* (the German Weimar Republic) came into being in 1919 following the end of the First World War. Switzerland's development took a different course: *die Schweizerische Eidgenossenschaft* or Old Swiss Confederacy was established in 1291, with formal separation from the Holy Roman Empire in 1648, and the creation of a federal Swiss state in 1848.

[2] See Rainer Schönhaar, *Novelle und Kriminalschema: Ein Strukturmodell deutscher Erzählkunst um 1800* (Bad Homburg: Verlag Gehlen, 1969), Winfried Freund, *Die deutsche Kriminalnovelle von Schiller bis Hauptmann* (Paderborn: Schöningh, 1975) and Claus Reinert, *Das Unheimliche und die Detektivliteratur*, Abhandlungen zur Kunst-, Musik-, und Literaturwissenschaft 139 (Bonn: Bouvier, 1973).

[3] This is also the case with some novellas of Poetic Realism. Annette von Droste-Hülshoff's *Die Judenbuche* (*The Jew's Beech*; Cologne: Anaconda, 2006 [1842]), Theodor Fontane's *Unterm Birnbaum* (*Under the Pear Tree*; Cologne: Anaconda, 2011 [1885]) and Wilhelm Raabe's *Stopfkuchen* (*Stopfkuchen*; Munich: dtv, 2010 [1891]) are often regarded as examples of the German-language detective story of the mid- and late nineteenth centuries.

[4] François Gayot de Pitaval, *Causes célèbres et intéressantes*, 20 vols (Paris, 1734–43); Julius Eduard Hitzig and Willibald Alexis, *Der neue Pitaval* (Leipzig: Brockhaus, 1842–90). See chapter 4 for additional discussion of Pitaval and chapter 1 for a discussion of the 'true crime' tradition in relation to twentieth-century German-language crime fiction.

[5] For example, Milanese reformer Cesare Beccaria's 1764 treatise *On Crimes and Punishments*, which employed Enlightenment notions to argue against torture and the death penalty, was translated into a number of languages and widely disseminated throughout Europe.

[6] Anja Katarina Weilert, *Grundlagen und Grenzen des Folterverbotes in verschiedenen Rechtskreisen* (Berlin: Springer, 2008), p. 92.

[7] 'Für den richterlichen Inquisator des reformierten, d.h. ohne Folter vorgehenden Inquisitionsprozeß verlor das Geständnis als Beweismittel nicht seine dominierende Rolle'; 'die poetische Wiederherstellung der gerechten Weltordnung'. Hans-Otto Hügel, *Untersuchungsrichter, Diebsfänger, Detektive: Theorie und Geschichte der deutschen Detektiverzählung im 19. Jahrhundert* (Stuttgart: J. B. Metzler-Poeschel, 1978), pp. 93 and 92. Hügel's groundbreaking examination of the history of popular German crime fiction is still, more than thirty years after publication, one of the most exhaustive attempts to reconstruct the development of this genre in the German-speaking countries of Europe. The bibliographic references alone, offered as they are against the backdrop of Hügel's discussions, make this book an invaluable source of information for scholars of the German-language crime story. All translations are my own unless stated otherwise.

[8] Hügel, *Untersuchungsrichter, Diebsfänger, Detektive*, p. 174.

[9] '"Prächtiger Fall!" rief er aus. "Eine Grenzlinie zwischen Absicht und Zufall, That und Unfall, wie die Schneide eines Rasiermessers"'. Adolph Müllner, *Der Kaliber. Aus den Papieren eines Criminalbeamten* (Leipzig: Reclam, n.d. [1828]), p. 61. *The Caliber*, trans. Mary W. Tannert and Henry Kratz, in Mary W. Tannert and Henry Kratz (eds), *Early German and Austrian Detective Fiction: An Anthology* (Jefferson: McFarland & Company, 1999), pp. 9–53 (p. 38).

[10] Jacques Barzun, 'Detection and the Literary Art', in Francis M. Nevins (ed.), *The Mystery Writer's Art* (Bowling Green: Bowling Green U. Popular Press, 1970), p. 249.

[11] Hügel, *Untersuchungsrichter, Diebsfänger, Detektive*, p. 129.

[12] Hügel, *Untersuchungsrichter, Diebsfänger, Detektive*, p. 138. The 1848 revolution failed due to the revolutionaries' lack of unity, allowing the ruling classes to reassert control very quickly. A number of liberals were forced into exile as a result.

[13] Hügel, *Untersuchungsrichter, Diebsfänger, Detektive*, p. 149.

[14] 'Temme versieht seinen Helden mit den Zügen eines idealen deutschen Beamten. Der Richter ist gekennzeichnet durch ein hohes Pflichtbewußtsein, das gleichermaßen die Rechte des Staates und der Bürger berücksichtigt . . . Durch die liberale Haltung der Hauptfigur, die realistische, aufklärende Darstellung der Probleme des Ermittlungsprozesses und die offen antireaktionäre politische Stellungnahme gewinnt die Richtergeschichte Temmes eine kritische Wirkung'. Hügel, *Untersuchungsrichter, Diebsfänger, Detektive*, p. 160.

[15] 'Ich habe ihn erschossen. Ich habe ihn mit ruhigem, kaltem Blute niedergeschossen. Er wollte mir nicht gehorchen. Er widersetzte sich mir . . . Es wäre für immer mit der amtlichen Autorität in dem Forst vorbei gewesen, wenn ich nachgegeben hätte . . . Ich bat Gott in meinem Herzen um Verzeihung, wenn ich eine Sünde dadurch beginge . . . Dann schoß ich ihn nieder.' Jodokus D. H. Temme, *Wer war der Mörder? Kriminalgeschichten* (Bielefeld: Pendragon Verlag, 2010), pp. 143–80 (p. 149). My translation.

[16] 'Es war die Überzeugung und die Wahrheit des furchtbarsten Fanatismus, des still und kalt und spitzfindig Grübelnden und dann zum Äußersten Fähigen.' Temme, *Wer war der Mörder?*, p. 149. My translation.

[17] Hügel, *Untersuchungsrichter, Diebsfänger, Detektive*, p. 160.

[18] 'Das Desintegrationsmotiv'. Hügel, *Untersuchungsrichter, Diebsfänger, Detektive*, p. 161.

[19] 'Das Verbrechen kann nur Unglück gebären. Warum am meisten für den Unschuldigen?' Temme, *Wer war der Mörder?*, p. 180. My translation. For further discussion of Temme's works, see chapter 4.

[20] 'Die "Indagations"-Geschichte: die Detektive auf der Spur des Verbrechers'; 'Die Entdeckungsgeschichte: die Detektive auf der Spur des Verbrechens'. Hügel, *Untersuchungsrichter, Diebsfänger, Detektive*, pp. 144 and 145.

[21] Hügel, *Untersuchungsrichter, Diebsfänger, Detektive*, p. 147.

[22] 'aber bei einem Herrn aus einer vornehmen adelichen Familie und noch dazu bei einem guten Konservativen, der seiner patriotischen Verdienste wegen einen Piepvogel in Knopfloch bekommen hat, da zieht man Glacéhandschuhe an! Der Herr Polizeirath hat die beiden Herren Brüder Heiwald vernommen, wie alle andern Menschenkinder; aber als Zeugen. Er ist endlich mit ihnen ein Herz und eine Seele geworden'. Carl Adolph Streckfuss, *Der Sternkrug. Criminal-Novelle* (Berlin: Brigl, 1870), p. 19. *The Star Tavern*, in Tannert and Kratz (eds), *Early German and Austrian Detective Fiction: An Anthology*, pp. 119–89 (p. 127).

[23] 'Ich sage nicht, daß ich einer bin, aber ich bitte Sie, mir nur soviel Vertrauen zu schenken, als Sie eben jedem Polizisten schenken würden'; 'Da würden Sie freilich wenig von mir hören, denn ich verabscheue die Polizei und noch mehr die Menschen, welche sich dazu herabwürdigen, Polizeispione zu werden'. Streckfuss, *Der Sternkrug*, p. 89. *The Star Tavern*, in Tannert and Kratz (eds), *Early German and Austrian Detective Fiction: An Anthology*, p. 159.

[24] 'Sie sind ein warmer Vertheidiger der Polizei; aber können Sie es billigen, wenn die Spione in Verkleidungen sich in das Innere der Familie einschleichen, wenn sie sich durch heuchlerische Freundschaft Vertrauen erschwindeln, um dann später ein vielleicht hingeworfenes, unbeachtetes Wort oder eine vertrauliche Mitteilung zum Verderben der nichts ahnenden Unglücklichen zu benutzen?' Streckfuss, *Der Sternkrug*, p. 90. *The Star Tavern*, in Tannert and Kratz (eds), *Early German and Austrian Detective Fiction: An Anthology*, p. 160.

[25] 'So wichtig die Entwicklungen auch waren, die die Detektiverzählung nach dem neunten Jahrzehnt des vorigen Jahrhunderts in Deutschland noch machte . . . hatte die Detektiverzählung zwischen 1860 und 1880 ihre Eigenständigkeit und die Ausbildung ihrer Form gewonnen. Der durchschlagende, seit 1890 eintretende Erfolg Conan Doyles traf in Deutschland auf eine in vielfacher Ausprägung schon bestehende Gattung'. Hügel, *Untersuchungsrichter, Diebsfänger, Detektive*, p. 174.

[26] The Holmes model was probably the single greatest foreign influence on European crime fiction of the turn of the century. Beyond the appeal of the Holmes-Watson duo, its popularity was partly to do with the mode of publication (short stories can be translated quickly and published easily in literary magazines abroad) and partly due to the sheer volume of stories.

[27] There were English translations of a few German-language stories, notably Grace Isabel Colbron's translations of some Groner novellas and novels, but the scope of their readership is unknown. There appears to have been no substantive German influence on the Anglo-American genre at this stage.

[28] See Dorothy L. Sayers, 'Introduction', in Dorothy L. Sayers (ed.), *The Omnibus of Crime* (New York: Harcourt Brace, 1929), pp. 9–38.

Select bibliography

Groller, Balduin, *Der Kasseneinbruch, Detektiv Dagoberts Taten und Abenteuer. Ein Novellen-Zyklus*, vol. 3 (Leipzig: Reclam, 1909). *The Vault Break-In*, trans. Mary W. Tannert and Henry Kratz, in Mary W. Tannert and Henry Kratz (eds), *Early German and Austrian Detective Fiction: An Anthology* (Jefferson: McFarland & Company, 1999), pp. 228–42.

Groner, Auguste, *Zwei Kriminalnovellen: Der Neunundsiebzigste. Die goldene Kugel* (Leipzig: Reclam, 1893). *The Golden Bullet*, trans. Mary W. Tannert and Henry Kratz, in Tannert and Kratz (eds), *Early German and Austrian Detective Fiction: An Anthology*, pp. 190–216.

——, *The Chronicles of Joe Müller, Detective*, trans. unnamed (Ignacio Hills Press Ebook, 2009).

——, *Warenhaus Groß & Komp* (Hamburg: Tredition, 2012).

Müllner, Adolph, *Der Kaliber. Aus den Papieren eines Criminalbeamten* (Leipzig: Reclam, n.d. [1828]). *The Caliber*, trans. Mary W. Tannert and Henry Kratz, in Tannert and Kratz (eds), *Early German and Austrian Detective Fiction: An Anthology*, pp. 10–53.

Puttkammer, Otto Ludwig Emil Freiherr von, *Der Todte von St. -Annas Kapelle. Ein Criminalfall* (Leipzig: Brockhaus Verlag, 1839), pp. 289–422. *The Dead Man of St. Anne's Chapel*, trans. Mary W. Tannert and Henry Kratz, in Tannert and Kratz (eds), *Early German and Austrian Detective Fiction: An Anthology*, pp. 55–117.

Streckfuss, Carl Adolph, *Der Sternkrug. Criminal-Novelle* (Berlin: Brigl, 1870). *The Star Tavern*, trans. Mary W. Tannert and Henry Kratz, in Tannert and Kratz (eds), *Early German and Austrian Detective Fiction: An Anthology*, pp. 119–89.

Temme, Jodokus D. H., *Wer war der Mörder? Kriminalgeschichten* (Bielefeld: Pendragon Verlag, 2010), pp. 143–80.

Westkirch, Luise, *Der Todfeind* (Dresen: Max Seyfert, 1912).

Further secondary reading

Barzun, Jacques, 'Detection and the Literary Art', in Francis M. Nevins (ed.), *The Mystery Writer's Art* (Bowling Green: Bowling Green U. Popular Press, 1970), pp. 248–62.

Colbron, Grace Isabel, 'The Detective Story in Germany and Scandinavia', *The Bookman*, 30 (September 1909–February 1910), 407–12.

Freund, Winfried, *Die deutsche Kriminalnovelle von Schiller bis Hauptmann* (Paderborn: Schöningh, 1975).

Hügel, Hans-Otto, *Untersuchungsrichter, Diebsfänger, Detektive: Theorie und Geschichte der deutschen Detektiverzählung im 19. Jahrhundert* (Stuttgart: J. B. Metzler-Poeschel, 1978).

Liang, Hsi-Huey, *The Rise of Modern Police and the European State System from Metternich to the Second World War* (Cambridge: Cambridge University Press, 1992).

Reinert, Claus, *Das Unheimliche und die Detektivliteratur*, Abhandlungen zur Kunst-, Musik-, und Literaturwissenschaft 139 (Bonn: Bouvier, 1973).

Sayers, Dorothy L., 'Introduction', in Dorothy L. Sayers (ed.), *The Omnibus of Crime* (New York: Harcourt Brace, 1929), pp. 9–38.

Schönhaar, Rainer, *Novelle und Kriminalschema: Ein Strukturmodell deutscher Erzählkunst um 1800* (Bad Homburg: Verlag Gehlen, 1969).

Skreb, Zdenko, 'Die neue Gattung: Zur Geschichte und Poetik des Detektivromans', in Viktor Zmegac (ed.), *Der wohltemperierte Mord. Zur Theorie und Geschichte des Detektivromans* (Frankfurt a. M.: Athenäum, 1971), pp. 35–96.

Spencer, Elaine Glovka, *Police and the Social Order in German Cities. The Düsseldorf District 1848–1914* (DeKalb: Northern Illinois University Press, 1992).

3

Austrian Crime Fiction: Experimentation, Critical Memory and Humour[1]

MARIEKE KRAJENBRINK

In recent decades, crime fiction in Austria has flourished in a variety of different forms. Like elsewhere in the German-speaking world, the genre has seen a veritable boom in Austria, where we find a lively crime fiction scene with festivals, readings and events, such as the annual *Wiener Kriminacht* (Viennese Crime Night) since 2002. Austrian crime authors have their own organization, the *AIEP Austria*, and have been strongly represented among awards such as the Friedrich Glauser Prize and the *Deutsche Krimipreis*.[2] Indeed, the introduction to a special issue on the Austrian crime novel in *Literatur und Kritik* in 2007 tells us that 'for a good twenty years, every second novel written in Austria has been a crime novel, either a real one, or one that somehow pretends to be'.[3] This is an interesting comment for two reasons: first, it indicates the sheer volume of contemporary production; secondly, it points to an openness of the genre and an increasing crossover between crime fiction and other forms of literature. Prominent literary authors such as Peter Handke, Gerhard Roth and Elfriede Jelinek have exploited the genre in highly sophisticated ways, whereas conversely, authors such as Wolf Haas and Heinrich Steinfest, who initially made their names in crime fiction, have more recently written novels that fall outside that category. One of the most interesting features of Austrian crime fiction is that we find so many subversive and/or playful variations: as Beatrix Kramlovsky puts it, 'the rules of the genre are often ambitiously broken, varied or satirized'.[4]

Given the huge growth and diversity of crime writing in Austria since the 1980s and particularly the 1990s, it is not possible for this chapter to provide a completely comprehensive survey. Instead, it will highlight some key characteristics and trends, and discuss works by representative authors. In order to gain a more sophisticated understanding of the crime genre in Austria, the chapter will focus in particular on the formal experimentation by early authors who would not consider themselves crime authors *per se*, before considering examples of more recent writers whose work increasingly defies categorization as either popular or highbrow literature.[5]

What, then, are the distinctive characteristics of Austrian crime fiction? Features include a marked sensibility for language, reflecting on its regional diversity, its ability to shape our perceptions and its representational limitations – in keeping with Austrian literature and traditions of language philosophy exemplified by

Ludwig Wittgenstein, Karl Kraus and Hugo von Hofmannsthal. These elements can manifest themselves in very different ways, for instance in the use of Viennese and other dialects, in a critical exposure of underlying but often unreflected ideological values carried by language, and in the 'joy of playing with language, using all the shades of ambiguity it offers'.[6] A further feature that feeds into crime fiction from the Viennese tradition of cabaret and satire is an ironic, subversive humour with touches of the surreal and a very specific quirkiness. The way in which one internet site markets Austrian crime fiction demonstrates how distinctive these elements are: 'New Austrian crime novels – off the wall and black as night. The wittiest and most outrageous crime novels are set in Austria.'[7]

Another key feature, more directly related to the crime genre and its critical potential for exploring social and political problems, is an intense engagement with Austrian society. Austrian crime fiction critically explores what otherwise remains hidden beneath tourist industry images that mask less palatable issues of right-wing populist radicalism and the legacy of Austria's role during the National Socialist era. The frequent use of such surface-subterranean tropes manifests itself in the exploitation of iconic settings, which allow both a digging up of the past and an exposing of the violence and neuroses lurking beneath the rural Alpine idyll and Vienna's splendorous charm. These tropes are visible in the work of authors such as Doron Rabinovici, whose novel *Suche nach M.* (*The Search for M*, 1997) draws on elements of crime fiction in an exploration of the continued impact of the Holocaust, and in historical crime novels, which have become increasingly popular in the last decade.[8] Writers such as Susanne Ayoub, Bettina Balàka and Andreas Pittler (see also chapter 7) combine an investigation of often contentious aspects of the twentieth-century past with critical societal commentary that sometimes ventures into the realms of memory studies. Unsurprisingly, psychology and psychoanalysis – of course born in Vienna – also form an important strand in Austrian crime fiction which, through the works of writers such as Edith Kneifl and Paulus Hochgatterer, interprets the surface-subterranean trope in challenging and nuanced ways. We will return to this topic when we explore Hochgatterer's work in more detail later.

Since the 1990s, the use of locale has become increasingly important in a number of crime novels and series. A frequent setting is the province, as seen in Alfred Komarek's popular series featuring the laid-back police inspector Polt (1998–), which explores regional identities within the framework of the *Weinviertel*, the famous wine-growing region north-east of Vienna or, more recently, in Claudia Rossbacher's 'Sandra Mohr' novels set in Styria (2011–). Manfred Wieninger's more politically engaged series features 'discount P. I.' Marek Miert in the dreary fictional town of Harland in the east of the country (1999–), while Kurt Lanthaler explores language and identity through his amateur detective, the truck driver Tschonnie Tschenett, who operates in the border area between Austria and Italian South Tyrol, with some dialogue also in Italian (1993–2002). In contrast, Vienna provides the setting for Stefan Slupetzky's Lemming, a former police detective turned private investigator, in a series that strongly references the historical background of many of the city's sites (2004–9). Bernhard Salomon sets his two novels with young reporter-investigator Albin Fischer among the iconic coffee-houses of Vienna and explores cross-border criminality between Austria and the nearby Czech Republic. The author literally explodes the myths associated with key tourist attractions when one of the coffee-houses is blown up in *Der zweite Mann* (The Second Man, 2006). We see a different side of Vienna in Ernst Hinterberger's detective Trautmann series, set in less privileged working-class areas and focusing on social critique (1998–2012). The contrast between Vienna's wealthy villas and the city's seedy underbelly, with excursions into the academic world, is explored in Martin Mucha's gritty series featuring philosopher P. I. Arno Linder, which draws on the tradition of hard-boiled crime fiction (2010–). Vienna is also the basis for Eva Rossmann's highly successful series, which brings together journalist and amateur detective Mira Valensky and Bosnian cleaning lady Vesna Krajner in an interesting variation of the Holmes-Watson constellation (1999–).

Strong female voices come to the fore not only in Rossmann's series, but also in Lisa Lercher's 'Mona and Anna' series (2001–) and in the novels of Amaryllis Sommerer. Indeed, women writers have long had a strong presence in Austrian crime fiction, as illustrated by the pioneering author Auguste Groner (1850–1929), who created the first police detective series in German-language crime fiction (see chapter 2). More recent contributions have included *Die Giftmörderinnen* (The Poison Murderesses, 1991) by the highly literary Elfriede Czurda, *Zwischen zwei Nächten* (Between Two Nights, 1991), which led Edith Kneifl to become the first Austrian and first female author to win the Glauser Prize in 1992, and *Weiße sterben selten in Samyana* (Whites Seldom Die in Samyana, 1986), by Christine Grän, the opening novel of a successful series featuring feisty gossip journalist and amateur detective Anna Marx.[9]

As Grän's novels show, popular crime fiction has at times adopted a light-hearted approach. As early as 1976, the highly successful TV series *Kottan ermittelt* (Kottan Investigates, 1976–84, ORF) presented a model that was to strongly influence crime writers in Austria. This cult series by Helmut Zenker and Peter Patzak is a satirical parody of police procedurals, in which crime plots and their resolution take a back seat to the slapstick and often surreal misadventures of the Viennese police protagonists. The police officers are portrayed as anti-heroes and figures of ridicule, which gives the series, without being overtly political, a markedly anti-deferential and anarchic flavour.[10] More recently, writers such as Wolf Haas, Thomas Raab and Heinrich Steinfest have adopted an equally playful approach to the genre, whilst authors such as Kurt Palm and Günter Brödl take the parodic mode to new heights, not least in their portrayal of Austria as a domestic tourist destination and of Austrians on holiday abroad.[11]

Literary experimentation with the crime genre: Handke, Roth, Lebert and Jelinek

Since the 1960s, a number of writers stand out for their experimentation with and development of the genre. As such, they are worthy of more individual exploration. This section examines how established literary authors deconstruct the crime novel formula and its underlying ideological and epistemological premises, or exploit the genre as a tool to set a plot in motion and thus give the narrative a certain framework, without restraining it with rigid conventions of closure. In such examples, the murder case and its resolution no longer take centre stage, but merely provide a basic structure in which anything can and does become possible. This ultimately leads to the dissolving of the genre and the creation of playful and subversive variations and transformations.

The turn towards formalist literary experimentation in the late 1960s and early 1970s finds expression in the early work of Peter Handke and Gerhard Roth. Neither author would see himself as crime writer nor would they be seen as such, but they are nonetheless important for the development of the genre in Austria. Both were members of the *Grazer Gruppe*, a loose association of authors that experimented with popular forms, such as the western, fantasy/horror, romance and the crime novel. The first work of Handke's to draw on the crime genre is *Der Hausierer* (The Peddler, 1967). This book is composed of two alternating sections, the first of which is presented as a formal analysis of the conventions of the crime genre in terms of a teleological dynamics of disruption and restoring of order, while the second part is composed of sentences typically found in crime novels – including quotations from Hammett and Chandler – but which do not form a recognizable plot. Similarly, Gerhard Roth's first experimentation with the genre, the English-titled *How to be a detective* (1972), defamiliarizes the model, presenting a highly fragmentary and decentred narrative. While this text contains many scenes typical of conventional crime narratives, its absurdist twists and turns, its chaotic structure and the increasing indeterminacy of the roles of detective, perpetrator and victim mean that conventional reading strategies are frustrated. In both cases, reading means looking for clues and coherence in a labyrinthine text that both foregrounds and frustrates the detection/construction of meaning.

Both authors continued to work with the genre in a way that was more recognizable, as shown by Handke's more conventionally suspenseful novel *Der kurze Brief zum langen Abschied* (*Short Letter, Long Farewell*, 1972), which echoes Raymond Chandler's *The Long Goodbye* (1953) and is set in the United States. Roth's *Der große Horizont* (The Big Horizon, 1974) and *Ein neuer Morgen* (A New Morning, 1976) explore fundamental questions about how we make sense of the world in a more coherent narrative framework, with frequent allusions to Chandler. We even find characters who identify completely with Philip Marlowe, believing themselves to be protagonists in American crime investigations; their entire interpretation of experience is predicated on an acceptance of the reality of this fictional model. Although not intended as crime novels, these narratives depend on an understanding of genre conventions if the reader is to appreciate the author's novelistic ambition. Crime elements serve to create a sense of fear and (paranoid) suspicion, a heightened perception in which every detail becomes a potential clue, without a closing elucidation being offered, thus pointing to a radical doubt of finding an objective truth.

Handke's last engagement with the genre was *Die Stunde der wahren Empfindung* (*A Moment of True Feeling*, 1975), which is set in Paris.[12] The basic impulse of what makes crime fiction so interesting for Handke is related to his concern with perception: the premise that things are not quite as they seem.[13] This is similar for Roth, who continued to develop his work with the crime genre, turning his attention to his native Austria. In Roth's case, however, there is a clear allegation that the authorities are deliberately concealing the truth, and his later writing in the cycle *Die Archive des Schweigens* (The Archives of Silence, 1980–91), influenced by Freud and Foucault, is increasingly concerned with uncovering what is hidden, particularly in relation to National Socialism. Roth's obsession with Austria's historical amnesia has made him an 'an investigator or a detective', set on revealing truths that the country preferred to ignore in the time he grew up.[14] For example, *Der See* (*The Lake*, 1995) explores the tensions of a father-son relationship to address questions of Austrian identity and its silenced past against the background of the disturbing rise in popularity of Jörg Haider's Freedom Party.[15]

Roth's work contains a strong critique of the patriarchal order, of ingrained injustices in every aspect of the criminal justice system and an interrogation of society itself, elements that are also key concerns of Nobel prize-winning author Elfriede Jelinek. Like Roth and Handke, Jelinek exploits the crime genre, combining the *Anti-Heimatroman* (anti-homeland novel) with the anti-detective novel. However, before turning our attention to this key author, it is useful to consider the work of Hans Lebert, which had a profound influence on Jelinek.

Lebert's novel *Die Wolfshaut* (Wolf's Skin, 1960) takes a hybrid form, which the author describes as 'a religious novel, hidden behind a ghost story, which is again hidden behind a rural crime story'.[16] Arguably, Lebert can be considered one of the originators of the *Anti-Heimatroman*, which has been of enormous importance in the development of Austrian literature since the 1960s. Where the traditional *Heimatroman* promotes a conservative vision of rural society and a reassuring sense of (patriarchal) order, the *Anti-Heimatroman* questions and undermines the premises of the original model, which had become tainted by its association with right-wing political ideology in the 1930s and 1940s. *Die Wolfshaut* also draws upon elements of the crime genre: there is a mystery to be investigated and the truth is brought to light, but justice is not achieved. Set in the early 1950s in a remote mountain village aptly named 'Schweigen' ('keeping silent' or 'silence'), this novel revolves around the dark secret of the murder of six foreign workers in the last days of the Second World War. One protagonist returns to the village in an attempt to find out why his father, who was forced to participate in the massacre, committed suicide. Assisted by another outsider, his investigations gradually uncover the truth in an atmosphere of brooding hostility. However, the main culprit, former Nazi Habergeier, now a member of the provincial parliament, remains unpunished. The reason why this novel has been so influential, and not just for Jelinek, is because it is one of the first novels to critically address the historical amnesia and the mechanisms of collective suppression of the Nazi past in Austria. Ultimately *Die Wolfshaut*, in frustrating expectations of a harmonious resolution typical of both the *Heimatroman* and the crime novel, reveals the dark side of the Alpine idyll and its attendant conservative-patriarchal values. There is profound cynicism about the possibility of justice and an indictment of the collective failure to face up to responsibility for Nazi crimes.

In many ways the novel was ahead of its time and the consolidation of its position as a seminal *Anti-Heimatroman* only really came with its successful re-publication in 1991, at a time in which – in the wake of the Kurt Waldheim affair – there was a greater public interest in the critical investigation of Austria's role in National Socialism. Jelinek calls Lebert's *Wolfshaut* one of the most important reading experiences of her life.[17]

An avid reader of crime fiction since her early youth, Jelinek is profoundly familiar with the genre, both in German and in English. In the early 1970s, she reviewed crime novels for the *Berliner Rundfunk*, and later for the Viennese magazine *Extrablatt*.[18] Like Handke and Roth, Jelinek is not a crime writer as such, but rather an author who experiments with multiple forms and genres. Nonetheless, her contribution to crime fiction is undeniable: in addition to combining the *Anti-Heimatroman* and anti-detective novel, Jelinek injects a new tone of radical feminist criticism to the crime genre. Furthermore, her fascination with language, already seen in Handke's and Roth's work, takes the form of, as the Nobel Prize presentation speech put it, 'tapping at language to hear its hidden ideologies', and is yet another manifestation of the deeply rooted Austrian concern with language philosophy.[19]

The novel in which Jelinek's experimentation with the crime genre is most prominent is *Gier* (*Greed*, 2000), which interestingly has the subtitle 'ein Unterhaltungsroman' (a novel designed to entertain). It expressly signals the connection to popular genre(s) and is at the same time deeply ironic, as this dense and complex novel, with its constantly repeated linguistic battering of violent sexual exploitation and (self-)humiliation requires quite some stamina on the part of the reader, and offers anything but easy and light entertainment.

The plot of *Gier* centres on country policeman Kurt Janisch, whose greedy desire is not only for women's sexual favours, but also for their possessions, especially their real estate.[20] Described as 'a good-looking and seemingly light-hearted man . . . just the sort we women like', his uniform serves him quite literally as camouflage.[21] None of the villagers, nor indeed the victims of his machinations, seem to suspect anything – not his wife, nor the sensitive Gerti, a middle-aged woman whose sexual desires he exploits in order to get his hands on her house, nor the sixteen-year-old Gabi, who throws herself at Janisch too, and whom he murders when she threatens to endanger his plans.

Obviously, casting a country policeman in the role of the murderer represents a crass reversal of traditional *Detektivroman* (detective novel) and *Polizeiroman* (police novel) conventions. Turning the local community's representative of the state from guarantor of justice and protector of the law into a cynical murderer implies a profound loss of trust in 'the system' and opens the door for a socio-political critique. Much of that critique is conveyed by means of the narrative voice, which time and again interrupts the action with a meandering intertextual, meta-reflexive and sarcastic commentary. In a parodic play with genre conventions, this voice allows the reader to reconstruct the details of the crime very early on, thus leaving little mystery as to the identity of the perpetrator. Within the fictional world, however, the novel's characters and the police fail to bring the truth to light, and the murder of Gabi remains unsolved in 'a world of silent witnesses'.[22] The suggestion is that the villagers do not have the courage to speak out, which in Jelinek's dense text, with its abundance of historical and political references, recalls collective attitudes towards Nazi crimes and contemporary xenophobic violence, in an Austria that Jelinek describes as 'the model child, which never did anything and never will do anything'.[23]

Jelinek provides a biting critique of deeply ingrained misogyny which is obviously represented by Janisch, but is also, and more disturbingly, internalized by the female characters. Instead of the conventional closure through the resolution of the crime and the prospect of justice being done, the end of *Gier* delivers another female casualty: Gerti dies of an overdose of barbiturates. Her suicide is directly attributable to Janisch, but it is clear that he will not be held accountable. The last sentence of the novel reads: 'It was an accident', a clear reference to the famous last sentence of Ingeborg Bachmann's *Malina*: 'It was murder.'[24] Thus, the novel inscribes itself into an Austrian female literary tradition of exposing (through a critique of language) systemic suppression of and violence against women, often connected to continued National Socialist attitudes. However, what is new in Jelinek's case is how she links this tradition with the use of popular forms.

Crime writing since 1995: Haslinger, Haas, Steinfest, Hochgatterer

Having looked at more experimental literary authors, it is time to explore more popular examples of the genre, and we will begin with Josef Haslinger's political thriller *Opernball* (Opera Ball, 1995). This novel, which immediately became a best-seller and was made into an award-winning TV film in 1998, also attracted praise from literary critics, for instance on the influential TV programme *Das literarische Quartett*. As such it successfully straddles the line between highbrow and lowbrow, combining sharp political critique with commercial success.

The novel opens with a poison gas attack that kills thousands of the guests at the opera ball, an annual highlight of the social calendar, which is broadcast live across Europe. The ball is a highly contested event associated with the establishment elite, which prompts protests by anti-establishment groups and thus generates many potential suspects. The opera house – a site with a long history dating back to the Austro-Hungarian Habsburg Empire – is deployed as an iconic image of Vienna and framed within a wider, critical portrayal of Austrian society and the more problematic aspects of Austria's past. Particularly interesting is the concern with the role of the media in contemporary society. The narrative is structured using a series of recordings with survivors, witnesses, police and suspects, made by the principle investigator in the text, a TV journalist, whose son, a cameraman, was among the victims of the attack. The culprits are early on revealed to be neo-Nazis. This structure with its multiple narrative voices and viewpoints denies the reader an overarching ordering consciousness or full closure. There is a strong sense of institutional collusion at various levels: the novel therefore does not propose a reassuring vision of the police or justice systems.

In terms of setting and space, Haslinger shows two faces of the city: the glittering tourist facade and what lies beneath its surface. As Souchuk observes,

> [t]he subterranean Karlsplatz station, with its late-night orgies and drug-addict-infested passageways, stands in stark contrast to the picturesque cultural centre overhead at street level. Indeed, the *Staatsoper*, site of Haslinger's deadly *Opernball*, is located right next to the subway station, and so . . . a space smaller than a city block . . . bears witness to the Viennese cultural dichotomy.[25]

This trope is widespread in Austrian crime fiction, denoting an equally widespread concern with the contradictions and hypocrisies inherent in Austrian social and political life. *Opernball* is viewed as one of the first crime novels to foreground this dichotomy, embracing the genre's potential for social critique. The novel's success marks a turning point in the development and reception of the genre, in that crime fiction was taken more seriously as a suitable vehicle for addressing social and political issues critically in Austria.[26]

Since *Opernball* there has been an enormous proliferation of the genre in Austria, with a concomitant range of settings, subject matter and modes. In recent decades, probably the most important creative and innovative impulse given to the genre was by Wolf Haas, born in 1960, who, with his playful approach to language, is widely regarded as having re-positioned the genre in Austria.[27] Before discussing his detective series, it is worth pointing out that Haas studied as a linguist, worked for two years as a *Lektor* at Swansea University in Wales, and wrote a highly regarded PhD on language philosophy and theory as the basis of the Vienna Group's 'Concrete Poetry' movement.[28] His creativity and playfulness with language were also an asset in his successful advertising career. These two strands illustrate both his serious academic concern with language and his commercial instinct for successful advertising slogans and campaigns.

Given this background, it is perhaps not surprising that Haas is notable for the sophistication with which he plays with language and literary style. One example of this play with language is that, in many instances, the solution to the crime case hinges on a linguistic ambiguity.[29] *Auferstehung der Toten* (*Resurrection*), the first volume in his highly acclaimed and popular series featuring the quirky detective Simon Brenner – an ex-police detective who is now a private investigator – was published in 1996. Brenner is a grouchy yet highly sympathetic underdog, who stumbles his way through the plot, frequently drawn in by chance and led by intuition, humanity and dogged perseverance. In a series marked by abundant use of irony and satire, one particularly innovative feature is the highly idiosyncratic narrative voice.

Haas brought the series to an end at the climax of the sixth novel, *Das ewige Leben* (Eternal Life, 2003), when the identity of the narrator is finally revealed just in time for him to die heroically by taking a bullet intended for Brenner. When Conan Doyle wanted to escape from the success of the Sherlock Holmes stories, he killed off the detective protagonist; when Haas wished to escape his own series, it was the narrator who was killed, not the detective. Just as popular demand induced Conan Doyle to revive Holmes, Haas brought back the narrator, but as a voice that persists after death, opening the novel *Der Brenner und der liebe Gott* (*Brenner and God*, 2009) with the words: 'My grandmother always used to say to me, when you die, your mouth will have to be killed off separately.'[30]

Haas employs a number of iconic locations across the country, which are used to address specific issues pertaining to Austria. These settings include centres of tourism, both in Vienna and in the Austrian countryside, and this brings us back to the common trope in Austrian crime fiction of the tension between appearance and reality, what lies behind the carefully constructed facade marketed to meet visitors' expectations. One of the best examples of the exposure of Austrian localities as part of a 'guilty landscape' is the invocation in *Auferstehung der Toten* of the hydroelectric works in Kaprun, a giant dam which in official discourse is glorified as a symbol of Austria's successful re-emergence after 1945, whilst in fact the Nazis had pushed the project forward using slave labour prior to that point. Haas makes reference to the murder of hundreds of these slave workers, thus exposing the dam as a block to memory and employing this site as a marker of Austria's problematic lack of critical engagement with its Nazi past and the return of the repressed.

An example of Haas's use of locale to engage in a critical yet witty fashion with topical problems in Austria can be found in *Silentium!* (Silentium!, 1999), which, set in Salzburg, links the cultural and touristic highlights of the city, like the Salzburg Festival, Mozart and the strong historical presence of the Catholic Church, with a current scandal involving child abuse within that church. Thus, once again, we see a dark reality behind the glittering facade presented to visitors and tourists. Although this summary may give the impression of a sombre narrative attention to such issues, Haas's style is very humorous, with liberal injections of slapstick comedy and Grand Guignol. We see this in a passage where a character gruesomely interrupts a love scene as he throws himself into the famous *Felsenreitschule* from a height. Even in the example referred to above of the dam, the references to the dark past are delivered in an irreverently comical style, where the target of the satirical humour is denial of responsibility.

Another very interesting and highly successful author of the same generation, noteworthy for his humour and for pushing the boundaries of the genre, is Heinrich Steinfest. Steinfest constructs surreal stories with whimsical and philosophical twists, moving away from the realism so strongly associated with the genre. He is able to make the most unlikely plots work convincingly, as in *Nervöse Fische* (Nervous Fish, 2004), where Viennese police inspector and avid Wittgenstein reader Lukastik is confronted with a mystery in which sharks in a pool on a hotel roof top have been used as the murder weapon. Steinfest's background as a painter is evident in his evocative style and frequent references to the visual arts, and he also makes frequent allusions to literature, such as the work of Thomas Bernhard and Raymond Chandler. Steinfest made his debut in 2000 with *Cheng. Sein erster Fall* (Cheng. His First Case), opening a series featuring the eponymous private investigator of Chinese descent, whose stories are set in modern-day Vienna and later in the German city of Stuttgart. In this first novel, Cheng rapidly loses one of his arms in a story that ultimately leads back to the legacy of the National Socialist past. Cheng, while identifiable as Chinese from appearances alone, is a fully acculturated Austrian whose lack of familiarity with Chinese culture and history give rise to many humorous situations in the novels. For instance in *Cheng*, his attempts to pose undercover as a Chinese businessman are frustrated when it turns out that all of the other characters he meets in this context speak Chinese and know considerably more about China than he does. This creation obviously confounds expectations based on ethnic appearance alone and challenges simplistic notions of what it means to be Austrian. Such questioning of Austrian identity is further pursued in ironic references to discourses on Austrians and Germans.[31] An example of this is found in one of the narrator's many lengthy digressions, where he considers Viennese attitudes towards guilt and innocence, perpetrator and victim, culminating in the highly sarcastic comment: 'The typical Viennese is, by the way, convinced that as a Viennese, one cannot at the same time be a Nazi; a passionate anti-Semite yes, a Catholic fascist yes, a democrat yes, but a Nazi, that's always a German.'[32]

In addition to the urban setting already discussed, the countryside also features, for instance in *Mariaschwarz* (Black Maria, 2008). The novel is set in the fog-enshrouded Alpine town of Hiltroff, a place described from the outset as one where many mysteries are to be found. Here, the enigmatic outsider Vinzent Olander relates to the local barman the story of why he came to this remote town: three years previously he had suffered a taxi accident in Milan in the course of which his daughter Clara disappeared, kidnapped by an onlooker. The accident was a set-up to kill the taxi driver, and the trace leads to Hiltroff, but in the intervening years Olander has come no closer to finding his daughter. Later, local children see what looks like a Loch Ness-type monster in the black lake *Mariaschwarz*, but when the lake is finally searched, the only sinister discovery is the skeletal remains of a woman who is identified as Clara's supposed kidnapper. This discovery brings in Viennese police detective Lukastik, who pursues the leads to Milan in an increasingly bizarre plot. He comes to wonder if there is even a case, whilst Olander's initial account of what happened in Milan reveals itself to be utterly unreliable. Ultimately the novel frustrates any expectation that a reliable truth can emerge, instead undermining the very idea of a stable connection between perception and reality. The novel knowingly plays with the crime genre, positioning this human drama against the backdrop of a profoundly mysterious universe, which mirrors itself in the blackness of the lake.

To conclude this section, we will examine a recent crime novel which is interesting because of the international profile it received as the winner of the European Union Prize for Literature in 2009, but also because of the way it reflects specifically Austrian concerns and anxieties: Paulus Hochgatterer's highly acclaimed and haunting *Die Süße des Lebens* (*The Sweetness of Life*, 2006). The professional background of the author, a prominent child psychiatrist who was involved in treating the victims in the Fritzl case in 2008, impacted significantly on his earlier novels and also has a strong bearing on this novel, his first foray into crime. While not having the degree of linguistic playfulness and dark humour found in other works already discussed, *Die Süße des Lebens* nevertheless deploys many of the features that are distinctive for the genre in Austria: an exposure of underlying misogynist and xenophobic attitudes that manifest themselves through the discourse used by characters; the *Anti-Heimat* tension between the idyllic surface of the touristic image and what lies underneath; an interest in the limits of individual perception and reason; a critical concern with violence and power, and with right-wing populist politics and the legacy of the National Socialist past. The murder serves as a novelistic pretext for a disturbing psychological portrayal of small-town life in modern Austria.

Set in a picture-postcard fictional provincial town around Christmas time, the novel opens with the shocking scene of a little girl rendered mute by the trauma of finding her grandfather brutally murdered. This calls to the scene the two figures who will serve as principal investigators, a psychiatrist, who is helping the little girl, a key witness, to speak again, and a police detective, who investigates the murder. Both are deeply disillusioned and flawed agents of society's management of deviant behaviour, who are all too aware of their limitations in keeping chaos, madness and evil at bay, and both at crucial junctures misinterpret or mishear important clues. The novel presents four different narrative voices in alternating chapters: the psychiatrist, the detective, a local priest and the impressionable younger brother of a youthful criminal. The latter two are both highly unstable and delusional, thus undermining even further the reliability of human perception. The psychiatrist character provides a mechanism by which the reader can see the range of neuroses that abound in this community: dysfunctional family relations; psychopathological violence against women, children and animals, to which society frequently turns a blind eye; and a narcissism breeding fascist mentalities among politicians. The detective's perspective exposes the failings of the judicial system in the face of a neo-Nazi attack on the local Moroccan restaurant and other instances of xenophobic violence in the town, as well as in dealing with juvenile delinquency more generally. The extract at the end of this chapter shows the oppressive provincial climate, where homophobia and xenophobia go hand in hand with a desire for the false and facile security offered by a fabricated idyll, echoed in the locals' sentimental escapist projections on Italy. Even the Nazi past, commodified as a tourist attraction, becomes part of this idyll, which can be read as a critique of the frequently sensationalist international fascination with this historical period. And yet, as the denouement of the novel suggests, the shadow of the Nazi era cannot so easily be dispelled, as we learn that the murder was motivated by a desire for retribution for a horrendous crime dating back to the Second World War.

As this chapter has shown, crime fiction is a thriving genre in Austria in which we find a great variety of approaches from a wide range of authors. Whilst this national output is still little known outside the German-speaking world, recent years have finally seen an increase in translation into English in particular. Following the success of Hochgatterer's *Sweetness of Life*, his second 'Kovacs and Horn' novel, *Das Matratzenhaus* (2010), was published in hardback with MacLehose Press as *The Mattress House* in 2012, with the paperback edition appearing a year later. From 2012 on, a number of Wolf Haas's 'Brenner' novels, a challenge for any translator due to their highly idiosyncratic use of language, appeared in the Melville International Crime Series (*Brenner and God* (2012), *The Bone Man* (2013), *Resurrection* and *Come, Sweet Death* (both 2014)). Andreas Pittler's historical crime novel *Zores* (2012) was also translated as *Inspector Bronstein and the Anschluss: Tsuris 1938* (2013) for the Californian Ariadne Press, which is planning translations of further volumes from Pittler's 'Bronstein' series, while a translation of Eva Rossmann's *Russen kommen* (2008) as *Goodness! The Russians Are Coming* is forthcoming from the same publishing house. While a specific Austrianness in mode and/or subject matter seems to be an important part of what makes these novels attractive to an international readership, and as such is highlighted on the publishers' websites, we see a different phenomenon in the recent revenge thriller *Die Totenfrau* (*Woman of the Dead*, 2014) by Bernhard Aichner, a best-selling action-packed page-turner using minimalist language in a rather breathless staccato style, for which the foreign rights were already sold before the original publication. The novel has appeared in English translation with Scribner/Simon and Schuster in the USA, and Orion/Weidenfeld & Nicholson in the UK. The (anticipated) international appeal in this case seems attributable to a distinct turn towards foreign fiction, with the ultra-tough female protagonist cast as Austria's answer to Stieg Larsson's Lisbeth Salander. It remains to be seen whether the diversity and versatility of crime fiction in Austria past and present will secure the stronger long-term international presence it merits.

* * *

Extract from Paulus Hochgatterer's *The Sweetness of Life*

Warmly wrapped up against the winter cold, Kommissar Ludwig Kovacs sips a beer outside a local Moroccan restaurant now free of attack from skinhead gangs since he began frequenting it. Kovacs still expects the business of the old man, recently found dead, to be resolved easily. Later, walking towards the half-frozen lake, his thoughts turn to Manolo's beach café, a favourite spot in his younger days, and the town's reactions when, following Manolo's accident, a returning local, Holdegger, opened a water-sports shop there.

In any case, there was no way Manolo was coming back from the dead. In his Corvette one sunny October morning, he had taken a bend on the Kanaltal motorway too quickly, careered effortlessly over the crash barrier, and landed in a river bed 150 meters below – a tributary of the Tagliamento. Some people considered this death in Italy to be highly romantic. They were probably the same individuals who used to bitch about Manolo's homosexuality: it's a good thing that faggot went back home to die. They were not bothered by the fact that Manolo was actually from Naples, about a thousand kilometres from the Kanaltal. Anyway, Holdegger did not seem to be queer, and the town was happy about that. In the few years since his return home, moreover, he had become one of the leading experts on the fish and bird populations of the lake, as well as on its climatic peculiarities. Fishermen and surfers would approach him for advice, and he had an excellent relationship with the wildlife observation centre. For those tourists who toyed with the idea of doing a dive, meanwhile, he devised a compendium of wild stories. He particularly enjoyed rubbishing the rumour about Nazi gold in the Toplitzsee, insisting that the treasures of the Third Reich had, in fact, disappeared almost within eyeshot of his shop: the transport ship, he claimed, had been scuttled at the foot of the Kammwand, then it disappeared under an avalanche triggered by a controlled explosion. On the back of his story people would sign up in droves; he would lead them to a fishing cutter which had sunk a good thirty years before, and announce that this was the pilot boat that the treasure ship had once followed. The boulders nearby were the result of the avalanche, he maintained. Nobody ever complained about these dives; on the contrary, there were so many enthusiastic testimonies from happy customers on Holdegger's web site that even the town council decided not to put the story straight.

In my line of work I'm seeking out the so-called facts, Kovacs thought, whereas people just want to be deceived. People always opt for what isn't true.

Paulus Hochgatterer, *The Sweetness of Life*, trans. Jamie Bulloch (London: MacLehose, 2008), pp. 79–80.

Notes

[1] Thank you to Jean Conacher, Gisela Holfter and Kate Quinn for their helpful reading of earlier versions of this chapter and also to Katharina Hall for her constructive comments, not least in the finishing stages.

[2] See *www.krimiautoren.at* (accessed 10 August 2015) and Sabina Naber, 'www.krimiautoren.at. Der österreichische Krimi im Plural', *Literatur und Kritik*, 417/8 (2007), 32–7.

[3] 'Seit gut zwanzig Jahren ist jeder zweite Roman, der in Österreich geschrieben wird, ein Krimi: ein echter oder einer, der immerhin so tut.' In Karl-Markus Gauß and Arno Kleibel (eds), 'Dossier: Der österreichische Krimi', *Literatur und Kritik*, 417/8 (2007), 23.

[4] Beatrix Kramlovsky, 'Show Your Face, oh Violence. Crime Fiction as Written by Austrian Women Writers', *World Literature Today*, 85 (2011), 13–15 (13).

[5] See also Arno Russegger, 'Ortspiele. Wortspiele. Aspekte kriminalistischen Erzählens in der österreichischen Gegenwartsliteratur', in Sandro M. Moraldo (ed.), *Mord als kreativer Prozess. Zum Kriminalroman der Gegenwart in Deutschland, Österreich und der Schweiz* (Heidelberg: Universitätsverlag Winter, 2005), pp. 75–98 (p. 75). Interestingly, Peter Plener and Michael Rohrwasser also suggest that '[t]he border between literary ambition and popular literature appears more porous in Austria, there are no such clearly demarcated leagues'. ['Die Grenze zwischen literarischem Anspruch und Unterhaltungsliteratur scheinen [*sic*] in Österreich durchlässiger, es gibt keine so deutlich voneinander geschiedenen Ligen.'] '"Es war Mord." Zwischen Höhenkamm, Zentralfriedhof und Provinz: Österreichs Krimiszene', *Der Deutschunterricht*, 2 (2007), 57–65 (58).

[6] Kramlovsky, 'Show Your Face', 15.

[7] 'Neue Österreich-Krimis – schräg und rabenschwarz. Die witzigsten und skurrilsten Krimis spielen in Österreich', *https://www.weltbild.at/1/7133/oesterreichische-krimis.html* (accessed 26 October 2014).

[8] See Dagmar C. G. Lorenz, 'In Search of the Criminal, in Search of the Crime. Holocaust Literature and Film as Crime Fiction', *Modern Austrian Literature*, 31/3–4 (1998), 35–48.

[9] See, for instance, Evelyne Polt-Heinzl, 'Frauenkrimis – Von der besonderen Dotation zu Detektion und Mord', in Friedbert Aspetsberger and Daniela Strigl (eds), *Ich kannte den Mörder, wußte nur nicht wer er war. Zum Kriminalroman der Gegenwart* (Innsbruck: StudienVerlag, 2004), pp. 144–70.

[10] See Friedbert Aspetsberger, 'Zu Helmut Zenkers TV-Krimi-Serie "Kottan ermittelt": In die Bilder abgesenkte FormKunst; mit Bildern hochgehaltener Realismus; Play-Back-Leben in der "Kapelle"', in Aspetsberger and Strigl (eds), *Ich kannte den Mörder*, pp. 240–89 (p. 273).

[11] See Palm's *Bad Fucking* (Bad Fucking, 2010) and Brödl's *Kurt Ostbahn: Hitzschlag* (Kurt Ostbahn: Heat Stroke, 1996).

[12] On Handke's use of the crime genre, see Marieke Krajenbrink, *Intertextualität als Konstruktionsprinzip. Transformationen des Kriminalromans und des romantischen Romans bei Peter Handke und Botho Strauß* (Amsterdam: Rodopi, 1996).

[13] See Richard Alewyn (quoting John le Carré, *A Murder of Quality*), 'Anatomie des Detektivromans', in Jochen Vogt (ed.), *Der Kriminalroman: Poetik – Theorie – Geschichte* (Munich: Fink, 1998), p. 70.

[14] Roth cited in Daniela Bartens, 'Topographien des Imaginären: Zum "Orkus"-Gesamtzykus unter Einbeziehung von Materialien aus dem Vorlass', in Daniela Bartens and Gerhard Melzer (eds), *Gerhard Roth: Orkus. Im Schattenreich der Zeichen* (Vienna: Springer-Verlag, 2003), pp. 39–68 (p. 65).

[15] See Marieke Krajenbrink, 'Unresolved Identities in Roth and Rabinovici: Reworking the Crime Genre in Austrian Literature', in Marieke Krajenbrink and Kate M. Quinn (eds), *Investigating Identities. Questions of Identity in Contemporary International Crime Fiction* (Amsterdam: Rodopi, 2009), pp. 243–60.

[16] Einen 'religiösen Roman, verborgen hinter einer Gespenstergeschichte, die sich wieder hinter einer bäuerlichen Kriminalgeschichte verbirgt', cited in Klaus-Peter Walter (ed.), *Reclams Krimi-Lexikon: Autoren und Werke* (Stuttgart: Reclam, 2002), p. 267. It is noteworthy that this hybrid novel is included in this crime encyclopedia.

[17] In her review, Jelinek calls *Die Wolfshaut* 'der erste radikal moderne Roman der österreichischen Nachkriegsliteratur' (the first radical modern novel of Austrian post-war literature) and 'eins der größten Leseerlebnisse meines Lebens'. 'Das Hundefell', *Profil*, 38 (1991), 108.

[18] See Verena Mayer and Roland Koberg, *Elfriede Jelinek. Ein Porträt* (Reinbek bei Hamburg: Rowohlt, 2007), p. 239.

[19] See *http://www.nobelprize.org/nobel_prizes/literature/laureates/2004/presentation-speech.html* (accessed 10 August 2015).

[20] See Andrea Kunne, *Postmoderne contre Coeur. Stationen des Experimentellen in der österreichischen Literatur* (Innsbruck: StudienVerlag, 2005), p. 302.

[21] 'Ein gutaussehender und scheinbar leichtherziger Mann, der Gendarm, wie er uns Frauen eben gefällt.' Elfriede Jelinek, *Gier* (Reinbek bei Hamburg: Rowohlt, 2004), p. 8. Elfriede Jelinek, *Greed*, trans. Martin Chalmers (London: Serpent's Tail, 2008), p. 4.

[22] 'Es ist eine Welt der stummen Zeugen ...' *Gier*, p. 418; *Greed*, p. 308.

[23] 'Österreich, das Musterkind, das nie etwas getan hat und getan haben wird.' *Gier*, p. 422; *Greed*, p. 311.

[24] 'Es war ein Unfall.' *Gier*, p. 462; *Greed*, p. 340; 'Es war Mord.' Ingeborg Bachmann, *Malina* (Munich: Piper, 1995), p. 695; *Malina. A Novel*, trans. Philip Boehm (New York: Holmes and Meier, 1990), p. 225.

[25] Anna Souchuk, '"Alles Ist Unter der Oberfläche Noch Lebendig": Penetrating the *Schöner Schein* through Satire in Josef Haslinger's *Opernball* and Robert Menasse's *Schubumkehr*', *Journal of Austrian Studies*, 46/1 (2013), 71–92 (79).

[26] See also Russegger, 'Ortspiele. Wortspiele', p. 76.

[27] See Peter Plener, '404 ding. Über die Kriminalromane von Wolf Haas', in Friedbert Aspetsberger (ed.), *Neues, Trends und Motive in der (österreichischen) Gegenwartsliteratur* (Innsbruck: StudienVerlag, 2003), pp. 107–39 (p. 107).

[28] Wolf Haas, *Sprachtheoretische Grundlagen der Konkreten Poesie* (Stuttgart: Akademischer Verlag, 1990).

[29] In the first novel of the series, Brenner is ironically hailed as 'der Duden-Detektiv'. See Plener, '404 ding', p. 144. On Haas and his use of language see also Sigrid Nindl, *Wolf Haas und sein kriminalliterarisches Sprachexperiment* (Berlin: Erich Schmidt, 2010) and Franz Haas, 'Aufklärung in Österreich. Die erhellenden Kriminalromane von Wolf Haas', in Moraldo (ed.), *Mord als kreativer Prozess*, pp. 127–34.

[30] 'Meine Großmutter hat immer zu mir gesagt, wenn du einmal stirbst, muss man das Maul extra erschlagen.' Wolf Haas, *Der Brenner und der liebe Gott* (Hamburg: Hoffmann und Campe, 2009), p. 7.

[31] For a compelling reading of Steinfest's Cheng novels, see Elke Sturm-Trigonakis, 'Der Wiener Privatdetektiv Markus Cheng – Charlie Chan in Österreich?', *Journal of Austrian Studies*, 45/1–2 (2012), 69–92.

[32] 'Der Wiener ist übrigens der Überzeugung, daß man als Wiener nicht gleichzeitig ein Nazi sein kann, leidenschaftlicher Antisemit ja, katholischer Faschist ja, Demokrat ja, aber ein Nazi, das ist immer ein Deutscher.' Heinrich Steinfest, *Cheng. Sein erster Fall* (Munich: Piper, 2007 [2000]), p. 206.

Select bibliography

Haas, Wolf, *Auferstehung der Toten* (Reinbek bei Hamburg: rororo, 2000). *Resurrection*, trans. Annie Janusch (London: Melville, 2014).

——, *Der Brenner und der liebe Gott* (Hamburg: Hoffmann und Campe, 2009). *Brenner and God*, trans. Annie Janusch (London: Melville, 2012).

Handke, Peter, *Der Hausierer* (Frankfurt a. M.: Suhrkamp, 1992 [1967]).

——, *Der kurze Brief zum langen Abschied* (Frankfurt a. M.: Suhrkamp, 2001 [1960]). *Short Letter, Long Farewell*, trans. Ralph Manheim (New York: New York Review of Books, 2009).

Haslinger, Josef, *Opernball* (Frankfurt a. M.: Fischer, 1995).

Hochgatterer, Paulus, *Die Süße des Lebens* (Vienna: Deuticke, 2006). *The Sweetness of Life*, trans. Jamie Bulloch (London: MacLehose, 2008).

Jelinek, Elfriede, *Gier* (Reinbek bei Hamburg: Rowohlt, 2004). *Greed*, trans. Martin Chalmers (London: Serpent's Tail, 2008).

Lebert, Hans, *Die Wolfshaut* (Hamburg: Europa Verlag, 2001 [1960]).

Pittler, Andreas, *Zores* (Vienna: Echomedia, 2012). *Inspector Bronstein and the Anschluss: Tsuris 1938*, trans. Vincent Kling (Riverside, CA: Ariadne Press, 2013).

Rossmann, Eva, *Russen kommen* (Vienna: Folio Verlag, 2008). *Goodness! The Russians Are Coming*, trans. Maria P. Bauer (Riverside, CA: Ariadne Press, forthcoming).

Roth, Gerhard, 'How to be a detective', in Gerhard Roth, *die autobiografie des albert einstein. Fünf Kurzromane* (Frankfurt a. M.: Fischer, 1982), pp. 133–53.

——, *Der See* (Frankfurt a. M.: Fischer, 2012 [1995]). *The Lake*, trans. Michael Winkler (Riverside, CA: Ariadne Press, 2000).

Steinfest, Heinrich, *Cheng. Sein erster Fall* (Munich: Piper, 2007 [2000]).

——, *Mariaschwarz* (Munich: Piper, 2010 [2008]).

Further secondary reading

Aspetsberger, Friedbert und Daniela Strigl (eds), *Ich kannte den Mörder, wußte nur nicht wer er war. Zum Kriminalroman der Gegenwart* (Innsbruck: StudienVerlag, 2004).

Brumme, Jenny, 'The narrator's voice in translation: What remains from a linguistic experiment in Wolf Haas's Brenner detective novels', in Suśanne M. Cadera and Anita Pavić Pintarić (eds), *The Voices of Suspense and their Translation in Thrillers* (Amsterdam: Rodopi, 2014), pp. 161–76.

Gauß, Karl-Markus and Arno Kleibel (eds), 'Dossier: Der österreichische Krimi', *Literatur und Kritik*, 417/8 (2007).

Henderson, Heike, 'Eva Rossmann's mystery novel "Russen kommen". The Russians Are Coming. New Crimes, Old Fears, and Intercultural Alliances', *Studia austriaca*, XX (2012), 25–32.

Krajenbrink, Marieke, 'Unresolved Identities in Roth and Rabinovici: Reworking the Crime Genre in Austrian Literature', in Marieke Krajenbrink and Kate M. Quinn (eds), *Investigating Identities. Questions of Identity in Contemporary International Crime Fiction* (Amsterdam: Rodopi, 2009), pp. 243–60.

Russegger, Arno, 'Ortspiele. Wortspiele. Aspekte kriminalistischen Erzählens in der österreichischen Gegenwartsliteratur', in Sandro M. Moraldo (ed.), *Mord als kreativer*

Prozess. Zum Kriminalroman der Gegenwart in Deutschland, Österreich und der Schweiz (Heidelberg: Universitätsverlag Winter, 2005), pp. 75–98.
Saur, Pamela S., 'Gerhard Roth's Orkus Novels *The Lake, The Plan, The Mountain*, and *The Stream* as Murder Mysteries', *Clues. A Journal of Detection*, 29/1 (2011), 61–70.
Schreckenberger, Helga, 'The Destruction of Idyllic Austria in Wolf Haas's Detective Novels', in Rebecca Thomas (ed.), *Crime and Madness in Modern Austria: Myth, Metaphor and Cultural Realities* (Cambridge: Cambridge University Press, 2008), pp. 424–43.
Stewart, Faye, *German Feminist Queer Crime Fiction: Politics, Justice and Desire* (Jefferson, NC: McFarland, 2014).

4

Swiss Crime Fiction: Loosli, Glauser, Dürrenmatt and Beyond

MARTIN ROSENSTOCK

Switzerland is where Sherlock Holmes dies. On 4 May 1891, he and Professor Moriarty meet on the brink of the Reichenbach Falls. In the ensuing struggle both men fall over the precipice, or so it subsequently appears. When Arthur Conan Doyle wrote this story, 'The Final Problem', in 1893 he believed that he had finally liberated himself from the burden Holmes had become.[1] This belief would prove false. Public and publishers clamoured for more stories, and ten years later Doyle resurrected his detective. It turns out that only Moriarty found his death at the bottom of the gorge. Holmes put his skills in Japanese martial arts to good use and foiled his opponent's attack. So not only does Holmes die in Switzerland, he also comes back to life there, never to die again, but rather to take his place amongst the immortals of crime fiction.

Swiss crime writing precedes Doyle's hero. Texts of this genre, inspired by French and German models, can already be found in the early nineteenth century and will be discussed briefly here. Detective fiction – whose narratives are organized around a central character's enquiry into a crime – appears in Switzerland later in the century and also owes a debt to forebears from abroad, mostly French and Anglo-Saxon this time. Swiss authors reshaped the genre for their native context; occasionally they wrote against foreign models. In all cases, Switzerland's culture and history left an impression and made Swiss detective fiction unique. Switzerland's two dominant figures during the genre's golden age, Friedrich Glauser and Friedrich Dürrenmatt, are the focus of this chapter. Their efforts allowed a Swiss genre tradition to emerge on whose themes and motifs contemporary writers can draw. A look at the work of two present-day Swiss crime writers will conclude the discussion.

The beginnings of Swiss crime fiction

With the rise of a bourgeois reading public a fascination with crime narratives develops in European societies. François Gayot de Pitaval's collection of court cases, *Causes célèbres et intéressantes*, published between 1734 and 1743, was a bestseller throughout the continent. The volumes became standard features not only on the shelves of legal professionals, but provided reading material for middle-class living rooms. Unsurprisingly, the *Pitaval* found emulators. In Switzerland, for instance, an account of the last criminals executed in Basel appeared in 1819, entitled *The Story of X. Hermann, F. Deisler, J. Föller und Jos. Studer, Sentenced to Death and Imprisonment by the Criminal Justice Court of Basel on 14 July 1819. Adapted from the Court Files and Published as a Warning.*[2] The narrative makes good on the title's cautionary gesture, detailing the criminals' misdeeds and their punishments: two are decapitated, the others branded and incarcerated for twenty-four years. Many similar accounts follow. A rival in scope to its French predecessor appears in 1865 when Jacob Senn publishes a volume that aims to combine diversion, exhortation and instruction: *The Most Interesting Crime Stories of Old and Recent Times: A Book to Entertain, Warn and Educate Both Young and Old, Adapted from the Existent Files and Edited by a High Judicial Official of Long Standing.*[3] This book has everything to offer from child theft to perjury and murder by poison.

The move from a factual account to a literary reworking of facts occurs in the latter third of the nineteenth century. The name most associated with this qualitative leap is Jodocus Donatus Hubertus Temme. Born in Westphalia in 1798, he reads law and pursues a career in the Prussian state bureaucracy. In 1848, however, he sides with the revolution. The state responds harshly. Over the following three years, Temme is arrested twice and charged with treason. Finally hounded from his post in 1851, he makes ends meet for another year and a half in Germany, before removing himself and his family to Switzerland. He secures a chair at the University of Zurich, but initially the position is unpaid, forcing him to live off his writing. Many of his stories and novellas revolve around crime, allowing him to draw on his professional knowledge. He spends the rest of his life in Switzerland, and by the time of his death in 1881 has become the most popular German-language crime writer.[4]

One of Temme's better-known works today is the novella *Der Studentenmord in Zürich* (The Murder of a Student in Zurich, 1872). The narrative is based on a true case, the 1835 murder of a German student who posed as an exiled member of a revolutionary group, but who may in fact have been a Prussian agent. The text features the well-established elements of reportage, such as quotes from the deceased's letters and official exchanges. It does, however, also employ more innovative elements. Like a classic detective story, Temme's novella begins with the discovery of the body. A detective is lacking, but nonetheless the text organizes the events into a mystery. The disembodied narrator provides forensic evidence, reports the depositions of witnesses, describes the milieu of the German expat community and introduces a host of shady characters, spies and agents provocateurs, con men and revolutionaries manqué. The reader follows an intelligence that is not merely recounting a crime, but is in fact trying to solve it. Implicitly, the novella constitutes a challenge to solve the mystery ahead of the narrator. As the genre develops in Switzerland and absorbs outside influences, this race towards the solution will, as elsewhere, become a central component of the formula. In *Der Studentenmord in Zürich* the race is already on, but a finishing line is lacking. The novella concludes with the murderer undiscovered. However, in the final two sentences the narrator claims that 'the files at one point contain a clue. It was not noticed', suggesting that he knows the killer's identity.[5] Temme's story thus sends the reader back to its beginning, so as to pay more attention on second perusal.

Carl Albert Loosli

Over the following decades the next evolutionary step occurs, from dramatized true crime to fictional narrative. Most of the writers who contributed to this development have been forgotten, some justly, others unjustly. For the future of the genre their usage of specifically Swiss locales and themes is key. The alpine landscape and the social backwardness it creates amongst its peasant population feature alongside illegal activities, such as smuggling, made possible through Switzerland's position as a neutral country amidst hostile European nations. The development reaches a temporary culmination in the work of Carl Albert Loosli, who will become the ancestral figure behind Glauser. A politically engaged journalist and writer with reformist convictions, Loosli takes issue with the cerebral nature of the genre's British form.[6] For him, Sherlock Holmes is only good for spoofing. In 'Die Geisterphotographie' (The Photograph of Ghosts, 1908) the Baker Street mastermind becomes Harlock Shelmes and Watson turns into Lawson. The parody, a twenty-page narrative depicting fraudulent occult practices in the upper middle class, is good-natured; in fact, with a few modifications the story might pass as one of Doyle's own. But Loosli's manipulation of genre conventions also suggests his awareness of their limitations. When he turns to crime fiction in earnest the result bears no resemblance to a Holmes story. In 1926, he writes *Die Schattmattbauern* (The Farmers of Schattmatt), first published in serial form in 1929 and 1930 and as a book in 1932. The novel, set in 1893, tells the story of how the life of Fritz Grädel, a successful farmer, disintegrates when his malicious father-in-law, Andreas Rösti, kills himself and disguises the suicide in such an ingenious manner that the suspicion of murder falls on his son-in-law. Grädel's lawyer Hugo Brand fulfils the role of quasi-detective and ultimately secures his client's release, after Grädel has spent four months in pre-trial confinement. The verdict of not guilty, however, is for want of evidence, not because Brand has proven the defendant's innocence. Grädel cannot live with this second-rate acquittal. He wastes away, has to be sent to a mental institution and dies there. Only years later does Brand find out the truth when Rösti's brother contacts him by letter and explains how the suicide could be staged so as to look like a murder.

In Loosli's text the detective figure can only manage a qualified success: he wins his court case, but can neither solve the mystery nor prevent the ruination of innocence. Brand is no Sherlock Holmes, and in Loosli's text, unlike in a classic detective story, the power of reason appears limited. This scepticism points ahead to Dürrenmatt's tortured detectives, to whom the world appears as a space of uncertainty in which the best laid plans fail. Dürrenmatt's philosophical concerns, though, are absent from Loosli's text. What dominates *Die Schattmattbauern* is a sense of the destructive forces of the human psyche and doubt regarding the ability or even the will of people in power to establish justice. Loosli paints a detailed picture of rural Switzerland in the last decade of the nineteenth century: the land stands on the brink of modernity – telephone wires are being installed, people are travelling and bringing a sense of the wider world to their communities – and yet society remains provincial. Grädel becomes the victim of his fellow citizens' susceptibility to rumour, of police mistakes and of a gruelling pre-trial confinement. *Die Schattmattbauern* is more than a detective or crime story. The text blends panoramic realism with psychological analysis and a call to reform. Loosli draws less on his knowledge of Edgar Allan Poe and Conan Doyle than on his experiences as a reporter and on the Swiss Biedermeier tradition, a literary school that depicted rural life and found its most accomplished practitioner in Jeremias Gotthelf. Despite exceeding the genre's scope, however, *Die Schattmattbauern* constitutes the point of origin for a tradition of modern Swiss detective fiction with literary ambition.

Friedrich Glauser

In Friedrich Glauser's debut *Wachtmeister Studer* (Sergeant Studer) novel, *Schlumpf Erwin Mord* (*Thumbprint*, 1935), the detective refers to a case in which 'a man had shot himself and disguised the suicide as murder'.[7] This is the central conceit of Loosli's novel, and in all likelihood Glauser is tipping his hat to the writer who had preceded him in the field.[8] Glauser is born in *fin de siècle* Vienna to a Swiss-Austrian couple. He loses his mother at the age of four, perhaps the root cause of many later problems. His life will be marked by restlessness, disease and self-destructive behaviour. He struggles through a number of educational institutions, finally earning his *Matura* – his high school leaving certificate – in Zurich, and in the last years of the First World War finds entry into Dadaist circles. In 1918, Glauser's father has him put under tutelage because of his morphine addiction. There follow periods in the foreign legion and Belgian coal mines, and finally a drug-related arrest and psychiatric treatment. In 1932, he is caught passing a forged prescription and is again institutionalized.[9] This time confinement may have been a blessing, for in the psychiatric clinic of Münsingen, Glauser creates the figure that will make his name, the down-to-earth Swiss detective Jakob Studer.[10]

While Glauser in many respects typifies the societal, economic and cultural upheaval that Europe underwent during the interwar period, Sergeant Studer is a man whose life may be buffeted by adverse surroundings, yet is never derailed.[11] Modelled on Georges Simenon's humane Inspector Maigret, Studer appears the image of constancy. He has been married, quite happily, for twenty-plus years, and is the father of two daughters. He likes a stiff drink and strong tobacco, and even smokes hashish during a North African trip, but never falls prey to these vices. His career has received some setbacks, yet he does not allow these to impact on his well-being and has now almost made it to retirement. By no means a parochial character, Studer speaks French and Italian, and he has studied with Edmond Locard and Hans Gross, criminology's leading lights. His perspicacity, though, remains hidden behind an unpretentious demeanour, and generally he cultivates a Swiss argot that enables him to mix easily with ordinary people. When Studer switches to High German it is in most cases not a good sign for his interlocutor. Acute, urbane and wise in the ways of the world, yet rooted in his Swiss heritage, the heavy-set man with the pointy nose is the first German-Swiss detective who captured the public's imagination to such a degree that he commands a following to this day. He is also amongst the first Swiss serial detectives. However, success comes too late. Glauser continues to write at a rapid pace, pushing himself harder perhaps than his depleted strength would allow. On 8 December 1938, the eve of his wedding to a nurse he met at Münsingen, he collapses and dies. He is only forty-two years old.

The 'Sergeant Studer' novels demonstrate an awareness of 1930s Swiss and European culture, and Glauser frequently draws on his experiences for plot material, setting or background. The sense of a country changing in modernity's flux, already present in Loosli's work, also pervades Glauser's. In the sergeant's first case, for which Glauser recast memories of working in a tree nursery, Studer marvels at how radio and advertising are enhancing the entrepreneurial spirit of a Swiss village. Yet while technology may be transforming business practices, the novels also show Swiss society as stable, and rarely to its own advantage: a veneer of respectability covers moral degradation. Connections secure ill-gotten gains and the privileged not only cheat those of little means out of their just deserts, but set them up as fall guys. By the same token, small-time criminals are mostly victims of economic and social circumstance and deserve decent treatment and a measure of forbearance. Studer, protector of the unfortunate, achieves more than the solution to a mystery. He functions as an agent of redemption for a society that requires purging of its vilest malefactors to retain a claim on the republican virtues of justice and equity for all. This theme of corruption and its removal will become a mainstay of Swiss detective fiction, featuring in Dürrenmatt's narratives and in those of his and Glauser's contemporary disciples.

While all five 'Sergeant Studer' novels are worth reading, the third, *Matto regiert* (*In Matto's Realm*, 1936), stands out as Glauser's most prescient analysis of Switzerland and Europe in the 1930s.[12] The deputy chief of the psychiatric clinic of Randlingen requests that Studer investigate the disappearance of his boss and one of his patients. Soon after, Studer discovers the body of the clinic chief, neck broken, at the foot of a ladder and, as in an Agatha Christie novel, everyone – doctors, patients, orderlies – is a suspect. But *Matto regiert* transcends the limits of a whodunit to become a parable of a world in crisis. One of the inmates, a scarred invalid of the Great War who writes prose poetry, has seen Matto, the spirit of unreason and, as the title implies, this spirit holds sway over Randlingen. Yet the clinic does not constitute a sealed-off locale in which the forces of madness are contained. Rather, the walls of the asylum are permeable; the poet's work suggests that Matto pulls the strings both inside and out.

In an open letter to Stefan Brockhoff, a pseudonym under which three German writers of detective fiction published, Glauser stated in 1937 that atmosphere is of key importance for a narrative, and in *Matto regiert* he acts on this belief, more successfully even than in his other novels.[13] The clinic's commanding windows signal surveillance, the labyrinthine cell corridors recall a prison more than a medical institution, and occasionally a turn of phrase will impart a sense of understated menace: birds, for instance, are not chirping or even cawing, but 'screamed in the fir trees' as if nature herself were giving voice to the inmates' misery.[14] Such language shows that Glauser's contact with the Zurich literary avant-garde left its mark, and in fact there is a surrealist quality to Randlingen, as if neurosis and paranoia had found architectural expression. The clinic's microcosm mirrors the world at large. Class warfare between personnel and administration is simmering below the surface, and the weak are victimized in both realms. The most harrowing example of wretched humanity is a man who killed his newborn because he lacked the money for its upbringing; society in turn has extended no aid, but rather locked him away.

Studer never becomes sovereign master of the situation. His own past comes back to cloud his judgement, and though he does arrive at the truth, in the process of detection he incurs guilt himself by contributing to the death of a blameless soul. Moreover, to stay the macrocosm's trajectory lies well beyond his powers. The alignment of the worlds outside and inside the asylum becomes abundantly clear in the scene provided as the extract at the end of this chapter. The detective and the deputy chief hear a Hitler speech on the radio. Before a huge crowd, the *Führer* takes credit for remilitarizing the Rhineland, and the doctor wonders where Matto's dominion ends. It does not end anywhere, the text implies. Glauser did not live to witness the triumph of unreason, but it seems probable that he would not have been surprised at the course of history.

Friedrich Dürrenmatt

From Glauser the baton passes to Friedrich Dürrenmatt and his first detective, Inspector Bärlach. While Glauser's hero, despite the occasional cold, is a man of rugged good health, Bärlach enters the stage a dying man. Cancer is eating away at his intestines and he will only solve two cases. Both men ply their trade in Bern, both are on the brink of old age and professionally both are lone wolves. Dürrenmatt certainly knew Glauser's work and made use of the imaginative space Studer had opened up on the Swiss literary scene. But Dürrenmatt's detective and his cases suggest a different set of preoccupations. While Glauser's world view is informed by economic, psychological and sociological paradigms, Dürrenmatt's take on 1950s Switzerland is coloured by the recent Second World War and the Holocaust, and is structured through his acquaintance with metaphysical and philosophical thought: his father was a protestant minister and he himself contemplated a dissertation on Søren Kierkegaard.[15] The technical aspects of criminology interest Dürrenmatt less. He follows Glauser in diagnosing corruption at the heart of Swiss society, but whereas the older writer's hero must confront the outcomes of, say, the unjust distribution of wealth, his successor's detectives face a world in which corruption may be the manifestation of radical evil. Confronted with such opposition, chances of success appear slim. Hence, a pessimism is present that finds expression in images of deterioration, of which Bärlach is not the only example.

When Studer investigated Matto's realm, he already felt the threat emanating from the larger country to the north. For post-war Switzerland, this threat seemed to have come and gone and the country to have escaped the effects of Nazism. Dürrenmatt's texts suggest that this view is naive, not to say wilfully blind: at the very least Switzerland's upper crust has been contaminated. The inspector knows the foe. During the interwar years, he pursued a career in Weimar Germany but returned home after a slap to the face of a Nazi bureaucrat had made him *persona non grata*. Now he will protect Switzerland from the lingering effects of a lethal belief system. In *Der Richter und sein Henker* (*The Judge and His Hangman*, 1950), Bärlach's first case, the concrete historical evil is only silhouetted in Bärlach's biography. In his second, *Der Verdacht* (*Suspicion*, 1951), the legacy of Nazism is literally present in Switzerland.

Gastmann, the criminal mastermind against whom Bärlach faces off in *Der Richter und sein Henker*, is Swiss-born, though he leads a rootless international existence. He enjoys connections to politics and industry that make him almost untouchable, and only via a roundabout method can the detective destroy his arch-enemy and establish justice. The case for which Bärlach seeks closure goes back decades. When both he and the criminal were young men, Gastmann killed a random person to prove to the detective that the orderless nature of reality and of interactions between human beings favour the criminal – 'that it's precisely this incalculable, chaotic element in human relations that makes it possible to commit crimes that *cannot* be detected'.[16] For Gastmann, human life is only material for an experiment, and over many decades the results have borne him out: Bärlach has been unable to prove his adversary's guilt. With time ticking away, the detective resorts to desperate measures. Both containing and utilizing chance occurrences, he establishes control over events and defeats nihilism. But the price is high, as he must sacrifice a good man and exact justice outside the realm of the law. The human being cuts a puny figure in this unstable world that is host to evil.

In *Der Verdacht* Inspector Bärlach is bedridden, recovering from an operation that has bought him another year, when he discovers that a prominent Swiss physician worked in a concentration camp and is responsible for countless deaths. Doctor Emmenberger used the opportunity Nazi Germany afforded him of indulging his sadistic inclinations. Now, with the war over, he has returned home and blended into the upper class. Incapable of ignoring evil, the frail old detective seeks out the monster who, like Gastmann, values only the gratification of his own impulses. Bärlach, however, is no match for Emmenberger, at least not physically. The doctor and his minions incarcerate the inspector, and his death by torture seems certain. But in the nick of time the quasi-mythical Jew Gulliver appears to save the day and exact vengeance for his people's suffering. Living on borrowed time, Bärlach is both driven and liberated by the proximity of death: he has not much time left to fight evil, and not much to lose should evil defeat him.

The Bärlach novels are morality tales set against the backdrop of Swiss feelings of vulnerability to Nazi infiltration. The inspector's world-weary decency casts out the corrupted members of society and re-establishes a precarious moral order. His victories signify the end of an era in Dürrenmatt's *oeuvre*. Time has run out for the detective and history has passed him by. Those next in line will not be allowed Bärlach's qualified successes.

Dürrenmatt turned again to the genre in the late 1950s, when he wrote a screenplay for a thriller about a child murderer. The film ends as one might expect, with a dead killer and a saved child. But when Dürrenmatt novelized the script, he introduced profound changes. The detective of *Das Versprechen* (*The Pledge*, 1958) is a failure, the riddle defies solution. In a short epilogue Dürrenmatt states that the text critiques the Enlightenment tradition the detective embodies: the world is more complex than the human mind can fathom. Inspector Matthäi has pledged to the victim's mother that he will find the murderer. The clues are few, but he pieces together a plan and purchases a petrol station at the side of a road which he knows the killer uses. A woman and her daughter live in an adjacent house, and the inspector's plan hinges on the assumption that the killer will single out the child as his next victim. This in fact occurs, but before he can strike, chance does: he dies in a car accident, unbeknownst to Matthäi, who is lying in wait. The killer's failure to appear destroys the logical edifice to whose vindication the detective has devoted his life. As a result, he descends into psychosis. In the Bärlach novels the detective's health is failing, yet two final efforts of rationality explain the world and check evil. In *Das Versprechen*, by contrast, the world's complexity exceeds human understanding, and reliance on reason leads to self-destruction.

The text underscores its awareness of the cultural values the detective represents via its structure. The narrative of Matthäi's failure is contained within a frame narrative and transmitted by a retired police officer. His listener is a fictionalized version of Dürrenmatt himself (who already appeared, thinly disguised, in *Der Richter und sein Henker*). *Das Versprechen* exploits the presence of a writer, not to say of the author, as a character for the consideration of genre conventions, of the relationship between author and text, and of fiction's status vis-à-vis reality. *Das Versprechen*, whose subtitle is *Requiem auf den Kriminalroman* (*Requiem for the Crime Novel*), thus becomes a meta-narrative about the crime genre as well as about the nature of fiction. In addition, the text's critique of totalizing claims as to the explanatory powers of rationality renders it an example of what years later, frequently in an Anglo-Saxon context, will come to be termed an anti-detective story, Thomas Pynchon's *The Crying of Lot 49* (1966) being one prominent example.[17]

Dürrenmatt was a prolific writer whose interests found expression in various formats and genres. He wrote successful plays, both dramas and comedies, as well as short narratives and novels that explore topics ranging from the dangers of modern science to the power dynamics of totalitarian regimes. The detective fades somewhat from his work after *Das Versprechen*, though Dürrenmatt kept a couple of unfinished projects featuring heirs to Bärlach and Matthäi in his desk drawer. Towards the end of his career, Dürrenmatt picked up one of these projects.[18] *Justiz* (*The Execution of Justice*), begun in the late 1950s, but not completed and published until 1985, is the complementary farce to the earlier tragedy. The broken-down detective of *Das Versprechen* has morphed into the narrator, the perpetually inebriated lawyer Felix Spät – a late-comer to the detective profession, as his surname, which means 'late' in German, already indicates. Not only is Spät late in entering the game, the case he investigates is literally late, an after-the-fact investigation into the realm of make-believe. His client is Dr h.c. Kohler, who shot an acquaintance, Professor Winter, in a crowded restaurant and was convicted and jailed for murder. Spät is to investigate the crime under the assumption that Kohler – whom the guests saw shooting the professor – is innocent. What seems like a parlour game soon turns serious. There are contradictions in the depositions of the witnesses and the murder weapon is missing. In addition, a likely suspect was present at the time of the shooting, the former Swiss national pistol champion Dr Benno. Fiction begins to supplant reality: Spät's investigation ruins Benno's reputation, who consequently hangs himself, which the authorities take as a confession of guilt. They reopen Kohler's case, and during a new trial Spät's fictitious version displaces the true course of events. Reality is rewritten and Kohler acquitted. Spät cannot countenance the perversion of justice to which he contributed and descends into alcoholism.

Perhaps not a single paragraph of *Justiz* was written with a straight face. Yet despite the narrative's zany tone, Dürrenmatt's late work stages a serious thought-experiment that engages with the Enlightenment tradition. The text queries theories of cognition as well as post-Kantian theorems on the philosophical status of fictions and hypotheses. Similar to *Das Versprechen*, *Justiz* puts Enlightenment thought to the test and finds it wanting. Beyond philosophical concerns Dürrenmatt's last detective novel also returns to other familiar ground. Switzerland abounds with corruption and greed to a point where a pimp appears as a comparatively decent character. The author indulges a penchant for the grotesque that characterizes many of his works.[19] There is a dwarfish heiress to an armaments empire who occasionally masquerades as a lawn gnome and is carried around by her outsized Uzbekistani bodyguards. She and other characters represent a society that has grown bizarrely deformed in its pursuit of wealth. The text traces the origins of the heiress's fortune back to the Middle Ages and thus pokes fun at self-aggrandizing Swiss myths about the country's heritage.[20] Dürrenmatt signs off from the genre with a text both facetiously humorous and utterly bleak. Not a single promise of the classic formula remains unbroken: the truth escapes the detective, and unlike in Matthäi's case where the criminal at least finds punishment through sheer chance, in *Justiz* the moral order remains in its fallen state.

The heirs: Schneider and Schaub

After Dürrenmatt had so vigorously explored his claim in the field of detective fiction during the 1950s, the genre experiences a decline in Switzerland over the following decades.[21] There are interesting texts, such as Adolf Muschg's *Mitgespielt* (Played Along, 1969) with its reflections of 1960s anti-authoritarianism, but in general the years until the early 1980s are lean. When the renaissance arrives, though, it does so with all the force of a new generation stepping onto the scene, just as Dürrenmatt's patriarchal figure bows out with his final effort. A comprehensive portrayal of the genre's last thirty years in Switzerland would exceed the scope of this chapter. Two highlights will have to suffice. These demonstrate that Glauser and Dürrenmatt have found worthy successors, who are aware of the tradition, of the themes that define Swiss detective literature and of the detectives that have preceded their own.

In 1993, Hansjörg Schneider introduced Peter Hunkeler, who is based in Basel. The inspector's first case revolves around the Turkish migrant worker Erdogan Civil and his discovery of a packet of diamonds in the city's sewage system. The stones give the narrative its title, *Silberkiesel* (Silver Pebbles). An international syndicate with a high-profile local businessman in its ranks is trying to apprehend Civil. Hunkeler must find the Turkish worker, protect him and his Swiss girlfriend, who works at a grocery market check-out, and expose the corruption that affluence and social rank disguise. Schneider chose a Glauser quote as an epigraph. In this quote Glauser emphasizes that the writer's task is to chronicle the quotidian and to render visible again that to which the reader has become so accustomed that he or she no longer perceives it. Schneider heeds this injunction. Despite the potentially glamorous theme of diamond smuggling, his text remains an eminently grounded piece of writing. The locales – a Turkish café, run-down tenement structures, the workers' changing room – smack of the everyday. The characters represent social reality, their aspirations lie within the scope of the normal, their anxieties are well known. This holds true for those who represent the law as well as for those who break it. The sole exception is the businessman whose turpitude approaches the pathological. As in Studer's cases, the sympathies lie with the underprivileged. Be they petty criminals, exploited foreign workers, women in low-wage jobs, even disgruntled policemen, theirs is an essential decency, and if they stray from the path of the legal or proper, these missteps result from unjust economic and social structures. Hunkeler frequently asks himself whether he is serving the right master, whether the police do not facilitate exploitation and suppression. In his darkest hours the fact that he, an old leftist, protects a bourgeois society causes him self-loathing.

Schneider has reinvigorated Swiss detective fiction with an agenda of social critique. Topical issues such as the plight of heroin addicts or the vulnerable status of immigrant communities feature alongside familiar motifs, particularly the moral bankruptcy of the country's elites. His inspector is a fighter for social justice and thus a worthy, though less sanguine, successor to Jakob Studer. To date, Hunkeler has used his skills in seven more cases, such as *Hunkeler und die Augen des Ödipus* (Hunkeler and the Eyes of Oedipus, 2010). A number of the novels have also been adapted for Swiss television.

Simon Tanner is a very different detective. Luckier with the ladies than is typical of Swiss detectives, Urs Schaub's hero is also better read than most. In particular, the detective knows Shakespeare act, scene and verse, but he is also familiar with Homer, Pascal and the German classics. Schaub's narratives abound with literary references. *Tanner*, the detective's 2003 debut, echoes the tradition of fairy tales and Romanticism. More explicitly, Dürrenmatt receives nods of acknowledgement. Like Matthäi, Schaub's detective is in search of a child murderer, and for Tanner too the search has become an obsession. After some years in Morocco, he has returned to Switzerland where the trail leads him to a rural village. Some of the characters, such as the matriarch of a rich local family and her dwarfish butler with his penchant for marionettes and literary puzzles, bear a strong resemblance to members of Dürrenmatt's cast of the outlandish. The theme of wickedness bred in the lap of luxury is also an old staple. But Schaub's text does not merely rehash themes and motifs; rather, it aligns them with elements unfamiliar in Swiss crime writing. The scepticism and metaphysical dread, so dominant in Dürrenmatt's *oeuvre*, are barely visible in the narrative of Tanner's hunt for the killer. On the contrary, and despite the text's fascination with the most lethal pathologies of the human psyche, Schaub's novel underscores the joys of existence and describes a world in which human effort can vanquish the threats to life and happiness. This optimism manifests itself in the detective's rather spectacular love life, but also in his immediate rapport with children and the celebration of food and drink. Life is worth living for Tanner and, fortunately, the intestinal cramps that plague him turn out not to be a symptom of the cancer from which Bärlach suffers, but of a dysfunctional pancreatic gland, easily fixed by an operation.

The text's emphasis on the moral calibre of simple people may also recall Sergeant Studer's cases. In this regard too, however, Schaub's text finds expression for the contemporary scene. Tanner's country is not beset by the depression-era grubbiness of Glauser's novels, and while there are large differences regarding people's financial circumstances, overall Switzerland has become affluent. People are also more emotionally expressive. Countrywomen enjoy dabbling in foreign cuisine, and gender relations have lightened. There is a touch of Hollywood dazzle to Schaub's text that is new to Swiss detective fiction. *Tanner* blends literary keenness with figures, themes and plot elements that have proven their entertainment value in an international arena. The text carries its erudition lightly and possesses the sheen of high-quality commercialism. The detective's victory in the showdown holds out the promise of more cases to come and, in fact, at the time of writing, Schaub has published three more novels featuring Simon Tanner, the most recent of which, *Der Salamander* (The Salamander), appeared in 2012.

After at least three generations, Swiss detective fiction has established itself as a feature of the country's literary scene. Without interruption, the line stretches from Loosli's engagement with the iniquities of the legal and penal systems, to

Glauser's narratives about a paladin of the disenfranchised and Dürrenmatt's ruminations on the nature of evil, to contemporary writers who have succeeded in finding their own voice. This tradition owes much to foreign influences, but is recognizable as something distinct. Most notable in this tradition are a sense of rationality's limitations and a current of social critique. The former is attributable in large measure to the country's position at the centre of a continent that during the twentieth century suffered much from the impotence of reason. The latter trait suggests that the genre fulfils a corrective function in Switzerland's culture, occasionally even a subversive one. Swiss detective fiction is often genre writing at its best: of literary quality, yet with popular appeal, engaged with topical social and cultural issues, yet articulate on themes of universal resonance.

* * *

Extract from Friedrich Glauser's *In Matto's Realm*

Sergeant Studer is sitting up with Dr Laduner, the deputy chief of the Randlingen psychiatric clinic, after a social gathering in the doctor's quarters. Studer is still trying to narrow down the list of suspects. In fact, the doctor himself is not above suspicion. With the radio playing in the background, Laduner holds forth on the pervasiveness of psychological disorders and the need to promote rational behaviour benefitting the community.

Perhaps Dr Laduner was lonely too? He had his wife, true, but there are certain things you can't discuss with your wife. He had colleagues, but what can you talk about with your colleagues? Shop! And with the doctors here? They regarded him as their teacher. Then one day a simple detective sergeant turns up in Dr Laduner's apartment. Dr Laduner seizes the moment and talks on and on at the said detective sergeant. And why not?

'He flings his paper streamers and War flares up...' Laduner repeated, and then fell silent. The military march faded out and a foreign voice filled the room. It was an urgent voice, but its urgency was unpleasant.

It said:

'Two hundred thousand men and women are gathered here to cheer me. Two hundred thousand men and women have come as representatives of the whole nation, which is behind me. Foreign states dare to accuse me of breaking a treaty. When I seized power this land lay desolate, ravaged, sick . . . I have made it great, I have made others respect it . . . Two hundred thousand men and women are listening to my words, and with them the whole nation is listening . . .'

Laduner slowly got up and went over to the shiny box from which the words were coming. A click, the voice fell silent.

'Where does Matto's realm end, Studer?' the doctor asked quietly. 'At the fence around Randlingen Clinic? You once talked about a spider sitting in the middle of its web. The threads reach out, they spread over the whole world. Matto flings his balls and his paper streamers . . .'

Friedrich Glauser, *In Matto's Realm* (1936), trans. Mike Mitchell (London: Bitter Lemon Press, 2005), pp. 205–6.

Notes

[1] See Arthur Conan Doyle, *Memories & Adventures* (London: Greenhill Books, 1988), p. 97.

[2] *Geschichte der Verbrecher X. Hermann, F. Deisler, J. Föller und Jos. Studer, durch das Kriminalgericht zu Basel den 14. Jul. 1819, theils zum Tode, theils zur Kettenstrafe verurteilt. Nach den Prozessakten bearbeitet und zur Warnung herausgegeben* (Basel: Schweighauser, 1819).

[3] Jacob Senn, *Die interessantesten Kriminalgeschichten aus alter und neuer Zeit: Ein Buch zur Unterhaltung, Warnung und Belehrung für Jung und Alt, nach den vorgelegenen Akten bearbeitet und herausgegeben von einem vieljährigen höhern Gerichtsbeamten* (St. Gallen: Altwegg-Weber, 1865).

[4] See also Jodocus Donatus Hubertus Temme, *Erinnerungen* (Leipzig: Keil, 1883).

[5] 'Die Acten enthalten einmal einen Fingerzeig. Er wurde nicht beachtet.' Jodocus Donatus Hubertus Temme, *Der Studentenmord in Zürich* (Zurich: Chronos Verlag, 2006 [1872]), p. 96. My translation.

[6] For a portrayal of the formative influences on Loosli's character and of his career as a writer and public figure, see Erwin Marti, *Carl Albert Loosli 1877–1959: Zwischen Jugendgefängnis und Pariser Bohème (1877–1907)* (Zurich: Chronos Verlag, 1996), *Carl Albert Loosli 1877–1959: Eulenspiegel in helvetischen Landen (1904–1914)* (Zurich: Chronos Verlag, 1999) and *Carl Albert Loosli 1877–1959: Im eigenen Land verbannt (1914–1959)* (Zurich: Chronos Verlag, 2009).

[7] 'Ein Mann hatte sich erschossen und den Selbstmord als Mord kamoufliert.' Friedrich Glauser, *Schlumpf Erwin Mord* (Zurich: Limmat Verlag, 1995), p. 37. My translation.

[8] See Edgar Marsch, 'Carl Albert Loosli und der Neue Schweizer Kriminalroman. Vom Justizroman zum Kriminalroman', in Edgar Marsch (ed.), *Im Fadenkreuz: Der neuere Schweizer Kriminalroman* (Zurich: Chronos Verlag, 2007), pp. 13–38 (p. 13).

[9] Glauser wrote about his addiction. The piece, entitled 'Morphium – Eine Beichte', has been collected in *Morphium und autobiographische Texte* (Zurich: Arche Verlag, 1980), pp. 121–36.

[10] See also Gerhard Saner's biography, *Friedrich Glauser: Eine Biographie* (Frankfurt a. M: Suhrkamp, 1981). Glauser's letters also make for interesting reading: Friedrich Glauser, *Briefe 1: 1911–1935* (Zurich: Arche Verlag, 1988) and *Briefe 2: 1935–1938* (Zurich: Arche Verlag, 1991).

[11] Studer also appears in a number of short stories, collected as *Wachtmeister Studers erste Fälle* (Sergeant Studer's First Cases) (Zurich: Arche Verlag, 1986). Glauser also wrote a detective novel that does not feature Studer, *Der Tee der drei alten Damen* (The Three Old Ladies' Tea, 1939), with Inspector Pilleviut as the detective.

[12] Matto already appears in Glauser's *oeuvre* in 1919 when he writes an expressionist theatre scene entitled 'Mattos Puppentheater' (Matto's Puppet Theatre), collected with other short pieces in Friedrich Glauser, *Mattos Puppentheater* (Zurich: Chronos Verlag, 1992), pp. 124–32. Like the later novel, the scene is set in a psychiatric clinic, but a detective does not appear.

[13] See Friedrich Glauser, 'Offener Brief über die "Zehn Gebote für den Kriminalroman"', in *Ich bin ein Dieb und andere Kriminalgeschichten* (Zurich: Limmat Verlag, 2008), pp. 118–29.

[14] 'schrien in den Tannen'. Friedrich Glauser, *Matto regiert* (Zurich: Limmat Verlag, 1995 [1936]), p. 17. My translation.

[15] For a consideration of the formative influences on Dürrenmatt's intellectual development, see his semi-autobiographical texts *Labyrinth* (Zurich: Diogenes Verlag, 1981) and *Turmbau* (Zurich: Diogenes Verlag, 1998) as well as the four volumes of *Gespräche* (Zurich: Diogenes Verlag, 1998).

[16] 'daß gerade die Verworrenheit der menschlichen Beziehungen es möglich mache, Verbrechen zu begehen, die *nicht* erkannt werden könnten'. Friedrich Dürrenmatt, *Der Richter und sein Henker, Der Verdacht* (Zurich: Diogenes Verlag, 1980), p. 68. *The Inspector Barlach Mysteries* (Chicago: The University of Chicago Press, 2006), p. 50.

[17] See William Spanos, *Repetitions: The Postmodern Occasion in Literature and Culture* (Baton Rouge: Louisiana State University Press, 1987), p. 24.

[18] One of these fragments is *Der Pensionierte* (The Pensioner) (Zurich: Diogenes Verlag, 1995), featuring Inspector Höchstettler. Dürrenmatt worked on this text in 1969, but abandoned it after a few chapters, apparently having lost control over the text's self-reflexive structure.

[19] Dürrenmatt's usage of the grotesque has received much attention. A good place to start is Werner Oberle's essay 'Grundsätzliches zum Werk Friedrich Dürrenmatts' and Reinhold Grimm's essay 'Parodie und Groteske im Werk Dürrenmatts', both published in W. Jäggi (ed.), *Der unbequeme Dürrenmatt* (Basel: Basler Druck- und Verlagsanstalt, 1962).

[20] For a more straightforward narrative of Switzerland's history, see Volker Reinhardt, *Geschichte der Schweiz* (Munich: C. H. Beck, 2006).

[21] See Paul Ott, *Mord im Alpenglühen: Der Schweizer Kriminalroman – Geschichte und Gegenwart* (Wuppertal: NordPark Verlag, 2005), pp. 66 ff. Ott's book is a comprehensive introduction to the genre.

Select bibliography

Dürrenmatt, Friedrich, *Das Versprechen* (Munich: Deutscher Taschenbuch Verlag, 1978 [1958]). *The Pledge*, trans. Joel Agee (Chicago: The University of Chicago Press, 2006).

——, *Der Richter und sein Henker, Der Verdacht* (Zurich: Diogenes Verlag, 1980 [1950; 1951]). *The Inspector Barlach Mysteries*, trans. Joel Agee (Chicago: The University of Chicago Press, 2006).

——, *Justiz* (Zurich: Diogenes Verlag, 1985). *The Execution of Justice*, trans. J. E. Woods (New York: Random House, 1989).

Glauser, Friedrich, *Der Chinese* (Zurich: Limmat Verlag, 1996 [1939]).

——, *Die Fieberkurve* (Zurich: Limmat Verlag, 1995 [1938]).

——, *Die Speiche* (Zurich: Limmat Verlag, 1996 [1941]).

——, *Matto regiert* (Zurich: Limmat Verlag, 1995 [1936]). *In Matto's Realm*, trans. Mike Mitchell (London: Bitter Lemon Press, 2005).

——, *Schlumpf Erwin Mord* (Zurich: Limmat Verlag, 1995 [1935]). *Thumbprint*, trans. Mike Mitchell (London: Bitter Lemon Press, 2004).

——, *Ich bin ein Dieb und andere Kriminalgeschichten* (Zurich: Limmat Verlag, 2008).

Loosli, Carl Albert, *Die Schattmattbauern* (Bern: Rotpunktverlag, 2006 [1926]).

Muschg, Adolf, *Mitgespielt* (Berlin: Suhrkamp Verlag, 1969).

Schaub, Urs, *Tanner* (Zurich: Pendo Verlag, 2003).

——, *Der Salamander* (Zurich: Limmat Verlag, 2012).

Schneider, Hansjörg, *Silberkiesel* (Zurich: Ammann Verlag, 1993).

——, *Hunkeler und die Augen des Ödipus* (Zurich: Diogenes Verlag, 2010).
Temme, Jodocus Donatus Hubertus, *Der Studentenmord in Zürich* (Zurich: Chronos Verlag, 2006 [1872]).

Further secondary reading

Bühler, Patrick, *Die Leiche in der Bibliothek: Friedrich Glauser und der Detektiv-Roman* (Heidelberg: Universitätsverlag C. Winter, 2002).
Crockett, Roger A., *Understanding Friedrich Dürrenmatt* (Columbia, SC: University of South Carolina Press, 1998).
Fringeli, Dieter, *Dichter im Abseits: Schweizer Autoren von Glauser bis Hohl* (Zurich: Artemis Verlag, 1974).
Jacksch, Eveline, *Friedrich Glauser: Anwalt der Außenseiter* (Bonn: Bouvier Verlag, 1976).
Ott, Paul, *Mord im Alpenglühen: Der Schweizer Kriminalroman – Geschichte und Gegenwart* (Wuppertal: NordPark Verlag, 2005).
Spycher, Peter, *Friedrich Dürrenmatt: Das erzählerische Werk* (Frauenfeld: Verlag Huber, 1972).
Tiusanen, Timo, *Dürrenmatt: A Study in Plays, Prose, Theory* (Princeton: Princeton University Press, 1977).

5

Der Afrika-Krimi: Africa in German Crime Fiction

JULIA AUGART

Over the past decades, the crime novel has developed from a form of purely entertaining mass literature to the most successful literary genre in the market,[1] and is being given increased attention and status in contemporary literary criticism. A subgenre of crime novels set in Africa existed relatively early on, with works by Agatha Christie, Edgar Wallace and Elspeth Huxley – the latter writing in the British crown colony of Kenya in the 1930s.[2] The 1970s finally saw the emergence of the German *Afrika-Krimi*: German crime fiction set in various African countries that integrates its setting into the action, plot, crime and depiction of investigators, victims and perpetrators. In addition to the crime and its resolution, many *Afrika-Krimis* present social problems or critique Western attitudes and behaviours towards Africa and Africans.

This chapter begins by placing the German *Afrika-Krimi* in the context of the contemporary German Africa novel, crime fiction and African crime fiction respectively. The *Afrika-Krimi* is then further explored through an analysis of crime genre elements such as setting, space, characters and crime, in order to provide an overview of the subgenre, as well as insights into a selection of primary texts.

The German Afrika-Krimi and its development

Africa is not just a popular literary topic;[3] African literature is also increasingly reviewed internationally. As a result, the German *Afrika-Krimi*, alongside African crime fiction, is the subject of growing attention and academic interest.[4] The *Afrika-Krimi*, a relatively new subcategory, thus forms part of a number of trends and offers the arguably restrictive crime genre, with its plot and character conventions, new opportunities to develop beyond purely entertaining suspense fiction.

Diverse tendencies are visible in the German *Afrika-Krimi*, which align with those Dirk Göttsche identifies in relation to the contemporary German Africa novel. Notably, some works project common stereotypes of Africa, while others embrace cultural difference, participate in postcolonial discourses, and provide opportunities to expose and disrupt attachments to outdated images and discourses about Africa, or to fashion these anew in the spirit of 'rewriting colonialism'.[5] In addition, the *Afrika-Krimi* can be classified alongside much loved *Regionalkrimis* (regional crime novels), such as the 'Eifel' series by Jacques Berndorf, the 'Allgäu' series by Volker Klüpfel and Michael Kobr, or the 'Brittany' novels of Jean-Luc Bannalec, to name just a few popular examples whose literary crime scenes are inseparable from a region or place.[6] The *Afrika-Krimi*, however, moves beyond the geographical boundaries of the *Regionalkrimi*, offering hitherto undiscovered and unexploited new spaces for crime narratives to unfold. Place and setting have become highly distinctive features, as Eva Erdmann argues in the larger context of contemporary international crime fiction.[7] Last but not least, it should be noted that the 'No. 1 Ladies' Detective Agency' series by Alexander McCall Smith, which has been an international best-seller since the 1990s and presents a romanticized, idealized and simplified image of Africa,[8] has opened the door for crime fiction from Africa by Deon Meyer, Pepetela and Helon Habila, among others.[9] As a result, Africa has attracted international attention and recognition as a crime setting, which has in turn led to the production of new crime fiction.

'African Crime Fiction refers to *crime, detective and mystery novels that are set in Africa or feature African characters*'[10] – so reads the definition of the University of Indiana's research project 'African Crime Fiction', which engages with the growing corpus of African crime novels. By contrast, in the foreword of their volume *Life is a Thriller: Investigating African Crime Fiction*, Anja Oed and Christine Matzke restrict their definition to 'crime fiction by African authors' and conclude that the African crime novel, like African literature more generally, is characterized by its social critique.[11] African crime fiction can thus be viewed as a fusion of entertainment and social criticism.[12] My own understanding of the concept 'German *Afrika-Krimi*' includes crime novels – thrillers, spy novels, historical crime novels, youth crime novels or crime short stories – written by German and German-speaking authors, and set on the African continent.[13] Crime novels set in German-speaking countries that feature African characters form a further subcategory. However, crime novels set in Africa that have no connection to the German-speaking world other than the national origin of their author belong to a broader definition of the German *Afrika-Krimi*.[14]

The first German *Afrika-Krimi* is Henry Kolarz's political thriller *Kalahari* (1977), which plays in Zimbabwe, Botswana and South Africa and features a kaleidoscope of characters from an African freedom fighter and South African mine owner to a German aid worker and Russian secret agents. Kolarz situates his crime novel against the backdrop of African independence movements and the Cold War, and outlines their impacts on Africa. At the same time, through its diamond-smuggling plot, the novel addresses the theme of raw commodities and their political sensitivity, which has played a significant role in Africa's relationship with its Eastern and Western partners from the colonial period to the present day. Although Joachim Warmbold accuses *Kalahari* of being unable to depict African landscapes and Africans accurately, this pioneering novel's sociopolitical engagement, its efforts to portray Africa and Africans positively, and its critical depiction of white South Africans and Russian politicians should be acknowledged.[15]

In spite of Kolarz's success – his second *Afrika-Krimi Die roten Elefanten* (The Red Elephants, 1981) was filmed for German television – relatively few *Afrika-Krimis* were published in the 1980s and early 1990s. Only in the mid-1990s is there an increase, with a concomitant development of the subgenre. Reasons for this growth include the rise of Africa in German literature,[16] as well as the emergence of the *Regionalkrimi* in the 1980s and its expansion in the 1990s.[17] Numbers have risen continuously since the turn of the millennium: more than half of the just over one hundred German *Afrika-Krimis* published to date appeared between 2010 and 2014.[18] Many of these novels have been published as e-books: they are significant for the genre in quantitative terms, but are sometimes of questionable quality.[19]

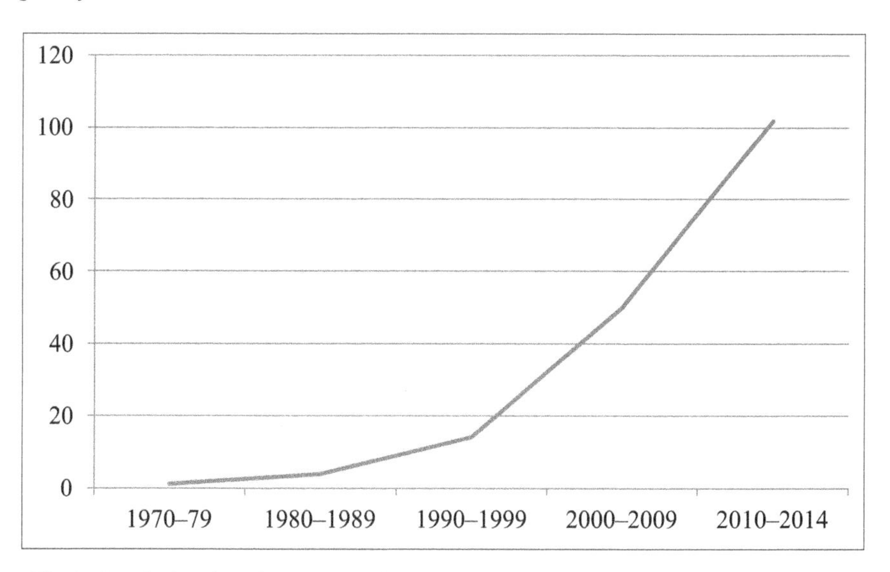

Fig 1. Graph showing the growth of German *Afrika-Krimis* between 1977 and 2014.

The first academic studies on the *Afrika-Krimi* also appeared in the 1990s, due to the growing interest in literary representations of Africa – inspired in part by postcolonial debates – as well as a more intensive academic engagement with the crime genre. Dieter Riegel, in his study *Africa in West German Crime Fiction* (1991), is the first to explore the subject, followed by Peter Bräunlein's '"Die Zähne blitzten weiß" – Afrika und Afrikaner/innen im Kriminalroman (Rassismus im Krimi)' ('"The Teeth Flashed White" – Africans in the Crime Novel (Racism in the *Krimi*)', 1996), which, while focusing on German *Afrika-Krimis*, does not explicitly identify them as a subgenre. Jochen Schmidt's wide-ranging study *Gangster, Opfer, Detektive* (Gangsters, Victims, Detectives, 2009 [1998]) examines a number of German *Afrika-Krimis*, but does not classify them as such,[20] while Göttsche, in his essay on German Africa novels, discusses some crime fiction, but without viewing it as a category. Only in 2013 is the subgenre finally defined and delineated, in a journal article on the investigator in the German *Afrika-Krimi*.[21]

The majority of authors who write *Afrika-Krimis* – with a few exceptions such as Bernhard Jaumann and Peter Höner – are not established writers and have other careers: Ulrich Wickert is better known as a television journalist than as a crime author, Christof Wackernagel is an actor, Horst Ehmke a German constitutional lawyer and politician, Martin Gutman a professor of theology, and Detlef Blettenberg and Lena Blaudez worked in the development aid sector before they started to write. Aptly, Andreas Alpes used to work as a journalist for the police and Eckard Mordhorst was a chief inspector. However, all of them have visited the African continent, whether as a tourist or for longer in a professional capacity, and have gathered impressions and experiences in various countries. They articulate or process these through their crime narratives and investigative protagonists, as Lena Blaudez elaborates:

> What I experienced and learned in Benin was unbelievably intense. The people, their way of life, the completely different priorities, the foreignness of being white and the slow assimilation into another culture – these things obviously affect you greatly. You develop a new way of looking, a wider perspective, which is further sharpened through the process of writing, through the attempt at formulation. And when you then experience incompetence, arrogance or bare-faced cynicism, and feel incredibly angry about the hypocrisy, sheer pragmatism, and political or economic calculation of institutions that are supposedly there to help the country, it sometimes really helps to say to yourself, I'll write down my thoughts about that. Of course, it's all very subjective, but it helps.[22]

Blaudez's need to explore her experiences in Africa arises from significant cultural and racial differences and the intensity of African life. At the same time, writing can function as a means of defusing or putting encounters and problems with the other culture into perspective, thereby serving as an outlet for emotions and sensations. By contrast, Swiss author Peter Höner tries to tell stories that show some of the difficulties created by mutual prejudice, which often make it hard to meet Africans on equal terms.[23] In Bernhard Jaumann's case, he simply knew from the beginning of his stay in Namibia that he would write about the country, as he had previously written about others.[24] Blaudez also reflects on the choice of the crime genre, which provides a good fictional framework for the experiences gained in Africa: 'Ultimately, the subject chooses the form. And the genre is so versatile: you can represent hard-hitting reality in an entertaining and exciting way using the tools of fiction, and the investigative case is always there to keep you engaged.'[25] In this way, German *Afrika-Krimis* help to articulate an intensively experienced realm, but also depict a new realm to the reader.

Many German *Afrika-Krimis* thus reflect the authors' views on Africa and are notable for detailed descriptions of lifestyle, customs or traditions, as well as the surroundings and their otherness in relation to Germany or Europe. The use of words, names or forms of address from different African countries and languages illuminate their respective ways of life. They create an authentic picture that moves beyond purely local colour, as the extract from Jaumann's *Steinland* (Stoneland, 2012) at the end of this chapter shows, with some *Afrika-Krimis* also providing a glossary of terms.[26] It is clear from these depictions that many of the authors love Africa, and represent Africa and Africans in a positive, often unprejudiced way. They reflect how Africa and Africans are seen and treated, and tend to present critical perspectives on Western policy in relation to Africa. Not all manage to paint a diverse picture, however: some authors remain imprisoned by clichés and stereotypes. Often, the central investigative figure can be viewed as the alter ego of the author, with each sharing the same professional interests, hobbies[27] and views on Africa, even when the novel is not explicitly factual, like Jürgen Alberts and Eckhard Mordhorst's *Leiche über Bord* (Body Overboard, 2008). One possible drawback of using the *Afrika-Krimi* to work through a sense of alienation or personal experience, or as a platform for critique, is that it may sometimes be lacking in suspense. Höner's Kenya novels have been criticized for being 'sedate', while Jaumann has been reproached for overly deliberate and dull crime plotting.[28]

The constituent elements of the German Afrika-Krimi

Like the crime novel more broadly, the *Afrika-Krimi* consists of constituent elements such as space or setting, main characters (investigators, victims and perpetrators), as well as the crime itself. These elements, however, are mostly placed in African contexts, as the examples below illustrate, emphasizing their particular contribution to the genre.

German *Afrika-Krimis* are set across almost the entire continent and portray all major regions. Only a few countries have not yet acted as a location, such as Djibouti or Niger. The most common setting is Kenya in East Africa, which has hosted seventeen *Afrika-Krimis* to date and is also one of the most popular countries depicted in German literature about Africa.[29] It is followed by Namibia and South Africa, which have eleven and nine novels respectively, if one counts Falk Guder's historical crime novel *Tod im Herrenzimmer* (Death in the Study, 2012) as a Namibia-*Krimi*. The latter is set in colonial Germany, but its investigative trail leads to *Deutsch-Südwestafrika* (German South West Africa), as Namibia was termed under German colonial rule from 1884–1915. All three countries – Kenya, Namibia and South Africa – are also preferred holiday destinations for Germans, which influence and inspire both writers and readers. Slightly further down the list, Morocco has six *Afrika-Krimis*, while Mali in West Africa has four. The Democratic Republic of Congo in Central Africa, with a total of six novels to date, is also increasingly being used as a setting, particularly in relation to its coltan metal industry.

Thirteen *Afrika-Krimis* are set in Germany, with either African characters or strong links with Africa. These are usually historical crime novels such as Ernst Georg Richter's *Das Kongo-Komplott* (The Congo Conspiracy, 2013) or contemporary crime novels such as Bella Fall's *Kein Sonnenaufgang in Afrika* (No Sunrise in Africa, 2002), which explores racism and the problems of African immigrants in Germany. In addition, there are novels that depict a fictitious Africa or African country, such as the Austrian writer Christine Grän's *Weiße sterben selten in Samyana* (Whites Seldom Die in Samyana, 1986), which makes generic use of the continent (see also chapters 3 and 6). Others show multiple countries, such as Karl Olsberg's thriller *Der Duft* (Fragrance, 2009), which plays in Uganda and the Republic of the Sudan, and Edi Graf's *Verschleppt* (Abducted, 2012), which moves from Germany to Namibia via Nigeria. A high number of novels also switch between European and African countries, or represent these locations in parallel, like Horst Ehmke's *Privatsache* (Private Affair, 2003), whose action takes place in Sierra Leone, Germany and Belgium.

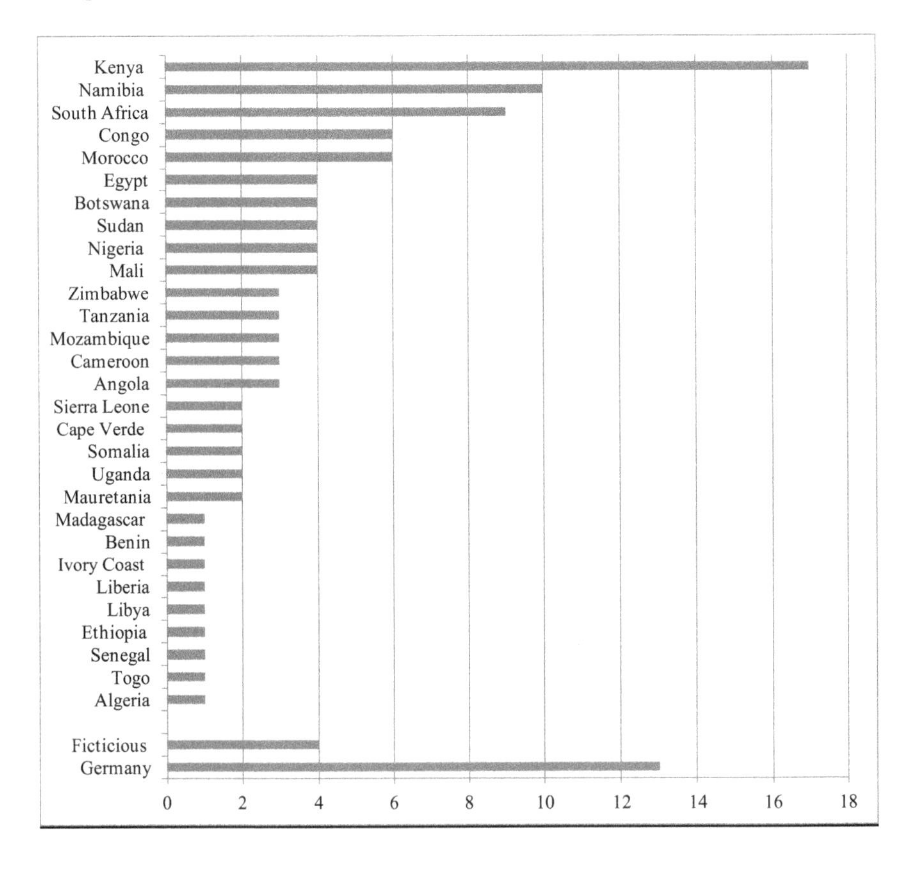

Fig 2. Table showing the number of *Afrika-Krimis* set in each country.

Most of the countries listed in figure 2 have a smaller number of German *Afrika-Krimis* to their name. Although the largest groupings of *Afrika-Krimis* correlate to countries or regions that are popular tourist destinations, this is not the only criterion. The high rate of German tourism in Namibia is partially linked to its former status as a German colony and to its complex postcolonial legacy in Namibia and Germany. The concentration of *Afrika-Krimis* set in this country is also due to author Bernhard Jaumann, who lived in Namibia for several years and consequently chose it as the setting for his 'Clemencia Garises' police series and his standalone *Geiers Mahlzeit* (Vulture's Meal, 2008).

Africa, which has been neglected in research on literary spaces,[30] serves as more than a backdrop in *Afrika-Krimis* – it also intensifies the puzzle of the crime and unsettles the reader through its representation.[31] In addition to the geographical location, the spatial dimensions in which *Afrika-Krimis* play out are significant – particularly isolated or bounded spaces such as a finite set of characters, in which the investigator seeks the criminal, or a locked room, as featured in Ralf Strackbein's *Wolkenmord. 12.000 Meter über Afrika* (Murder in the Clouds – 12,000 Meters above Africa, 2012), which depicts a murder being committed and then solved in an airplane flying high over the continent. Another significant notion is Africa as an 'unknown space' – one that is unfamiliar to the reader or has yet to be discovered – which contributes both to the heightening of suspense and to a sense of mystification within the narrative. The partial inaccessibility of Africa, even today, offers crime novels plenty of potential.

In the context of crime genre conventions, the roles of both investigating and non-investigating figures are significant. In particular, the figure of the investigator[32] occupies a central role in the crime novel and its narrative. The reader can identify with the investigator and he/she also functions as a representative of the reader-as-investigator in the solving of the crime. German police detectives investigating in Africa are rare, as they do not have the jurisdiction to operate there. Only in *Leiche über Bord* do we see two German police investigators being sent to Abidjan in Ivory Coast in order to solve a murder on board a German freighter – in other words, officially on German territory. By contrast, Hannes Nygaard's *Fahrt zur Hölle* (The Way to Hell, 2013) shows Superintendent Lüders operating in Kenya and Somalia in an undercover capacity, while Detlef Wolff's police inspector in *Katenkamp in Kenia* (Katenkamp in Kenya, 1983) is tasked with running a training programme for Kenyan police, but gets involved in investigating two murder cases. Conversely, *Afrika-Krimis* set in Germany feature mainly German police investigators operating on their own professional terrain, as seen in Fall's *Kein Sonnenaufgang in Afrika*, Richter's *Das Kongo-Komplott* and Stefan Winges's *Mord im Afrika-Klub* (Murder in the Africa Club, 2010).

Detectives or private investigators are also a popular investigative type on the African continent and are usually sent by their German clients, as seen in Detlef Blettenberg's *Land der guten Hoffnung* (Land of Good Hope, 2006), in which the private investigator offers insights into South Africa's post-apartheid society while searching for the kidnappers of a ship-owner's daughter. In Carsten Stenzel's thriller *Douala* (Douala, 2012), a private investigator travels to Cameroon, but, like the country's indigenous pygmies, falls into the hands of neo-colonial slave traders. The 1990s Kenyan crime trilogy by Peter Höner features Swiss private investigator Jürg Mettler, who stays on in Kenya after his first job, and fights crime together with his friend, the Kenyan police inspector Tetu Njoroge.

The largest group of investigators is made up of a diverse set of amateur detectives, who are often pulled accidentally into a case[33] and are frequently associated with the thriller genre, in which the investigator cannot always accurately be separated from the figure of the victim. The amateur detective, journalist or agent – all already employed in investigative occupations – usually encounter their crimes in the course of other inquiries. Investigative journalists include Anna Marx in Grän's *Weiße sterben selten in Samyana* and Edi Graf's radio journalist Linda Rohloff, who repeatedly gets involved in cases in Germany that lead to different African countries such as Kenya, South Africa or Nigeria. In C. B. Stoll's *Der Viktoria-Report* (The Victoria Report, 2012), Mara Podolski uncovers the criminal activities of a German food producer in Tanzania and Germany, and in Peter Zeidler's *Abschied in Casablanca* (Farewell in Casablanca, 2000), German federal intelligence agent Sembritzki searches for poison-gas factories reputedly located in Morocco. Other amateur detectives include a film director in Blettenberg's *Harte Schnitte* (Hard Cuts, 2005), a female psychotherapist in Andreas Albes's thriller *Die Insel* (The Island, 2002), an economic adviser in Wolfgang Mock's *Der Flug der Seraphim* (The Flight of the Seraphim, 2003) and two management consultants in Olsberg's *Der Duft*. In Ehmke's *Privatsache*, the main protagonist is a technician and aid worker. Lena Blaudez features a female photographer in her crime novels and Christof Wackernagel's investigator in *Der Fluch der Dogon* (The Curse of the Dogon, 2012) is a carpenter.

Apart from a few exceptions, the investigators operating in Africa are German and offer German readers the possibility of identification. However, as investigators they are fundamentally outsiders,[34] especially as they are working outside their own country and cultural sphere. They are marked out as other by their appearance, but also by their investigative methods and views. As Blaudez's protagonist points out: 'I am white. I am a foreigner.'[35] At the same time these investigators set themselves apart from their fellow countrymen, who visit Africa as tourists. As Höner's private investigator Mettler emphasizes: 'He is not a tourist . . . He is not here on holiday.'[36] However, they usually work closely with a partner and their discussions allow the reader to gain information from their observations or preliminary conclusions.[37] Sometimes *Afrika-Krimis* will depict culturally diverse teams, which are frequently designed to show the investigators as equals with equal rights.[38] Thus Wolff's Katenkamp works closely with and learns from Kenyan police inspector Shikuku, while Jaumann's police inspector Clemencia Garises collaborates with her police colleagues and *Allgemeine Zeitung* reporter Claus Tiedtke. Investigators' lovers sometimes become confidants who replace their colleagues, as in the case of Blaudez's photographer Ada Simon or Höner's private investigator Mettler, whose girlfriend often criticizes his investigations, but describes herself as his assistant.[39]

In contrast to investigators in the *Afrika-Krimi*, non-investigative figures such as victims or perpetrators are African and German or European respectively. Yet crime novels set in Germany or Europe, which are classified as *Afrika-Krimis* due to their African characters rather than setting, feature victims who are almost always African. Notably, differences between victims are represented in a way that is anchored in reality. Thus, if the narrative features a white murder victim, his or her higher status and the priority given to the investigation are emphasized, as seen in the novel *Katenkamp in Kenia*, or Jaumann's two novels *Die Stunde des Schakals* (*The Hour of the Jackal*, 2010) and *Steinland*. The perpetrator – usually a murderer – is often the most inconspicuous character and as a suspect sets the wheels of deception in motion.[40] Criminal figures – not necessarily the perpetrator, but often also clients – are frequently situated in the political elite and in business or management circles.[41] In Kolarz's *Die roten Elefanten*, poaching and ivory-smuggling crimes are never solved, because the African elite needs to be protected. The author alludes here to rumours about the involvement of a former Kenyan first lady in ivory smuggling during the 1970s. Similarly, in Jaumann's *Steinland*, a political minister responsible for intimidation and murder is not publicly exposed. Authors also regularly show white (Western) criminals in action or cooperating with African partners. In Höner's novels, fictional Kenyan gold trading is linked to the Swiss banking mafia, showing corruption on both sides. In Ehmke's *Privatsache*, a former aid worker organizes human trafficking between Sierra Leone and Europe, while novels presenting cases of poaching often have white or Western financial backing, which facilitates the export of the product abroad.

The plot of the crime novel centres on the unexplained crime and its solution.[42] As in the traditional crime novel,[43] murder is the most common transgression in the German *Afrika-Krimi*, which shows African spears, poison or a coconut used alongside Kalashnikovs as murder weapons. In Wolff's *Katenkamp in Kenia*, two murders – those of a Kenyan prostitute and a German tourist – require solving. In Jaumann's *Die Stunde des Schakals*, murders of former secret agents from the apartheid era are under investigation, while in the novel *Steinland*, the suicide of a farmer is presented as murder and thereby politicized. The theme of kidnapping is also addressed in various crime novels, alongside the hijacking of ships. The latter is depicted in crime novels set in Somalia, such as Nygaard's *Fahrt zur Hölle* and Gérard Schwyn's *Die Piraten von Somalia* (The Pirates of Somalia, 2010), which explore the problem of piracy in the Horn of Africa. The kidnapping of people is featured in Blettenberg's *Land der guten Hoffnung*, set in South Africa, and Jürgen Schmidt-Ravens's *Mord in der Kasbah* (Murder in the Casbah, 2006), which shows the abduction and release of a millionaire's daughter in Morocco. Ehmke's *Privatsache* and Graf's *Verschleppt* explore the trading of African girls and the forced prostitution of female Africans in Europe.

Many of the crime novels address crimes that are largely specific to Africa and thus reinforce the reductive and mainly stereotypical images of Africa presented in the international media. These crimes include poaching and the illegal trade of elephant ivory, rhinocerous horn and animal furs, as *Die roten Elefanten* illustrates when the Kenyan anti-poaching unit uncovers a complex smuggling network. Other crime novels explore illegal mining and the export of raw materials and natural resources, such as tropical timber in Blaudez's work, but a more common focus is on diamonds or gold, as in Lüders's *Gold im Gilf Kebir* (Gold in the Gilf Kebir, 2001), or more recently on coltan metal from Congo in Stieglitz's *Coltan* (Coltan, 2014), among others. In *Der Fluch der Dogon*, Wackernagel draws attention to the illegal export of African artworks and shows how sacred masks from Mali are sold in high-class German art galleries. Other crimes include food production scandals, such as those featured in Stoll's *Viktoria-Report*, and illegal pharmaceutical experiments in Stuhr's *Die Miene des Todes* (The Mine of Death, 2010), which simultaneously describes the exploitation of Zimbabwean mine workers and their use as subjects in medical experiments. In Olsberg's action-packed thriller *Der Duft*, two management consultants uncover secret experiments with an illegal scent on gorillas in Uganda and are able to thwart a terrorist plot using this deathly fragrance.

These crime novels therefore do not simply engage with African themes and crimes, but also with social problems that lend them a wider meaning. Occasionally, novels draw on the stereotype of a magical-spiritual Africa, such as Hilliges's *Die dunkle Macht [Afrikas]* (The Dark Power [of Africa], 2001); further examples include some voodoo scenes in Blaudez's work and Wackernagel's representation of Dogon's magical powers. Other novels, however, make an effort to revise this image of Africa by depicting normal, everyday life, and representing individuals and cultures as equal. In the case of Peter Höner's work, this has led to commonalities between Kenyan and Swiss cultures being highlighted rather than differences.[44]

In their Kenya crime novels, Höner and Wolff formulate a critique of tourism at the point when mass tourism is just taking off. Already in 1983, Wolff explores the tourist industry's negative manifestations, such as sex tourism and sexual exploitation, and in the 1990s, Höner portrays the behaviour of tourists and expats critically, drawing parallels with former colonial masters. The crime novels of Ehmke and Blaudez – the latter herself an aid worker in West Africa for a number of years – repeatedly question development aid practices and include the depiction of corrupt aid workers. The focus on crimes such as the export of raw materials and natural resources, pharmaceutical experiments and the production of toxins can be read as a critique of the neo-colonial exploitation of Africa. Alternatively, many German *Afrika-Krimis* are keen to present a different, non-judgemental depiction of Africa, to discuss racism or discrimination, and to criticize existing, collective prejudices against Africa and Africans.

The Namibia novels of Bernhard Jaumann are historical *Afrika-Krimis* that form part of a growing trend of historical Africa novels[45] and historical crime novels.[46] In *Die Stunde des Schakals*, Jaumann merges the historically documented murder of white apartheid opponent and independence fighter Anton Lubowski in 1989 with a set of fictitious murders in the present. These murders, of South African secret service agents, eventually lead to the closure of the unsolved Lubowski case. Historical facts and Jaumann's view of how events might have unfolded are presented through the memories of his fictitious characters. The novel thereby portrays the country at the time of apartheid and its struggle for independence, but also shows a present-day Namibia, whose society is still divided twenty years later.[47]

Thus far, Jaumann's *Steinland* is the only German *Afrika-Krimi* that has engaged directly with postcolonial issues.[48] The novel explores the current land reform programme in Namibia, which aims to redistribute farmland whose ownership may have been continuous since colonial times. At the same time, it uses flashbacks to outline the history of a German family and its farm since the beginning of German settlement in the nineteenth century. These sequences show how the Rodensteins built up and tended their farm, 'Steinland' (Stoneland), over generations and – as the extract at the end of the chapter clearly shows – regard this land as their own. Through the act of bestowing German names on the property and its features, they override earlier African names and affiliations and make the land into their 'personal possession'.[49] In the novel, the farm is to be expropriated and allocated to previously disadvantaged population groups as part of the land reform. The owner of the farm shoots himself, but his suicide is covered up by his family and neighbours, who pretend that he was shot during an ambush on the farm in order to delay or prevent the expropriation. Eventually, the 'murder' is solved, along with the reason for the expropriation order: the Minister for Land and Resettlement has a personal interest in the farm, and ultimately, as is shown in a disillusioned dénouement, everything stays as it is – neither the politician is exposed nor the farm expropriated. The question of how land reform is to be carried out peacefully and fairly also remains open and indicates the difficulties Namibia has with its colonial legacy. Both crime novels by Jaumann thus place the crimes of the past alongside the crimes of the present, and show how the origins of current crimes lie in the past of apartheid or colonialism.

Conclusion

As its development over the past forty years shows, the German *Afrika-Krimi* has evolved into an independent subgenre within the larger genre of crime fiction. *Afrika-Krimis* follow conventional crime narrative structures, adapting elements such as setting, characters and crimes in accordance with their respective African contexts and in their choice of critically aware themes. In part, the *Afrika-Krimi* conforms to media stereotypes of a continent shaped by disaster and criminality through its choice of genre and themes: some crime novels reproduce common prejudices or, as Göttsche shows, combine stereotypical German fantasies about Africa with disaster plots.[50] Nonetheless, many *Afrika-Krimis* do make an effort, as Roth already argues in 2001, to provide a positive and diverse portrait of Africa using an 'unprejudiced eye'.[51] In their themes and topics, authors also often show that they are concerned with more than the crime and its resolution. In their representations of African life, they allow the reader to gain an insight into the continent and its diverse cultures, and illuminate the problems faced by African countries, as well as the role of the West, in a nuanced way. In the process they question aspects of the tourist industry, development aid and the exploitation of Africa by Western industrial nations, as well as exploring issues such as racism, prejudice and stereotypical modes of thought. Thus, Oed and Matzke's assertion in relation to African crime novels – that they are fundamentally linked by their strong emphasis on social criticism – also holds good for many German *Afrika-Krimis*, allowing them to be viewed positively as 'crime with a message'.[52]

* * *

Extract from Bernhard Jaumann's *Steinland*

Detective Inspector Clemencia Garises and her colleague Tjikundu visit a farm called 'Steinland' (Stoneland), in order to interview Mrs Rodenstein about the apparent murder of her husband and the kidnapping of her son. The investigation is set against the backdrop of the land reform programme, which aims to redistribute land to Namibian citizens formerly disadvantaged by colonialism, and has created tensions between the government and rich, white farmers such as the Rodensteins.

'Mevrou Rodenstein is outside in the garden.'

Mrs Rodenstein wore work clothes and veld-shoes made from kudu leather. She was in the process of pruning some bare-looking bushes. When she noticed Clemencia and Tjikundu, she lowered the pruning scissors and said: 'You have to do it in winter. Before the shoots become succulent again.'

'To everything its season', said Clemencia. Winter wasn't over by a long stretch. But even if by a miracle everything were to sprout and bloom tomorrow, there was nothing more important to Mrs Rodenstein right now than the garden.

As if she had guessed Clemencia's thoughts, she said: 'It won't help anyone to let the work slide. Quite the opposite. I owe it to the family to make sure everything keeps running smoothly. This is our home.'

She cut off a withered branch and added, 'for now'.

'Do you want to move?'

'Want?' Mrs Rodenstein laughed bitterly. 'The government has sent us a compulsory purchase order. Our farm has been chosen to pass into the ownership of the previously disadvantaged as part of land reform. Because it's suitable for that purpose, says the justification. Everything that belongs to the whites and is moderately thriving is suitable. And we're not the only ones in the area who are going to be dispossessed.'

'But you'll receive compensation?' asked Tjikundu.

'If by compensation you mean that we'll be paid a couple of dollars per square metre, then yes. But what do we get for the sweat used to build up this farm? What about everything we planted in this garden and coaxed into life? What about the sunsets we won't be able to see any more from the veranda? And the happiness and suffering of generations? The memories we carry here with us every day?'

And what about the people who also lived and worked here, but who weren't even entitled to be buried on this land? Clemencia knew that this question was on the tip of Tjikundu's tongue. She touched him lightly on the arm. No, not now. After all, they weren't here to discuss the land reform, but to investigate a criminal case.

Bernhard Jaumann, *Steinland* (Berlin: Kindler Verlag, 2012), p. 60. Chapter and extract translated by Katharina Hall.

Notes

[1] Christine Matzke and Susanne Mühleisen (eds), *Postcolonial Postmortems. Crime Fiction from a Transcultural Perspective* (Amsterdam and New York: Rodopi, 2006), p. 1 and Eva Erdmann, 'Nationality International. Detective Fiction in the Late Twentieth Century', in Marieke Krajenbrink and Kate M. Quinn (eds), *Investigating Identities: Questions of Identity in Contemporary International Crime Fiction* (Amsterdam and New York: Rodopi, 2009), pp. 11–26 (p. 11).

[2] For example, Agatha Christie's *Death on the Nile* (1937) and Elspeth Huxley's *Murder on Safari* (1938).

[3] See Dirk Göttsche, 'Rekonstruktion und Remythisierung der kolonialen Welt: Neue historische Romane über den deutschen Kolonialismus in Afrika', in Michael Hofmann and Rita Morrien (eds), *Deutsch-afrikanische Diskurse in Geschichte und Gegenwart: Literatur- und Kulturwissenschaftliche Perspektiven* (Amsterdam and New York: Rodopi, 2012), pp. 171–95 (p. 171).

[4] Lenny Picker, 'Beyond that Lady Detective', *Publisher's Weekly*, 29 August 2011, *http://www.publishersweekly.com/pw/by-topic/new-titles/adult-announcements/article/48474-beyond-that-lady-detective-african-crime-fiction.html* (accessed 20 August 2015); Matzke and Mühleisen (eds), *Postcolonial Postmortems*, p. 1.

[5] See Dirk Göttsche, 'Zwischen Exotismus und Postkolonialismus. Der Afrika-Diskurs in der deutschsprachigen Gegenwartsliteratur', in M. Moustapha Diallo and Dirk Göttsche (eds), *Intertextuelle Texturen. Afrika und Deutschland im Reflexionsmedium der Literatur* (Bielefeld: Aisthesis, 2003), pp. 161–244 (p. 161).

[6] Jochen Schmidt, *Gangster, Opfer, Detektive: Eine Typengeschichte des Kriminalromans* (2nd edn; Hillesheim: KBV Verlag, 2009 [1998]), p. 971.

[7] See Erdmann, 'Nationality International', p. 12.

[8] See Effi Bettinger, 'Riddles in the Sands of Kalahari: Detectives at Work in Botswana', in Matzke and Mühleisen (eds), *Postcolonial Postmortems*, pp. 161–79 (p. 161).

[9] See Picker, 'Beyond that Lady Detective'.

[10] Sarah Keil, 'Guide to the African Crime Fiction Project', *http://libraries.iub.edu/guide-african-crime-fiction-project* (accessed 20 August 2015), emphasis in original.

[11] Anja Oed and Christine Matzke (eds), *Life is a Thriller. Investigating African Crime Fiction* (Cologne: Rüdiger Köppe Verlag, 2012), p. 10.

[12] Oed and Matzke, *Life is a Thriller*, p. 10.

[13] Most of the authors of German-language *Afrika-Krimis* are German. There are a few Swiss writers, such as Peter Höner, and Austrian works such as Gerhard Roth's *Der Strom* (The Current, 2002).

[14] For example, Erich Loest's *Waffenkarussell* (The Weapons Carousel), written under the pseudonym Hans Walldorf, was published in East Germany in 1968. This crime novel is set in Nigeria and England, and features a Scotland Yard investigator. The novel therefore does not fit my narrower definition of a German *Afrika-Krimi*.

[15] Joachim Warmbold, *'Ein Stückchen neudeutsche Erd'. Deutsche Kolonial-Literatur. Aspekte ihrer Geschichte, Eigenart und Wirkung, dargestellt am Beispiel Afrikas* (Frankfurt a.M.: Haag & Herchen, 1982), p. 198.
[16] Göttsche, 'Zwischen Exotismus und Postkolonialismus', p. 161.
[17] Schmidt, *Gangster, Opfer, Detektive*, p. 984.
[18] This data has been gathered in the course of my research project.
[19] The novels of Angelika Friedmann do not offer convincing portrayals of Kenyan journalists and investigators, and their wide-ranging discussions on injustice and the unequal distribution of property in the world are very Germanocentric.
[20] In the section 'Fremdgänger', he explores crime novels with crime scenes outside Germany, which he presents as a discrete group. Schmidt, *Gangster, Opfer, Detektive*, p. 1005.
[21] See Julia Augart, 'Der reisende Detektiv. Ermittler im deutschen Afrikakrimi', *Acta Germanica. German Studies in Africa*, 41 (2013a), 42–55.
[22] 'Das, was ich in Benin erlebt und erfahren habe, war unglaublich intensiv. Die Leute, die Lebenshaltungen, die ganz anderen Prioritäten, die Fremdheit als Weiße und das langsame Hineinwachsen in eine andere Kultur, das bewirkt natürlich viel für einen selbst. Man entwickelt einen neuen Blick, einen größeren Blickwinkel, der auch durch das Aufschreiben wieder geschärft wird, durch den Versuch, zu formulieren. Und wenn man dann Inkompetenz und Arroganz erlebt oder blanken Zynismus und sich wahnsinnig ärgert über Heuchelei, puren Pragmatismus und politisches oder wirtschaftliches Kalkül von Institutionen, die angeblich dazu da sind, dem Land Nutzen zu bringen, da tut es einfach ganz gut, sich zu sagen, ich schreibe jetzt mal auf, was mir dazu einfällt. Das ist natürlich ganz subjektiv, hilft aber.' Lena Blaudez, afterword to *Spiegelreflex. Ada Simon in Cotonou* (Zurich: Unionsverlag, 2005), p. 247; trans. by Katharina Hall.
[23] Sonja Lehner, *Schwarz-weiße Verständigung. Interkulturelle Kommunikationsprozesse in europäisch-deutschsprachigen und englisch- und französischsprachigen afrikanischen Romanen (1970–1990)* (Frankfurt a.M.: Verlag für Interkulturelle Kommunikation, 1994), p. 236.
[24] See Anon, 'Wenn Fantasie Historie greifbar macht', *Allgemeine Zeitung*, 18 February 2011, *http://www.az.com.na/kultur/wenn-fantasie-historie-greifbar-macht.122096.php* (accessed 20 August 2015).
[25] 'Das Sujet wählt die Form, letztendlich. Und das Genre ist so vielseitig: Man kann knallharte Realität mit Mitteln der Fiktion unterhaltsam und spannend darstellen, es gilt immer den roten Faden des Falls, der einen dranbleiben lässt.' Lena Blaudez, *Farbfilter. Ada Simon in Douala* (Zurich: Unionsverlag, 2006), p. 282, trans. by Katharina Hall.
[26] For example, Bernhard Jaumann adds a glossary at the end of each of his novels explaining Namibian-German expressions, which derive mainly from Afrikaans.
[27] See Schmidt, *Gangster, Opfer, Detektive*, p. 1011 and Augart, 'Der reisende Detektiv', 52.
[28] Peter Bräunlein, '"Die Zähne blitzten weiß" – Afrika und Afrikaner/innen im Kriminalroman (Rassismus im Krimi)', *Die Horen. Zeitschrift für Literatur, Kunst und Kritik*, 182 (1996), 31–57 (43); Bruno Arich-Gerz, 'Bernhard Jaumann und seine Namibia-Prosa', 2012, *http://culturmag.de/rubriken/buecher/bernhard-jaumann-und-seine-namibia-prosa/54816* (accessed 20 August 2015).
[29] See Julia Augart, 'Kenia in der deutschen Literatur. Ein Überblick über die verschiedenen Werke und ihre Relevanz hinsichtlich einer interkulturellen Germanistik (in Kenia)', in Shaban Mayanja and Eva Hamann (eds), *Schwerpunkte der DaF-Studiengänge und*

Germanistik im östlichen Afrika (Göttingen: Universitätsverlag Göttingen, 2014), pp. 149–70 (p. 150).

[30] Bruno Arich-Gerz, Kira Schmidt and Antje Ziethen (eds), *Afrika – Raum – Literatur. / Africa – Space – Literature. Fiktionale Geographien. / Fictional Geographies* (Remscheid: Gardez Verlag, 2014), p. 14.

[31] Peter Nusser, *Der Kriminalroman* (3rd edn; Stuttgart: Metzler Verlag, 2003 [1980]), p. 45.

[32] The term 'detective' is frequently used in literature on crime fiction without making any distinction between police inspector, private investigator or amateur detective. I therefore use the neutral term of 'investigator' here and distinguish where possible between the different types of investigator in the rest of the chapter.

[33] Nusser, *Der Kriminalroman*, p. 39.

[34] See Dieter Riegel, 'Africa in West German Crime Fiction', in Eugene Schleh (ed.), *Mysteries of Africa* (Bowling Green: Bowling Green State University Popular Press, 1991), pp. 50–64 (p. 51).

[35] 'Ich bin eine Weiße. Ich bin eine Fremde.' Blaudez, *Spiegelreflex*, p. 71.

[36] 'Er ist kein Tourist . . . Um Ferien zu machen, ist er nicht hier.' Peter Höner, *Rafiki Beach Hotel* (Zurich: Limmat Verlag, 1990), p. 54.

[37] See Nusser, *Der Kriminalroman*, p. 43.

[38] See also Julia Augart, '(Inter)Cultural Investigations. Kenya in German Crime Fiction', *Journal for Studies in Humanities and Social Sciences*, 2/1 (2013), 104–16.

[39] Höner, *Rafiki Beach Hotel*, p. 226.

[40] Nusser, *Der Kriminalroman*, p. 37.

[41] Nusser, *Der Kriminalroman*, p. 37.

[42] Nusser, *Der Kriminalroman*, p. 22.

[43] Nusser, *Der Kriminalroman*, p. 23.

[44] See Julia Augart, '"Fühlt man sich wohler, gescheiter, zivilisierter? – Kommen die Weißen deswegen nach Afrika?" – Zur interkulturellen Begegnung in Peter Höners kenianisch-Schweizer Krimitrilogie', *Acta Germanica. German Studies in Africa*, 36 (2008), 91–104.

[45] Göttsche, 'Rekonstruktion und Remythisierung der kolonialen Welt', p. 172.

[46] See Barbara Korte and Sylvia Paletschek, 'Geschichte und Kriminalgeschichte(n): Texte, Kontexte, Zugänge', in Barbara Korte and Sylvia Paletschek (eds), *Geschichte im Krimi. Beiträge aus den Kulturwissenschaften* (Cologne: Böhlau, 2009), pp. 7–27 (p. 7).

[47] Namibia achieved independence in 1990; see also Julia Augart, 'Vexierbild Vergangenheit. Bernhard Jaumanns Namibia Krimi *Die Stunde des Schakals*', in Andreas Erb (ed.), *Bernhard Jaumann: Tatorte und Schreibräume – Spurensicherungen* (Bielefeld: Aisthesis Verlag, 2015), pp. 131–51.

[48] However, Jaumann's forthcoming novel *Der lange Schatten* (The Long Shadow, 2015) also explores German colonial crimes in the context of current, controversial debates about Herero and Nama skulls kept in Germany and their repatriation to Namibia.

[49] 'persönlichen Besitz'. Bernhard Jaumann, *Steinland* (Munich: Kindler Verlag, 2012), p. 49.

[50] Göttsche, 'Zwischen Exotismus und Postkolonialismus', p. 179 onwards.

[51] 'vorurteilsfreien Blick'. Wilhelm Roth, 'Die Globalisierung des Krimis. Kriminalromane über und aus der Dritten Welt', 10 December 2001, *http://astm.lu/die-globalisierung-des-krimis/* (accessed 20 August 2015).

[52] Oed and Matzke, *Life is a Thriller*, p. 11.

Select bibliography

Alberts, Jürgen and Eckhard Mordhorst, *Leiche über Bord. Ein Tatsachenroman* (Munich: Heyne Verlag, 2008).
Blaudez, Lena, *Spiegelreflex. Ada Simon in Cotonou* (Zurich: Unionsverlag, 2005).
——, *Farbfilter. Ada Simon in Douala* (Zurich: Unionsverlag, 2006).
Blettenberg, Detlef, *Land der guten Hoffnung* (Bielefeld: Pendragon Verlag, 2006).
Ehmke, Horst, *Privatsache* (Frankfurt a.M.: Eichborn, 2003).
Fall, Bella, *Kein Sonnenaufgang in Afrika* (Munich: Frauenoffensive, 2002).
Graf, Edi, *Verschleppt* (Meßkirch: Gemeiner Verlag, 2012).
Grän, Christine, *Weiße sterben selten in Samyana* (Reinbek bei Hamburg: Rowohlt Verlag, 1986).
Guder, Falk, *Tod im Herrenzimmer* (Bremen: Kellner Verlag, 2012).
Höner, Peter, *Rafiki Beach Hotel* (Zurich: Limmat Verlag, 1990).
——, *Elefantengrab* (Zurich: Limmat Verlag, 1992).
——, *Seifengold* (Zurich: Limmat Verlag, 1995).
Jaumann, Bernhard, *Die Stunde des Schakals* (Munich: Kindler Verlag, 2010). *The Hour of the Jackal*, trans. John Brownjohn (Oxford: Beaufoy Publishing, 2011).
——, *Steinland* (Munich: Kindler Verlag, 2012).
——, *Der lange Schatten* (Munich: Kindler Verlag, 2015).
Kolarz, Henry, *Kalahari* (Frankfurt a.M.: Krüger Verlag, 1977).
——, *Die roten Elefanten* (Berlin: Ullstein Verlag, 1981).
Nygaard, Hannes, *Fahrt zur Hölle* (Cologne: Emons Verlag, 2013).
Olsberg, Karl, *Der Duft* (Berlin: Aufbau Verlag, 2009).
Strackbein, Ralf, *Wolkenmord. 12.000 Meter über Afrika* (Siegen: Magolves-Verlag, 2012).
Stieglitz, Peter, *Coltan* (kindle edition, 2014).
Stuhr, Michael, *Die Miene des Todes* (Stuttgart: Thienemann Verlag, 2010).
Wackernagel, Christof, *Der Fluch der Dogon* (Hamburg: edition nautilus, 2012).
Wolff, Detlef, *Katenkamp in Kenia* (Reinbek bei Hamburg: Rowohlt Verlag, 1983).
Zeidler, Peter, *Abschied in Casablanca. Sembritzki auf Mission in Marokko* (Zurich: Arche Verlag, 2000).

Further secondary reading

Arich-Gerz, Bruno, 'Bernhard Jaumann und seine Namibia-Prosa', 2012, *http://culturmag.de/rubriken/buecher/bernhard-jaumann-und-seine-namibia-prosa/54816*.
Augart, Julia, '"Fühlt man sich wohler, gescheiter, zivilisierter? – Kommen die Weißen deswegen nach Afrika?" – Zur interkulturellen Begegnung in Peter Höners kenianisch-Schweizer Krimitrilogie', *Acta Germanica. German Studies in Africa*, 36 (2008), 91–104.
—, 'Der reisende Detektiv. Ermittler im deutschen Afrikakrimi', *Acta Germanica. German Studies in Africa*, 41 (2013), 42–55.
—, '(Inter)cultural Investigation: Kenya in German Crime Fiction', *Journal for Studies in Humanities and Social Sciences*, 2/1 (2013), 104–16.
—, 'Vexierbild Vergangenheit. Bernhard Jaumanns Namibia Krimi *Die Stunde des Schakals*', in Andreas Erb (ed.), *Bernhard Jaumann: Tatorte und Schreibräume – Spurensicherungen* (Bielefeld: Aisthesis Verlag, 2015), pp. 131–51.

Bräunlein, Peter, '"Die Zähne blitzten weiß" – Afrika und Afrikaner/innen im Kriminalroman (Rassismus im Krimi)', *Die Horen. Zeitschrift für Literatur, Kunst und Kritik*, 182 (1996), 31–57.

Keil, Sarah, 'Guide to the African Crime Fiction Project', *http://libraries.iub.edu/guide-african-crime-fiction-project*.

Matzke, Christine and Susanne Mühleisen (eds), *Postcolonial Postmortems. Crime Fiction from a Transcultural Perspective* (Amsterdam and New York: Rodopi, 2006).

Oed, Anja and Christine Matzke (eds), *Life is a Thriller. Investigating African Crime Fiction* (Cologne: Rüdiger Köppe Verlag, 2012).

Picker, Lenny, 'Beyond that Lady Detective', *Publisher's Weekly*, 29 August 2011, *http://www.publishersweekly.com/pw/by-topic/new-titles/adult-announcements/article/48474-beyond-that-lady-detective-african-crime-fiction.html*.

Riegel, Dieter, 'Africa in West German Crime Fiction', in Eugene Schleh (ed.), *Mysteries of Africa* (Bowling Green: Bowling Green State University Popular Press, 1991), pp. 50–64.

6

Der Frauenkrimi: Women's Crime Writing in German

FAYE STEWART

Towards the end of the twentieth century, the shelves of German bookstores began to fill up with a popular new subgenre of crime novel written by, about and for women: it was aptly dubbed the *Frauenkrimi* (women's crime novel).[1] The robust male investigators and culprits of yore took feminine forms in stories that contest social inequality and celebrate new constructions of gender and sexuality. In contrast with the female characters who often occupy the more passive roles of victims and witnesses in earlier crime stories, the active women driving *Frauenkrimi* narratives lead investigations, solve murders, avenge injustices, and plot and commit gruesome crimes themselves. They sometimes work alone and sometimes in collaboration with male or female partners, and they engage in flirtations and relationships with men or women or occasionally both. At the time of their appearance, *Frauenkrimis* by writers such as Christine Grän, Doris Gercke, Edith Kneifl and Ingrid Noll challenged established notions about who could write successful crime stories, what female characters could do in mysteries and which social issues these novels could address. This subgenre, which has arguably become a genre in its own right, brings new perspectives to the representation of gender and sexuality in popular fiction.

The birth and instantaneous popularity of feminist crime novels by women is evidence of a paradigm shift in the late twentieth century, both in Germany and beyond. This literary trend was inspired in part by Anglo-American feminist mystery writers – including Marcia Muller, Katherine V. Forrest, Sara Paretsky, Sarah Dreher, Marion Foster, Val McDermid and Sue Grafton – whose work was not only successful with English-speaking readers, but also quickly appeared in German translations that attracted devoted audiences. Though *Frauenkrimis* participate in such cross-cultural trends, they additionally document and respond to specific social conditions and changes in and around the German-speaking world, bearing witness to a postmodern scepticism towards accepted ideas of nation, culture and identity. Political shifts leftward since the 1960s, threats of terrorist violence in the 1970s and the end of the Cold War with the fall of the Berlin Wall and German unification in 1989 and 1990 brought about a growing mistrust of political ideologies and overarching claims to greater truths. The move away from a national individualism and towards European integration produced increasingly transnational notions of ethnicity, citizenship and language, together with a backlash in the form of racist and neo-fascist violence. The legacies of the anti-establishment 1968 generation gave rise to a flourishing left-leaning, do-it-yourself popular culture and the proliferation of politically engaged cultural studies methodologies, feminist theory and queer approaches in the academy. From the mid-1970s onward, the women's and gay rights movements shifted greater attention to social divisions and inequalities and the institutions that uphold and police them. This historical context created fecund conditions for the mainstream production and reception, beginning in the 1980s, of overtly political, female-centred narratives that broke with generic traditions and tried out new forms of expression.

Literary and publishing contexts

When considering the large number of women crime writers who began to publish in the late twentieth century, one might be tempted to ask: how can we explain the previous dearth of female crime authors? Scholars cite a number of reasons. Feminist critics point out that not only is the crime genre largely a male-dominated literary tradition – both in terms of its authors' identities and in the gendered representations it projects – but that the search for truth and the desire to re-establish social order at the heart of the genre are inherently patriarchal endeavours.[2] It should therefore come as no surprise that the conventional portrayal of the detective is male-embodied, and also that the feminine is often aligned not with the solution but rather with the problem of the crime. A number of scholars examine the connections between gender and genre, pointing out that women authors, particularly those whose work offers strong female figures, have done more than simply change the gender of the traditional detective and rewrite the narratives with a focus on women: they have additionally emancipated their texts from male-centred language and logic in order to empower their feminine protagonists and antagonists.[3] On the other hand, as chapter 2 of this volume demonstrates, women like Auguste Groner had already been publishing crime stories in German since the nineteenth century, although their contributions often went unrecognized or received less publicity than male-authored texts. Indeed, women's writing has traditionally been undervalued and, until recent decades, it has all too often been dismissed as either exclusively addressing women's concerns and therefore uninteresting to mainstream readers, or as merely autobiographical and not of wider social significance.

The connections between German crime fiction and female writers can be traced back to the mid-nineteenth-century literature of Annette von Droste-Hülshoff. A landmark text, Droste-Hülshoff's novella *Die Judenbuche* (*The Jew's Beech*, 1842) can be regarded as an early German murder mystery, narrating the background, discovery and investigation of the unexplained killing of a Jewish merchant in a Westfalian village. The novella contains a study of the cultural milieu of a late eighteenth-century society with an unruly populace and ineffectual justice system around the time of the French Revolution. *Die Judenbuche* emphasizes the significance of gender and ethnic identities – particularly in its portrayals of bigotry, anti-Semitism, oppression and abuse – in the social context of violent crimes. However, Droste-Hülshoff's text remains unmentioned in some histories of the genre, perhaps because its author was female, or perhaps because the police detective plays a minor role and the mystery remains unsolved, therefore troubling a categorization of the text as crime fiction.

From the 1920s onwards, mystery fiction flourished in Britain and the United States with the emergence of the 'cosy' and 'hardboiled' crime subgenres, elements of which are later taken up by *Frauenkrimi* authors. The British cosy, popularized by Golden Age writers such as Dorothy L. Sayers, Margery Allingham and Josephine Tey, typically has an amateur sleuth, a limited number of characters and an insular social setting where the characters have shared histories and everyone is a suspect. The trailblazing Agatha Christie created a female series heroine, Miss Marple, a nosy spinster who solves mysteries confounding local police through her intellect and shrewd eye for detail. Following in Miss Marple's footsteps are amateur *Frauenkrimi* detectives who investigate murders in small communities, sometimes while vacationing in the countryside or travelling abroad. Like cosies, many German *Frauenkrimis* use humour and thematize guilt and complicity, but contain more sex and violence than their gentler British predecessors.

In the United States, writers like Dashiell Hammett and Raymond Chandler popularized hardboiled or *noir* fiction, which usually features a private detective investigating a large number of characters in a gritty urban lower- or middle-class setting where masculinity, brutality and humanity's dark sides take centre stage. Like their hardboiled ancestors, *Frauenkrimis* often highlight violence and protagonists with marginal social status who confront – but are sometimes unable to eradicate – decadence and depravity. Their robust detectives are sexually active, drink heavily and can be volatile. Unlike the hardboiled novel, however, *Frauenkrimis* rewrite gender dynamics by redistributing narrative power positions and destabilizing sexualized notions of women as submissive, threatening or merely confounding. Thus, German women writers like Doris Gercke in *Weinschröter, du mußt hängen* (*How Many Miles to Babylon*, 1988) depict gruesome crimes in quaint, small towns or pastoral idylls reminiscent of the settings of British cosies, or, like Pieke Biermann in *Potsdamer Ableben* (Potsdam Demise, 1987), conjure violent urban environments navigated by tough and defiant detectives like those of American hardboiled classics. Gercke and Biermann became two of the first and best-known representatives of the feminist *Frauenkrimi* wave, but it is important to note that this wave was in fact preceded by several pioneering German women writers whose work prior to the 1980s showed greater continuity with male-centred traditions of crime writing.

From the 1950s on, female authors participated increasingly in the production of German-language mysteries. Three successful early women writers of crime fiction were Alexandra Becker, Irene Rodrian and Ingeburg Siebenstädt, who published stories with male perpetrators and investigators, worked with male co-authors and published under male pseudonyms. Together with her husband Rolf, Becker authored two series of short crime plays adapted for radio, *Dickie Dick Dickens* (Fatty Dick Dickens) and *Gestatten, mein Name ist Cox* (Greetings, My Name is Cox), beginning in the 1950s. Set in 1920s Chicago and contemporary London, the Beckers' series evoke the conventions of Anglo-American crime fiction, particularly *noir* and the hardboiled, with their incisive, satirical depictions of gangsters, anarchy and the struggles of police and private detectives to stop violent crime and maintain order. Irene Rodrian's debut *Tod in St. Pauli* (Death in St. Pauli, 1967), a gritty vengeance story starring a freshly released convict, made her the first woman to be awarded the prestigious Edgar Wallace Prize. Rodrian was also the first female thriller writer to gain success and recognition in the mainstream literary market, and she went on to publish over twenty more crime novels, including several mysteries with pronounced feminist themes. Like Rodrian, East German author Ingeburg Siebenstädt was extremely prolific. Beginning with *Der Überfall* (The Assault, 1967), she published dozens of mysteries during and after German division under the pseudonym of Tom Wittgen. With her cosy, insular social settings and interest in the lives of everyday working people, Siebenstädt gained a reputation as the 'Agatha Christie of the GDR' and, in 1994, was awarded the *Ehren-Glauser* (Honorary Glauser) by the German crime writers' association *Das Syndikat* (The Syndicate) for lifetime achievement. Many of the early novels by these trailblazing women did not, however, engage consistently with feminist themes.

The advent of the *Frauenkrimi* in the 1980s and 1990s was the culmination of other literary trends and developments both in and beyond German-speaking Europe. Particularly in West Germany in the 1960s and 1970s, there was a cultural tendency to portray crime not as an occasional deviation from social norms perpetrated by a few aberrant individuals, but rather as a fundamental societal problem engendered by institutionalized structural injustice, the roots of which could be traced to imperialism, colonialism, fascism and their legacies. With its relentless critique of power relations in post-war German society, the left-wing *Soziokrimi* (social crime story) – also known as the *Politkrimi* (political crime story) or *Neuer Deutscher Krimi* (new German crime story) – can be viewed as a predecessor of the *Frauenkrimi*. Feminist crime also participates in the anti-fascist and liberation discourses of the post-1968 era, interrogating inequalities in connection with social hierarchies and social expectations. In the wake of these movements, the 1980s witnessed a major change in the visibility of women crime writers and the politics of the texts they were writing. The clever and sometimes sarcastic titles of early feminist mysteries by Lydia Tews, Helga Riedel, Susanne Thommes, Claudia Wessel and Rodrian communicate their authors' commitment to re-examining traditional gender roles and offering compelling female characters. Tews's first crime novels, *Sie sind ein schlechter Bulle, gnädige Frau* (You're a Bad Cop, Ma'am, 1982) and *Leichen brauchen kein Make-up* (Corpses Don't Need Makeup, 1984), appeared around the same time as Riedel's *Einer muss tot* (Someone Must Die, 1983), Thommes's *Altweibersommer* (Old Women's Summer, 1984) and the lesser-known Wessel's self-published *Es wird Zeit* (It's about Time, 1984). Rodrian increasingly addressed feminist concerns in her psychosocial mysteries, from *Küsschen für den Totengräber* (Kiss for the Gravedigger, 1974; see chapter 1) to *Schlagschatten* (Sharp Relief, 1983) and *Das Mädchen mit dem Engelsgesicht* (The Girl with the Angel Face, 1986).

The feminist *Frauenkrimi* was thus born in West Germany and Austria in the mid- to late 1980s, with the near-simultaneous appearance of several novels that not only offered female heroines who fought against sexism, but also celebrated left-leaning political strategies that aimed for social justice and espoused anti-establishment, anti-racist and anti-imperialist perspectives. The *Frauenkrimi* wave began around 1986, a year that saw the publication of Austrian author Christine Grän's debut *Weiße sterben selten in Samyana* (Whites Seldom Die in Samyana) and West German activist Corinna Kawaters's second mystery, *Zora Zobel zieht um* (Zora Zobel Moves In). Grän's journalist heroine Anna Marx has her first crime-solving adventure in Samyana, a fictitious country in southern Africa, where she investigates colonial legacies of white Eurocentrism and racism against black Africans (see also chapter 5). The overweight gossip columnist Anna Marx went on to become a cult figure, starring in several more volumes, including *Marx ist tot* (Marx is Dead, 1993), which won the esteemed Marlowe Prize awarded by the German Raymond Chandler Society. Appearing in the same year as Grän's debut was the second instalment in Kawaters's left-wing series featuring the autonomous rebel Zora Zobel, named in honour of the militant feminist group *Rote Zora* (Red Zora), in which author Kawaters was active, and which took credit for multiple terrorist attacks against sex shops, pharmaceutical companies and state institutions from the 1970s to the 1990s. *Zora Zobel zieht um* is the sequel to the feminist-inflected crime novel *Zora Zobel findet die Leiche* (Zora Zobel Finds the Body, 1984), but the second book is noteworthy because it bears the subtitle *Frauenkrimi*, has an almost exclusively female cast (with the exception of a male murder victim) and heralds feminist collaboration. Biermann's 1987 *Potsdamer Ableben* was also the first in a series and, like Gercke's 1988 debut *Weinschröter, du mußt hängen*, depicts female police officers as positive role models working in law enforcement to protect female and child victims of abuse and sexual violence. Biermann's *Potsdamer Ableben* features a diverse squad of Berlin homicide officers under the leadership of Chief Inspector Karin Lietze: her police team includes male, female, heterosexual and homosexual officers, as well as a Jewish secretary, who cooperate to defend the weakest members of society. While Biermann's novels, with their rotating narrative perspective, consistently heroicize the police force as a model of coalitional justice, Gercke's first book concludes with detective Bella Block's resignation from the police department, which she rejects due to the rampant sexism she perceives among her colleagues, as shown in the extract at the end of this chapter. Later instalments in Gercke's 'Block' series depict the protagonist working as a private detective.[4]

Another trend in this feminist mystery wave was the psychological crime thriller, which women writers adapted by narrating the background and commission of crime from the point of view of a female perpetrator. The *Frauenkrimi* thus takes up an existing trend in German crime literature, the casting of the main character in a career outside law enforcement or detective work, and combines it with an investigation of the social and psychological conditions that produce scenarios of violence and vengeance. Early examples of this variant include Sabine Deitmer's short story collections *Bye-bye, Bruno* (1988) and *Auch brave Mädchen tun's* (Even Good Girls Do It, 1990), Ingrid Noll's *Der Hahn ist tot* (*Hell Hath No Fury*, 1991), and works by Austrian writers such as Edith Kneifl's *Zwischen zwei Nächten* (Between Two Nights, 1991) and Elfriede Czurda's *Die Giftmörderinnen* (The Poison Murderesses, 1991). These authors share an interest in exploring women's motives for committing murder and other transgressions, often against male victims. At the same time, they investigate the social contexts in which criminality unfolds, stressing the institutionalization of bigotry and misogyny and thereby suggestively hinting that their fictional women's wrongdoings are logical – if not justifiable or defensible – reactions to the oppression and abuse they have suffered in late twentieth-century society. For instance, Deitmer's *Bye-bye, Bruno*, which bears the evocative subtitle *Wie Frauen morden* (How Women Murder), is a collection of fifteen stories about murderesses who creatively and often gruesomely do away with the men in their lives. These male victims are quite unsympathetic: because they pose obstacles to the women's independence and freedom, they seem entirely deserving of the bloody ends they meet, and the reader can easily imagine that the world would be better off without them. Healthy doses of humour and satire permeate these texts. A number of perpetrator crime novels, like Kneifl's *Zwischen zwei Nächten*, also stress the experiences of women who love other women or are coming out as bisexual or lesbian. These queer crime stories link representations of such characters with broader critiques of patriarchal order, domestic violence and the limitations of the law in defending the vulnerable citizens who most need its protection.

Scholars and critics note that, with the advent of women's crime writing as a mainstream phenomenon in the late twentieth century, visible changes rapidly took place in the literary scene. In her book on German and French crime novels by women, Nicola Barfoot identifies a clear shift during this era: 'The late 1980s saw a major change in the quantity and type of attention being paid to women writers in Germany, with gender suddenly becoming a significant issue in the publication and reception of the crime novel.'[5] Barfoot sees this trend as both international in scope and having distinctly German dynamics: as her comparative analysis suggests by placing German feminist crime novels of the 1990s side by side with contemporary French works, there were shared and diverging currents between the two literary traditions. A 1989 article called 'Marlowes Töchter' (Marlowe's Daughters) in the news magazine *Der Spiegel* also notes this change in the domestic market, brought about by 'a host of female detectives who are competing with the conventional, punchy and acerbic-masculine professional sleuths in crime novels of late'.[6] The *Spiegel* article treats English- and German-language texts as part of the same phenomenon, discussing the American Sara Paretsky alongside the German Gercke and the Austrian Grän, though it does suggest that the former preceded and probably influenced the development of the latter.

As indicated at the beginning of this chapter, the successful feminist crime novels of Anglo-American women like Paretsky and her contemporaries, including Sue Grafton, Katherine V. Forrest and Barbara Sjoholm Wilson, played a critical role in inspiring the German-language *Frauenkrimi*.[7] Translations of mysteries by these popular English-speaking authors appeared with German publishers like Rowohlt and Argument, found a rapidly growing European readership and stimulated the development of home-grown variants of the genre. In addition to introducing English writers to German readers, Rowohlt and Argument – together with mainstream publishers like Fischer and women's publishers like Orlanda and Frauenoffensive – also participated in the evolution of the *Frauenkrimi* from a trend into a genre of its own with the dissemination of feminist, lesbian and socially critical texts. Rowohlt was an early promoter of crime novels by successful authors like Rodrian, Grän and their contemporaries Susanne Billig, Uta-Maria Heim and Christine Lehmann. Rowohlt also brought out Biermann's feminist short story crime collection, *Mit Zorn, Charme, und Methode: oder: Die Aufklärung ist weiblich!* (With Wrath, Charm and Method: or: Enlightenment is Feminine!, 1992), which features feminist crime stories by authors from East and West Germany as well as Austria and Switzerland.[8] Argument contributed to the development and popularization of the genre with the 1988 creation of Ariadne, a series dedicated exclusively to feminist crime novels by female authors. Although Ariadne's first volumes were primarily translations from English, today the series emphasizes German-language novels by contemporary authors such as Merle Kröger, Monika Geier and Anne Goldmann, in addition to the aforementioned Lehmann, whose first three feminist mysteries originally appeared with Rowohlt in the late 1990s and were republished by Ariadne in the 2000s.

In addition to these developments in the publishing industry, the establishment of professional organizations also helped to nurture and promote the work of female mystery authors. The model for this was 'Sisters in Crime', founded in 1987 in the United States by Paretsky and other Anglo-American writers to combat sexism in the crime genre and in the profession through networking, publicity, collaboration and mutual support. *Mörderische Schwestern* (Murderous Sisters), originally founded in 1996 as the German branch of 'Sisters in Crime', has been an independent group based in German-speaking and European nations since 2007. The group, which promotes women's mysteries by organizing writing workshops and facilitating exposure to professional investigations, has regional branches in Germany, Austria and Switzerland; sister organizations in France, Spain and Great Britain; and alliances with non-gender-specific groups for German-language crime writers, like *Das Syndikat*, founded in 1986. Due in large part to the work of the *Mörderische Schwestern* and their allies, the twenty-first century has seen the creation of a hotly debated *Frauenkrimipreis* (Women's Crime Prize) and yearly *Frauenkrimifestivals* (women's crime festivals), which have contributed to the unprecedented availability and recognition of women's mystery fiction.

Social and political contexts

The *Frauenkrimi* engages intertwined cross-cultural discourses and flows, locating feminist concerns in distinctively Germanic contexts. It comments on the gendering of power and violence in the law, the state and the media, and it imagines ways in which social transformation and political change can be brought about through coalitional activism and feminist-lesbian-queer solidarity. Embedded within the *Frauenkrimi*'s negotiation of misogyny and heteronormativity, one also finds an analysis of the histories, geographies and cultural traditions of contemporary German-speaking nations.

German-language women's crime writing provides literary evidence of the wide-ranging changes in both Germany and Austria that have transformed perceptions and representations of women, gender roles and sexual minorities in the last half century. As one might assume from the name, *Frauenkrimis* spotlight gender and sexuality, but they also cast a critical eye on other facets of modern life by analysing identity constructions within larger contexts. The genre thus performs literary interventions into contemporary discourses and debates. *Frauenkrimis* develop feminist critiques of local and national politics, capitalism and socialism, globalization, mass media and the arts, and ideas about identity and belonging. The genre's focus on women is visible in the crimes it typically features, which highlight violence and injustices inflected by gender and sexuality, such as rape, domestic abuse, hate crimes and institutionalized sexism. But beyond its interests in challenging gender discrimination and empowering women, the *Frauenkrimi* is also centrally concerned with exploring the rights of and protection for children, minorities and other marginalized groups. Many of its authors have a history of political engagement and activism: for instance, Kawaters was indicted for her involvement in terrorist attacks with the feminist group *Rote Zora*, Biermann served as a mouthpiece for the prostitute rights movement and Kneifl worked with an inter-ministerial task force on women's affairs. The protagonists in their works come from a range of sociocultural backgrounds – they are unemployed rebels and radical feminists, police officers and prostitutes, small-town housewives and globetrotting students, wealthy architects and bohemian artists – and build coalitional alliances in order to address the injustices they witness. They offer insights into social problems and visions of social transformation, developing theories of effective individual and political action.

Although German-language crime fiction is often described as a Western phenomenon – that is, it did not come about as a well-defined genre in the GDR for a variety of reasons – the political atmosphere in its socialist counterpart certainly affected social developments and cultural forms in West Germany. East German women were theoretically equals in the socialist state, where they were encouraged to be active in the workforce and had access to abortions and childcare. However, in reality, women still largely did 'women's work' both in public and in private. Their career options were typically limited to traditionally feminine professions like teaching and secretarial work; it was possible, but uncommon, to find a female police officer or inspector (the GDR television series *Polizeiruf 110* (Police: Dial 110) was groundbreaking in featuring a female police detective in the 1970s, Lieutenant Vera Arndt – see chapter 8). And, while women were increasingly working outside the home, they were still performing the majority of domestic duties, a phenomenon often referred to as the *Doppelbelastung* (double burdening) of women. Although, perhaps due to censorship, East German authors made fewer significant contributions than Western writers to the early development of women's mystery writing and the feminist *Frauenkrimi*, their political situation appears in both East and West German narratives critiquing sexism in the socialist state. For example, in the short story 'František' (1992), GDR author Barbara Neuhaus reflects on the gender discrimination that a female East German police officer tolerates in order to succeed and advance her career. Neuhaus follows in the footsteps of the socialist feminist Christa Wolf who, in stories like 'Selbstversuch' (Self-Experiment, 1973), examined the obstacles facing women who attempted to gain equal footing to men in the socialist state and its workforce. Another feminist crime writer from the GDR is Dagmar Scharsich, whose debut *Die gefrorene Charlotte* (The Frozen Charlotte Doll, 1993) spins a tale of border-crossing and conspiracy in divided Berlin, highlighting the experiences of and limitations faced by straight and gay East German women during the collapse of the Iron Curtain. In West German texts such as Biermann's *Potsdamer Ableben* and its sequels *Violetta* (*Violetta*, 1990) and *Herzrasen* (Racing Heart, 1993), readers also find representations of women in the Eastern Bloc before and after the fall of the Wall: Biermann's series follows activists in a West Berlin prostitute rights group, who declare solidarity and work together with their counterparts in Eastern Europe to gain recognition, protection, respect and independence.

On the other side of the divided German-speaking world, the left-wing 1968 student movement and the sexual revolution of the 1970s encouraged women to pursue college educations, careers and financial independence. This was slower to happen in socially conservative Austria than in West Germany, where sexism and misogyny were longer lived, as we see in Kneifl's representation of the specifically Austrian dynamics of gender-based oppression in *Zwischen zwei Nächten* and many of her later novels. Kneifl's works are reminiscent of the writing of Austrian feminists Ingeborg Bachmann and Elfriede Jelinek, who criticize the subtle manifestations of everyday gendered violence in late twentieth-century Austria (see chapter 3). Two other successful Austrian crime writers, Lisa Lercher and Angelika Aliti, also position strong women as investigators of social injustice in places as different as inner-city Vienna and the Styrian countryside. In West Germany, the left-wing squatter scene of the 1980s lured rebellious and disenchanted young people with protests against the growing middle class. Finding inspiration in role models such as Gudrun Ensslin and Ulrike Meinhof, two of the first RAF (Red Army Faction) terrorists, these movements encouraged the participation of women in political activism and leadership. These political shifts and constellations find expression in the voices of the squatters, anarchists, militant feminists, ex-convicts and unemployed rebels who populate Kawaters's 'Zora Zobel' novels. At the same time, the increasing appeal of left-wing and egalitarian ideas, embodied by the Green Party, helped to change the popular conception of politics – and professional work – as a white man's world. A number of mysteries by West German authors before and after unification imagine women effecting political change by playing active roles in local and state institutions like law enforcement and social work. Sexism and corruption in politics, the police force and related professions are critiqued in feminist crime series by Biermann, Gercke, Alexandra von Grote and Maria Gronau. Access to a safe and egalitarian education is another common concern for feminist mystery writers, who explore institutionalized sexism and sexual abuse in schools and universities in works such as Thea Dorn's *Berliner Aufklärung* (Berlin Enlightenment, 1994) and Lehmann's 'Lisa Nerz' series, particularly *Harte Schule* (School of Hard Knocks, 2005).

The second-wave women's movement and the gay rights movement in West Germany and Austria gained support and momentum in the 1970s and 1980s by organizing around the issues of abortion, prostitution, pornography and homosexuality. In early *Frauenkrimis*, these matters surface in the work of Biermann, who not only argues for prostitute rights and promotes sexual diversity in her series featuring Karin Lietze and the Berlin homicide division, but also deals with AIDS in the short story '3'21"' (1992) in her edited collection *Mit Zorn, Charme, und Methode*. AIDS also comes up as a motive for killing in Manuela Kay's short story 'Scheißbullen' (Crap Cops), published in the anthology *Queer Crime: Lesbisch-schwule Krimigeschichten* (Queer Crime: Lesbian-gay Crime Stories, 2002). Edited by Lisa Kuppler, *Queer Crime* includes four other mysteries by German-speaking women writers as well as intrigues involving bisexuals and transsexuals. With half of its collection featuring female characters who love other women, Ariadne is noteworthy for including lesbian texts under the broader category of feminist crime fiction, thereby promoting the mutual interests of feminist and lesbian cultures and politics. Two Ariadne publications from the early 1990s were among the first lesbian mysteries in German: in Kim Engels's *Zur falschen Zeit am falschen Ort* (In the Wrong Place at the Wrong Time, 1991), four gay and straight women go on vacation together and become embroiled in an international intrigue, and in Gabriele Gelien's *Eine Lesbe macht noch keinen Sommer* (One Lesbian Does Not Make a Summer, 1993), a young lesbian solves the mystery of her disappearing mail, which ultimately involves her in the investigation of a child pornography trafficking ring. Ariadne further supports the diversification of women's crime writing by publishing books featuring bisexual detectives like the macho Lisa Nerz in Lehmann's series, child protagonists like the girl sleuth in Ann Camones's *Verbrechen lohnt sich doch!* (Crime Does Pay!, 1994) and bicultural investigators like Katrin Kremmler's German-Hungarian adventurer, Gabriella Müller. As these examples indicate, the 1990s and early 2000s have seen the increased representation of sexual and other minorities in the crime genre.

Another pivotal political development of the twentieth and early twenty-first centuries has been the foundation and expansion of the European Union. A number of German feminist crime novels address this transnational transformation by featuring German protagonists who travel to or live in other European countries, thus introducing cultural variations and differing political situations to a German-language readership. In *Die Häupter meiner Lieben* (*Head Count*, 1993), Ingrid Noll examines relationships between Germans and Italians at the moment when the structure of the European Union was crystallizing. Maria Gronau's *Weibersommer* (Women's Summer, 1998) explores the differences between German, French and Corsican politics, while *Weiberschläue* (Women's Shrewdness, 2003) depicts the ways in which the fall of the Berlin Wall has facilitated international crime, such as organ trafficking between Eastern and Western Europe. Karin Rick's *Furien in Ferien* (Furies on Vacation, 2003) suggests that women in Greece have a long way to go before they can attain the gender equality they have in Austria. In two mysteries set in Budapest, *Blaubarts Handy* (Bluebeard's Cell Phone, 2001) and *Pannonias Gral* (Pannonia's Grail, 2004), Katrin Kremmler analyses the differences between German and Hungarian cultures and especially the social limitations still faced by women and lesbians in post-socialist Europe.

In the midst of these wide-reaching transformations, the ongoing success story of the German-language *Frauenkrimi* is evidence of the intimate relationships among social changes, national contexts, publishing industries and popular literary tastes. Although pioneering female authors like Groner, Droste-Hülshoff, Rodrian and Siebenstädt published crime fiction prior to the 1980s, the work of Grän, Kawaters, Biermann, Gercke, Deitmer and others represents a new era of crime writing, one that continues to this day. German feminist crime fiction plays an important social role in questioning existing forms of order and promoting democratic ideals, suggesting the significance of gender and sexual equality to the overall health of contemporary society. It imagines a social order in which every citizen's actions count, in which it does not take a police officer or a professional detective to right transgressions. In many *Frauenkrimis*, like the popular works of Kneifl and Noll, female figures address social problems by perpetrating crimes. These texts definitively assert that women are not always passive or victims, nor does feminist culture require them to be positive role models, but that they can and do commit violent, gruesome – and often gratifying – acts. With nuanced, entertaining and politically charged narratives that offer intriguing visions of social justice, women writers continue to make a mark on German-language culture.

Established writers of the feminist *Frauenkrimi* like Gercke, Kneifl and Noll still garner fans with their novels, several of which have been adapted into television and film series. Twenty-first-century feminist crime authors are likely to work in both literary and visual media: Merle Kröger, the prize-winning author of *Grenzfall* (Borderline Case, 2012), is a distinguished documentary filmmaker, while Thea Dorn and Astrid Paprotta, who became famous as crime novelists, have since written screenplays for the popular television series *Tatort* (Crime Scene; see chapter 8).[9] This is also true of the prolific Petra Hammesfahr, whose numerous acclaimed novels and screenplays make her one of the best-known contemporary mystery writers. Popular crime authors like Christine Lehmann, Charlotte Link and Nele Neuhaus have been recognized for their work in other genres as well, including radio plays, romance and young adult books, psychological novels and non-fiction. These successful women are promoting, updating and expanding the growing genre of crime fiction, and they are in good company with the likes of Monika Geier, Uta-Maria Heim and Eva Rossmann, among many others writing and gaining widespread recognition today.

* * *

Extract from Doris Gercke, *How Many Miles to Babylon*

Hamburg police detective Bella Block has been asked to investigate an anonymous report alleging that two recent suicides in the village of Roosbach were in fact murders. She accepts the assignment because she has a summer house in Roosbach and can enjoy the idyllic countryside from the comfort of her blooming garden. Bella is eager for a break from the city, from her daily routine, and especially from her colleagues, among whom she is the only female detective.

She pondered the evening and realized that the investigation wasn't going to be as easy as she'd hoped. After twenty years in police service, she'd learned to pay attention to her gut feelings whenever she took over a new case. She had always been affected by the lives of the people she persecuted.[10] She knew there was a causal relationship between the structure of this society and its steadily increasing crime rate. None of her coworkers suspected what she herself was barely aware of: that her exceptional commitment stemmed from a hidden feeling of complicity, as if she were responsible for the kind of social conditions which drove parents to physically abuse their children. Whenever she started on a new case she imagined that, on solving it, she would find a way out for delinquents. This rarely happened: Apart from the fact that the system was complacent and virtually static, eventually she always had to hand her cases over to a judge or public prosecutor. Yet during the period of investigation, of identity checks and speculation, she was driven by the belief that this time she would make a difference. Gradually, though, her perspective changed and it grew increasingly difficult for her to work. Bella traced this change in attitude back to the time when she and her team had visited the Museum of Criminology. An exhibit of sodomy-rape had aroused collective disgust and indignation – or so she thought. Shortly afterward, she had overheard her male coworkers talking about it. She'd never had any illusions about the moral integrity of cops; because they continually dealt with society's margins and with brutality they, too, were on the extreme edge of the social spectrum – one in which violence was gratuitous. She had learned to live with the fact that they were a bunch of misanthropes. But when she heard them revelling in the gory details of that exhibit Bella simply couldn't accept it as everyday professional cynicism. At that point she had started to view her fellow officers in a different light. They continued to be polite when they had to deal with Bella, but from that point on an uneasy tension altered the previously friendly work atmosphere. Now she understood why regulations demanded that detectives not be left alone with women during the course of an interrogation. And she realized that the high divorce rate among detectives – twice the national average – wasn't just the result of irregular working hours.

Doris Gercke, *How Many Miles to Babylon*, trans. Anna Hamilton (Seattle: Women in Translation, 1991), pp. 27–9.

Notes

[1] *Frauenkrimi* translates literally as 'women's crime novel', but is also often understood as 'feminist crime novel'. Definitions of the term lay greater or lesser emphasis on the gender identities of the writer, subject and intended audience, as well as on the texts' politics. See Nicola Barfoot, *Frauenkrimi/polar féminin: Generic Expectations and the Reception of Recent French and German Crime Novels by Women* (Frankfurt a. M.: Peter Lang, 2007) and chapters by Sabine Deitmer ('Anna, Bella & Co.: Der Erfolg der deutschen Krimifrauen', pp. 239–53) and Sabine Wilke ('Wilde Weiber und dominante Damen: Der Frauenkrimi als Verhandlungsort von Weiblichkeitsmythen', pp. 255–71) in the anthology by Carmen Birkle, Sabina Matter-Seibel and Patricia Plummer (eds), *Frauen auf der Spur: Kriminalautorinnen aus Deutschland, Großbritannien und den USA* (Tübingen: Stauffenburg, 2001).

[2] For discussions of gender dynamics in the crime fiction genre, see the following critical texts: Gabriele Dietze, *Hardboiled Woman: Geschlechterkrieg im amerikanischen Kriminalroman* (Hamburg: Europäische Verlagsanstalt, 1997); Teresa L. Ebert, 'Ermittlung des Phallus. Autorität, Ideologie und die Produktion patriarchaler Agenten im Kriminalroman', in Jochen Vogt (ed.), *Der Kriminalroman: Poetik – Theorie – Geschichte* (Munich: Wilhelm Fink, 1998), pp. 461–85; and Kathleen Gregory Klein, *Women Times Three: Writers, Detectives, Readers* (Bowling Green, OH: Bowling Green State University Popular Press, 1995).

[3] See Anja Kemmerzell, 'Was ist ein Frauenkrimi?', *Ariadne Forum*, 4 (1996), 5–6, and 'Über die Rezeption von Frauenkrimis', *Ariadne Forum*, 5 (1997/8), 128–9; and also Sally R. Munt, *Murder By the Book? Feminism and the Crime Novel* (London: Routledge, 1994).

[4] The 'Bella Block' novels were also adapted into a successful, long-running crime television series that aired on ZDF, but there are significant differences between Gercke's Block and the television character: the latter returns to the police force.

[5] Barfoot, *Frauenkrimi/polar féminin*, p. 72.

[6] 'einer Schar weiblicher Detektive, die in Kriminalromanen neuerdings den hergebrachten, schlagkräftigen und herbmännlichen Profischnüfflern Konkurrenz machen'. 'Marlowes Töchter', *Der Spiegel*, 1 (1989), 148–50 (148).

[7] Many scholars date Anglo-American feminist crime as an identifiable trend to the early 1980s, with the detective series debuts of Sue Grafton (*'A' is for Alibi*, 1982) and Sara Paretsky (*Indemnity Only*, 1982). Two of the earliest lesbian sleuths were born in the writing of Barbara Sjoholm Wilson (*Murder in the Collective*, 1984) and Katherine V. Forrest (*Amateur City*, 1984). Other popular feminist and lesbian crime fiction authors of the era whose work appeared in German translation include Marian Foster, Sarah Schulman and Val McDermid.

[8] Biermann's anthology includes prominent authors such as the (West) German Sabine Deitmer and the Austrian Edith Kneifl, in addition to the Austrian Helga Anderle; the Swiss Milena Moser; and Germans from the West, such as Birgit Rabisch and Elke zur Neiden; as well as from the East, such as Bärbel Balke, Barbara Neuhaus and Gudrun Küsel.

[9] Paprotta's *Die ungeschminkte Wahrheit* (The Unvarnished Truth, 2004) and Dorn's *Die Hirnkönigin* (The Brain Queen, 1999) both won the *Deutscher Krimi Preis*. Paprotta has also written for the television crime series *SOKO Wismar*.

[10] Author's note: the original German text uses the term 'verfolgte', which the published translation renders as 'persecuted'. In this context, however, 'pursued' or 'prosecuted' would be a more accurate translation.

Select bibliography

Biermann, Pieke, *Potsdamer Ableben* (Berlin: Rotbuch, 1987).

——, *Violetta* (Berlin: Rotbuch, 1990). *Violetta*, trans. Ines Rieder and Jill Hannum (New York: Serpent's Tail, 1996).

—— (ed.), *Mit Zorn, Charme, und Methode: oder: Die Aufklärung ist weiblich!* (Frankfurt a. M.: Fischer, 1992).

Deitmer, Sabine, *Bye-bye, Bruno. Wie Frauen morden* (Frankfurt a. M.: Fischer, 1988).

Gelien, Gabriele, *Eine Lesbe macht noch keinen Sommer* (Hamburg: Argument, 1993).

Gercke, Doris, *Weinschröter, du mußt hängen* (Hamburg: Verlag am Galgenberg, 1988). *How Many Miles to Babylon*, trans. Anna Hamilton (Seattle: Women in Translation, 1991).

Grän, Christine, *Weiße sterben selten in Samyana* (Reinbek bei Hamburg: Rowohlt, 1986).

——, *Marx ist tot* (Reinbek bei Hamburg: Rowohlt, 1993).

Gronau, Maria, *Weiberlust* (Berlin: Schwarzkopf & Schwarzkopf, 1995).

Kawaters, Corinna, *Zora Zobel zieht um* (Giessen: Focus, 1986).

Kneifl, Edith, *Zwischen zwei Nächten* (Vienna: Wiener Frauenverlag, 1991).

Lehmann, Christine, *Der Masochist* (Reinbek bei Hamburg: Rowohlt, 1997).

Noll, Ingrid, *Der Hahn ist tot* (Zurich: Diogenes, 1991). *Hell Hath No Fury*, trans. Ian Mitchell (London: HarperCollins, 1996).

——, *Die Häupter meiner Lieben* (Zurich: Diogenes, 1993). *Head Count*, trans. Ian Mitchell (London: HarperCollins, 1997).

Rodrian, Irene, *Tod in St. Pauli* (Munich: Goldmann, 1967).

Further secondary reading

Barfoot, Nicola, *Frauenkrimi/polar féminin: Generic Expectations and the Reception of Recent French and German Crime Novels by Women* (Frankfurt a. M.: Peter Lang, 2007).

Birkle, Carmen, Sabina Matter-Seibel and Patricia Plummer (eds), *Frauen auf der Spur: Kriminalautorinnen aus Deutschland, Großbritannien und den USA* (Tübingen: Stauffenburg, 2001).

Guenther-Pal, Alison and Arlene A. Teraoka, '"God, How Idyllic": The German Countryside and the Abject of Enlightenment in Doris Gercke's *Weinschröter, du mußt hängen* (1987)', *Women in German Yearbook*, 27 (2011), 150–75.

Pailer, Gaby, '"Weibliche" Körper im "männlichen" Raum: Zur Interdependenz von Gender und Genre in deutschsprachigen Kriminalromanen von Autorinnen', *Weimarer Beiträge* 46/4 (2000), 564–81.

Sieg, Katrin, 'Postcolonial Berlin? Pieke Biermann's Crime Novels as Globalization Critique', *Studies in 20th & 21st Century Literature* 28/1 (2004), 152–82.

——, 'Women in the Fortress Europe: Feminist Crime Fiction as Antifascist Performative', *differences*, 16/2 (2005), 138–66.

Stewart, Faye, 'Dialogues with Tradition: Feminist-queer Encounters in German Crime Stories at the Turn of the Twenty-first Century', *Studies in 20th & 21st Century Literature*, 35/1 (2011), 114–35.

——, *German Feminist Queer Crime Fiction: Politics, Justice and Desire* (Jefferson, NC: McFarland, 2014).

Tielinen, Kirsimarja, 'Ein Blick von außen: Ermittlungen im deutschsprachigen Frauenkriminalroman', in Bruno Franceschini and Carsten Würmann (eds), *Verbrechen als Passion: Neue Untersuchungen zum Kriminalgenre, Juni Magazin für Literatur und Politik*, 37/38 (2004), 41–68.

Vogel, Marianne, 'Ein Unbehagen an der Kultur: Zur Kriminalliteratur deutschsprachiger Schriftstellerinnen in den 90er Jahren', in Ilse Nagelschmidt, Alexandra Hanke, Lea Müller-Dannhausen and Melani Schröter (eds), *Zwischen Trivialität und Postmoderne: Literatur von Frauen in den 90er Jahren* (Frankfurt a. M.: Peter Lang, 2002), pp. 49–67.

7

Historical Crime Fiction in German: the Turbulent Twentieth Century

KATHARINA HALL

According to Ray Browne, historical crime 'has developed into the fastest growing type of crime fiction' in English-language markets, and a similar boom has been visible in German-language contexts over the last two decades.[1] While this subgenre is often associated with temporal settings such as the medieval era, due to the early influence of Ellis Peters's 'Brother Cadfael' series (1977–94) and Umberto Eco's *The Name of the Rose* (1980), historical crime fiction by German-language authors has focused on the more recent, turbulent history of the twentieth century: the First World War (1914–18), the collapse of the German and Austro-Hungarian empires (1918), the Weimar Republic (1919–33), National Socialism (1933–45), Austrian annexation (1938), the Second World War (1939–45), Allied Occupation (1945–49), the division of Germany and the Cold War (1949–90), the student movement of the 1960s, the terrorist movement of the 1970s, and the fall of East Germany (the GDR) and reunification (1989–90).

The flourishing of the historical crime novel (*der historische Krimi*) is exemplified by the 'Inspector Kappe' or 'Es geschah in Berlin' (It Happened in Berlin, 2007–) series, created by crime writer Horst Bosetzky in conjunction with the publisher Jaron. Penned by a group of authors under Bosetzky's editorship, the series has used its *Kettenroman* (chain novel) format to create a twenty-six part historical epic that, thus far, follows Berlin police inspector Hermann Kappe, and later his police inspector nephew Otto Kappe, from 1910 to 1960. Iris Leister's *Novembertod* (November Death, 2008), shows Hermann Kappe encountering communists and right-wing radicals as the imperial order makes way for the Weimar Republic in 1918. Horst Bosetzky's *Mit Feuereifer* (With Zeal, 2011) explores the persecution of homosexuals under National Socialism against the backdrop of the 1936 Berlin Olympics, while Petra Gabriel's *Kaltfront* (Cold Front, 2014) sees Hermann and Otto wrestle with Cold War complexities and the East German *Stasi* (*Staatsicherheitsdienst*; state security service) in 1956. The series also examines legacies of the past: Horst Bosetzky's *Auge um Auge* (Eye for an Eye, 2014), set in 1954, traces a murder back to the crimes of a former Nazi doctor. The Kappe novels are thus a substantial project that utilize the genre to 'investigate' twentieth-century German history, creating 'eine Kriminalgeschichte der Zeit' (a crime narrative or criminal history of the time), with Berlin as the symbolic centre of events.[2]

Reunification, following forty years of division into East and West Germany, has undoubtedly fuelled the surge in historical crime fiction: the events of 1989–90 prompted a sustained re-evaluation of Germany's 'double past' of fascism and communism, as well as wide-ranging public discussions about guilt, victimhood and memorialization.[3] Historical milestones such as the fortieth anniversary of the 1968 student movement (2008) or the twentieth anniversary of the fall of the Berlin Wall (2009), and controversies over the trials of Nazi perpetrators (such as Sobibór death-camp guard John Demjanjuk in 2010–11) and the future of the *Stasi* Archive in 2007[4] have also stimulated public interest in the historical legacies of the twentieth century. Collectively, these have created a market receptive to cultural products that address the past, with German-language crime writers recognizing the commercial and literary possibilities of a mass audience keen to explore history from a German, Austrian or Swiss perspective – not least as certain eras have had a distinctly criminal dimension that dovetails with the genre's thematic concerns. The capacity of the authoritarian state and its representatives for criminality and persecution (National Socialist Germany; communist East Germany), the criminal actions of individuals or extremist groups against the state or those deemed 'other' (political assassins, left-wing terrorists,[5] right-wing neo-Nazis) and the subsequent responses of the state (tighter security measures and laws; court trials) provide rich material for the historical crime author's pen. Such narratives have usefully been termed *Verarbeitungskrimis*: crime narratives that engage with or work through difficult aspects of the German past.[6]

The forms and functions of historical crime novels in German

German-language historical crime writers employ a variety of formats that perform diverse functions. Some opt to write standalone novels. An early example is Hans Hellmut Kirst's satirical crime novel *Die Nacht der Generale* (*The Night of the Generals*, 1962), which depicts a psychopathic SS general as a murderous symbol of the rampaging, criminal Nazi regime.[7] More recently Richard Birkefeld and Göran Hachmeister's *Wer übrig bleibt, hat recht* (To the Victor the Spoils, 2002) features a Nazi policeman investigating a series of murders in Berlin at the end of the war, while Christa Bernuth's *Innere Sicherheit* (Internal Security, 2006) explores the motives of West German, left-wing terrorists and the refuge some of these were given by the GDR. All of these texts exploit a particular freedom conferred by the standalone: not having to safeguard the investigative figure for the next novel in the series allows authors to create uncompromising narratives with radical plots or dénouements. Thus, *Die Nacht der Generale* shows Grau, the investigator hunting the Nazi murderer, paying for his efforts with his life. Unequal power relations and the criminality of the regime doom his attempts to achieve justice. *Wer übrig bleibt, hat recht* overturns genre conventions by depicting an investigator with whom the reader cannot identify: Kalterer is a Nazi policeman, a perpetrator of atrocities in the east, and evades justice at the end of the novel by murdering former concentration camp inmate Haas to secure a new identity for himself after 1945.[8] *Innere Sicherheit* ends with the flight of policeman Martin Beck with former terrorist Nina from the GDR to an uncertain future that denies narrative closure. Equally unsettling is Andrea Maria Schenkel's standalone *Tannöd* (*The Murder Farm*, 2006), which transposes a genuine 1920s crime to a secretive rural community in the 1950s in order to thematize the suffering of slave labourers during the Nazi era and a post-war reluctance to engage critically with the past.

Other crime writers create ambitious historical crime series with an epic sweep. Andreas Pittler uses Protestant-Jewish-Viennese policeman David Bronstein to explore twentieth-century Austrian history, with the added innovation that four of the novels move back in time from 1934 to 1913, thereby simultaneously excavating the past and tracing the causes of future historical events. *Tacheles* (Plain Talking, 2008) plays in 1934 at the time of the failed Nazi *Juliputsch* (July Rebellion); *Ezzes* (Good Advice, 2009) in 1927 in the run-up to the *Julirevolte* (July Revolt, triggered by the acquittal of right-wingers in the Schattendorf trial); *Chuzpe* (Impudence, 2010) in 1918, as the monarchy crumbles, and *Tinnef* (Useless, 2011) in 1913 as the Redl spying affair unfolds. Volker Kutscher's prize-winning 'Gereon Rath' series, which has sold 650,000 copies in Germany to date, begins with *Der nasse Fisch* (The Wet Fish, 2007), set in 1929.[9] The fifth instalment, *Märzgefallene* (The March Fallen, 2014) has reached 1933, and like the novels before it, uses police inspector Rath's cases to undertake an in-depth investigation into the complexities of the Weimar period and of National Socialism's rise.

By contrast, some historical series examine key periods from a present-day perspective, so that 'geschichtliche Aufklärungsarbeit' (historical investigative work) is carried out in addition to the criminal investigation,[10] thereby foregrounding issues such as memory, justice and guilt. Bernhard Schlink, author of the best-selling novel *Der Vorleser* (*The Reader*, 1995), began his literary career with crime novels featuring Gerhard Selb, a former Nazi state prosecutor turned private investigator after the war. The first, *Selbs Justiz* (*Self's Punishment*, 1987), is an ecological crime novel that explores the Nazi past,[11] while the second and third, *Selbs Betrug* (*Self's Deception*, 1992) and *Selbs Mord* (*Self's Murder*, 2001), examine the legacies of terrorism and the collapse of the GDR. The trilogy thus seeks to provide an insight into three key periods of twentieth-century German history, as well as their continuing effects.

Lastly, the incorporation of German history into series that thematize diverse issues is widespread. Here, authors target a broad readership by engaging with a range of social, political and historical questions, rather than identifying themselves as purely historical crime writers. Wolfgang Schorlau's 'Georg Dengler' private-eye series features investigations about the pharmaceutical industry, global resource conflicts and post-traumatic stress disorder, but also explores the fall-out from the GDR's collapse in *Die blaue Liste* (The Blue List, 2003),[12] Nazi crimes in *Das dunkle Schweigen* (Dark Silence, 2005) and the right-wing violence that marred the 1980 *Oktoberfest* in *Das München-Komplott* (The Munich Plot, 2009). Nele Neuhaus's *Tiefe Wunden* (*The Ice Queen*, 2009), the third in the 'von Bodenstein and Kirchhoff' police procedural series, uses the present-day killing of an old woman to illuminate the role of female perpetrators during the Nazi era and the theme of Jewish vengeance. An earlier example is provided by Friedrich Dürrenmatt's crime novel *Der Verdacht* (*Suspicion*, 1951): the second of the Swiss 'Bärlach' novels shows the ailing police inspector on the trail of a former Nazi concentration camp doctor (see also chapter 4 on Swiss crime).

What are the larger purposes and functions of such historical crime novels? Anna Richardson, analysing Jewish-American author Michael Chabon's historical crime fiction, posits that 'the reader is invited to apply his or her knowledge of the Holocaust in combination with the problem-solving skills required by crime narratives in order to . . . hopefully find some cultural resolution within the narrative solution'.[13] In the context of the novels under discussion, readers may indeed be invited to apply their knowledge of twentieth-century European history along with their deductive skills to the text. However, the extent to which any 'cultural resolution' to complex historical events can be found via the dénouement is debatable: the power of many historical crime novels resides precisely in the moral, ethical or judicial questions that they leave open. Such novels often contain a dual narrative, in which closure is delivered in relation to the main criminal investigation, but larger questions are deliberately left unresolved to encourage continued reflection.

This kind of twofold narrative, which simultaneously grants and refuses closure, is visible in barrister and crime writer Ferdinand von Schirach's *Der Fall Collini* (*The Collini Case*, 2010), a courtroom drama in which tool-maker Fabrizio Collini admits to killing German industrialist Hans Meyer, but refuses to explain why. This *Kriminalroman* focuses on the murderer's motive, and in the process thematizes the failure of West German law to adequately deliver justice for Nazi crimes due to the so-called Dreher Law of 1968.[14] The latter was a seemingly innocuous law, whose statute of limitations allowed large numbers of former Nazis to evade justice, including the novel's murder victim. Thus, while the reader is provided with the solution to the question of Collini's motivation (his frustration at the state's failure to punish Meyer led him to dispense Old Testament-style justice), the larger questions of how the Dreher Law came to be so easily approved and how many Nazi criminals subsequently evaded justice remain open. The law and post-war attitudes to National Socialism are thus put on trial and found wanting. On publication, *Der Fall Collini* reignited discussion about how successfully Nazi crimes had been addressed in legal contexts, and in January 2012, Minister of Justice Sabine Leutheusser-Schnarrenberger cited the novel when announcing an independent commission to examine the Federal Ministry of Justice's engagement with the Nazi past.[15] The text is given further resonance by the author's family background: he is the grandson of Nazi Hitler Youth leader Baldur von Schirach.[16]

Many writers, including professional historians, journalists and lawyers, employ the historical crime narrative for pedagogical purposes. In historian and author Christian von Ditfurth's view, 'a historian is the perfect criminal investigator' as 'every murder is historical; its cause always lies in the past'.[17] Accordingly, his investigator Dr Josef Maria Stachelmann is a historian specializing in National Socialism, who uses his professional skills to investigate cases linked to that period. In *Mann ohne Makel* (*A Paragon of Virtue*, 2002), Stachelmann is asked by the police to help solve a series of revenge murders by a Jewish survivor of the Holocaust, while *Lüge eines Lebens* (Lifelong Lie, 2007) shows him uncovering a perpetrator's past while researching the Buchenwald concentration camp. In both cases, Stachelmann's historical knowledge provides the author with a means to educate the reader about the role of the police in Nazi persecution, the Nazi theft of property from Jewish-German citizens and the activity of *Einsatzgruppen* (execution task forces) in Poland. Some writers, as noted by Julian Preece in relation to Schorlau's *Blaue Liste*, also include a bibliography and a commentary on the process of researching the novel, which both assures readers of its historical veracity and allows them to deepen their historical knowledge after finishing the text.[18]

A number of German-language historical crime novels illuminate the findings of key historical studies or movements. Birkefeld and Hachmeister's *Wer übrig bleibt, hat recht* is shaped by the historical turn towards perpetrator studies in the 1990s, such as Christopher R. Browning's *Ordinary Men* (1992), which focuses on perpetrator motivation and the factors that led supposedly 'ordinary' Germans to help implement the Holocaust.[19] The authors' nuanced portrayal of Nazi policeman-perpetrator Kalterer, which encourages an understanding of his motivations (ambition, careerism and peer pressure), contrasts with the symbolic depictions of perpetrators as psychologically impaired monsters in the earlier novels of Dürrenmatt and Kirst. Birkefeld and Hachmeister's portrait of a Nazi society in which denunciations are carried out for personal rather than ideological ends also echoes the work of historians such as Robert Gellately.[20] Similarly, Pierre Frei's *Onkel Toms Hütte, Berlin* (*Berlin*, 2003), set during Allied Occupation, is a hybrid serial killer/detective novel that shows both the influence of the 1970s *Alltagsgeschichte* (history of everyday life) movement in detailing the morally complex lives of Germans under National Socialism, and the debates on German wartime suffering that re-emerged at the turn of the millennium.[21]

Historical crime novels are also utilized for political or ideological ends, as is seen in East German novels whose post-war murderers are revealed to be former Nazis masquerading as East German citizens. Gerhard Harkenthal's *Rendezvous mit dem Tod* (A Date with Death, 1962) shows the successful capture of one such imposter and ends by warning East German readers that they must be vigilant against the continued spread of fascism from West Germany. More recent Nazi-themed crime novels can be viewed as engaging collectively in 'memory contests': their contrasting literary representations of the past form part of an ongoing process by which individual, national and political identities are negotiated in the present.[22] Thus, crime novels such as those by Birkefeld and Hachmeister and von Schirach, which critique the post-war failure to adequately punish Nazi criminals, take up a broadly left-wing position. Others send mixed messages, such as Schlink's *Selbs Justiz*, which condemns the post-war silence about the Nazi past, before having its private detective push the murderer, a former Nazi, off a cliff. The unacknowledged consequence of this dénouement is that the villain cannot be placed on trial, thereby allowing the silence about his war-time crimes to continue.[23] Similarly, Frei's *Onkel Toms Hütte, Berlin* highlights the persecution of Jews under National Socialism, but risks privileging German suffering over Jewish suffering through its sustained focus on German women who fall victim to a serial killer during Allied Occupation. Anne Chaplet's *Russisch Blut* (Russian Blood, 2006) foregrounds the rape of German women by Soviet soldiers and the issue of *Vertreibung* (the expulsion of Germans from the eastern territories at the end of the war), but glosses over Nazi crimes and the Holocaust, thereby aligning itself with revisionist, post-war discourses through a selective remembering of the past.

Following this broad overview, the chapter now turns to a more detailed analysis of two examples of German historical crime fiction, which have been selected for their quality and their exploration of two important periods of history. The first, Hans Fallada's *Jeder stirbt für sich allein* (*Alone in Berlin*, 1947) is a *Kriminalroman* (crime novel) set during the Nazi era, while the second, Simon Urban's *Plan D* (*Plan D*, 2011), is a *Detektivroman* (detective novel) and alternative history set in a 2011 East Germany. While published over sixty years apart, these texts support Lee Horsley's assertion that 'crime and detective fiction can readily be combined with the transformative mode of satire', allowing authors to critique 'the corruption and misconduct of establishment figures' and 'to lash the crimes and vices of their own age'.[24]

Hans Fallada's Jeder stirbt für sich allein (Alone in Berlin)

This standalone novel by Hans Fallada (the pseudonym of Rudolf Ditzen, 1893–1947), was published shortly after the Second World War in 1947 by Aufbau, later to become the biggest GDR publisher, and again in the 1960s by Rowohlt in West Germany. Its sales were steady but unspectacular until it was rediscovered by American publisher Melville House, which introduced the text to the English-speaking world in 2009. The translation achieved critical and commercial success, and led Aufbau to publish a new unabridged German edition in 2011, after the original manuscript was located in its archives.[25]

Typically viewed as a resistance novel, *Jeder stirbt für sich allein* is also a historical novel. Although written just after the period it describes – from 1940 to 1946 – it portrays a Nazi state whose political and social structures were obliterated in 1945, and so are already of another era. By extension, the author's adoption of the *Kriminalroman* model – tracing the story of a crime from its inception to its conclusion while exploring the motivation of the criminal – positions the text as a historical crime novel, albeit an ironic one.[26] In this instance, the 'crime' is distributing anti-Nazi postcards to incite civil disobedience – an act of treason punishable by death – and the 'criminals' are a middle-aged, working-class couple, Anna and Otto Quangel, politicized by the death of their soldier son in France.

The narrative's darkly humorous satirical tone further unsettles such categorizations, showing how notions of law, criminality and justice are systematically perverted by the National Socialist state. Far from being criminals, the Quangels are the victims of a corrupt, criminal regime, whose police enforce the state's ideological persecution of its Jewish-German citizens and those who attempt political opposition. The *Kriminalroman* provides the perfect framework in which to explore these issues and their Kafkaesque ironies.

Written in less than a month in October 1946, just before the author's own death, the 500-page novel is a stylistically uneven but compelling portrait of Nazi society that retains a startling sense of immediacy. The Quangels' story is based on the genuine case of Elise and Otto Hampel, who were sentenced to death for distributing seditious postcards by Nazi judge Roland Freisler and were executed on 8 April 1943. Fallada was given access to the couple's *Gestapo* (*Geheime Staatspolizei*; secret state police) file by the poet and future GDR culture minister Johannes R. Becher, and while changing some factual details, hoped to capture 'die innere Wahrheit' (the inner truth) of their story.[27] Given that Fallada was writing for a sponsor – Becher and the Russian Occupation authorities – one might expect the novel to conform to the ideals of Soviet, anti-fascist literature, but apart from the final chapter, which foreshadows East German socialist realism in its depiction of 'the boy' working on the land and looking hopefully to the future, it does not do so.[28] Instead, Fallada offers a nuanced depiction of 'kleinen Leuten' (little people), who oppose the regime in a modest way and do not fit the model of heroic resistance fighters, because their relation to the Nazi regime is too complex and contradictory.[29]

Otto Quangel is a working-class foreman in a furniture factory, who, along with his wife, voted for Hitler after experiencing unemployment in the early 1930s. He is not a member of the Nazi Party, because the inequality of Nazi society, which rewards party members regardless of merit, offends his sense of fairness. However, until their son was killed in action, he and Anna were members of the Nazi *Arbeiterfront* (Workers' Front) and *Frauenschaft* (Women's Organization) respectively, and were willing to overlook 'the suppression of all other political parties, or things that they had condemned as merely excessive in degree, or too vigorously carried out, like the persecution of the Jews'.[30] When Anna takes in their Jewish-German neighbour Frau Rosenthal, Otto refuses to let her stay longer than one night, and when Frau Rosenthal later commits suicide, he tells Anna that they must pretend that they barely knew her. This groundbreaking characterization of resisters as former *Mitläufer* ('fellow travellers' who went along with the regime) and as morally nuanced individuals anticipates the *Alltagsgeschichte* movement of the 1970s, which saw historians researching the 'history of everyday life' to understand the complexities of living in Hitler's dictatorship. As historian Detlev Peukert notes, in the process of such research 'the stereotypes of the utterly evil fascist and the wholly good anti-fascist dissolve . . . Black and white becomes grey on grey. The everyday lives of simple "ordinary people" turn out to be far from simple and ordinary.'[31]

While Part 1 of the novel focuses on the Quangels' 'criminalization' (their decision to write seditious postcards following the death of their son), the acquisition of their 'weapons' (postcards, pen and ink) and their first 'crime' (leaving a postcard in the stairwell of an office building), Part 2 introduces the *Gestapo* investigators who will track them down and deliver them to the Nazi judicial system.[32] Their inclusion makes the novel the earliest post-war example of a subset of crime novels featuring a 'Nazi detective' – an investigative figure working as part of the National Socialist police force, army or paramilitary organizations.[33] Instead of showing the Nazi policeman as an efficient, heroic investigator – as advocated by the Nazi Propaganda Ministry in 1940[34] – Fallada's policemen make a number of errors, break procedural rules to appease superiors or gain promotion, carry out brutal interrogations in the infamous Prinz-Albrecht-Strasse cells and murder innocent suspects to conceal their own failings. In short, they are presented as members of a criminal organization that violates the rights of citizens, thereby echoing the 1946 Nuremberg International Military Tribunal's judgement of the *Gestapo* and the later findings of historians such as Robert Gellately.[35]

The novel's most nuanced portrait of a policeman is Inspector Escherich, who works on the case almost continuously from the discovery of the first postcard to after the Quangels' arrest. Escherich knows that the postcards pose no real threat to the regime, as most will be immediately handed in, and that the culprit will either make a mistake or give himself away. However, his superior, *SS Obergruppenführer* (senior group leader) Prall, is impatient to see results and this pressure leads Escherich to frame petty criminal Enno Kluge by tricking him into a false confession. As the extract at the end of this chapter shows, Escherich uses his position in the power hierarchy to keep his deputy inspector from objecting to this manoeuvre. The truth has become secondary and when Kluge outlives his usefulness, Escherich lures him to a night-time meeting, shoots him and records his death as suicide. The Nazi policeman is thus explicitly figured as a murderer.

However, Escherich is also the only policeman in the novel to undergo a moral epiphany. When his superiors briefly take him off the case and place him in the custody of the SS, he is shown experiencing fear properly for the first time. Once reinstated, the memory of his mistreatment allows him to empathize with Otto Quangel and to recognize the criminality of the Nazi authorities' actions. Escherich now regrets catching the Quangels in the service of the regime and is further confronted by Otto about the reality of his role: 'You're working in the employ of a murderer, delivering ever new victims to him. You do it for the money; perhaps you don't even believe in the man. No, I'm certain you don't believe in him. Just for money, then.'[36] The moral crisis engendered by this statement leads Escherich to commit suicide.

Inspector Escherich's depiction is the exception to the rule. The other *Gestapo* and SS characters are shown upholding Nazi ideology without significant ethical concerns. Aside from Otto Quangel, Anna Quangel and Enno Kluge, the state is responsible for the deaths of Trudel Hergesell (the former fiancée of the Quangels' son), her husband Karl Hergesell, Lore Rosenthal (the Quangels' Jewish-German neighbour) and Ulrich Heffke (Anna's brother). All are ordinary German citizens criminalized by the state through their association with the Quangels or for ideological reasons. Although the novel uses the figure of Dr Reichhardt, Otto's cultured cellmate, to assert that the Quangels' resistance was worthwhile, this question is complicated by the deaths of the Hergesells and Heffke, who come to the attention of the *Gestapo* only because of their personal links to the Quangels. The novel also shows how those who find the Quangels' postcards are placed at risk: for example, a doctor hiding his Jewish wife becomes the unwelcome recipient of the authorities' attention when a postcard is found in his practice. The remaining 275 postcards appear to have had no positive impact, failing in their mission to create a mass opposition movement: all but eighteen are handed in to the *Gestapo* by terrified citizens.

The tone of the novel's last section, 'The End', is ambiguous. On the one hand, the narrative is given closure through the Quangels' nobility in their courtroom trials and in prison, and by the hopeful outcome of the final chapter: the future of Kuno Borkhausen, a petty criminal's son, looks bright following his adoption by Eva Kluge, the only figure in the novel to successfully challenge the regime by leaving the Nazi Party. Her willingness to see the best in Kuno and her refusal to judge him on the basis of his father's criminality signals a break with the biological determinism of the Nazis. On the other hand, the price paid by the Quangels and those caught up in their actions linger on in readers' minds. The narrative's refusal to gloss over the unintended negative consequences of resistance for the Hergesells and for Heffke results in a complex reading experience that defies easy textual interpretation.

Simon Urban's Plan D

Simon Urban's debut crime novel, *Plan D* (2011), is an alternative history in which the reunification of East and West Germany has not yet taken place and the Berlin Wall still stands. The year is 2011: East German *Volkspolizei* (People's Police) captain Martin Wegener is called to the outskirts of East Berlin, where former political advisor Albert Hoffmann has been found hanging from a pipeline that exports Russian gas across the German–German border. As the murder is politically sensitive, West German police detective Richard Brendel is seconded to the investigative team. Its brief is to solve the case ahead of crucial economic talks between West German Chancellor Oskar Lafontaine and East German head of state Egon Krenz.[37]

In contrast to *Jeder stirbt für sich allein*, *Plan D* uses the *Detektivroman* model: the narrative's focus is on the investigation, with the murderers' identities revealed only at the end. However, like Fallada, Urban adopts a satirical approach to life under a repressive regime – in this case a 60-year-old GDR dictatorship teetering on the brink of bankruptcy. He also draws inspiration from alternative histories such as Robert Harris's *Fatherland* (1992) and Michael Chabon's *The Yiddish*

Policeman's Union (2007), which use crime narratives to anchor their fantasy scenarios. *Fatherland* depicts Nazi Germany in 1964 following Hitler's victory in the Second World War. Like Urban's Wegener, *Kripo* (criminal police) inspector Xavier March investigates the death of an old man with past links to the regime and uncovers dangerous state secrets. *The Yiddish Policeman's Union* opens in an alternate present in which three million Jews escaped the Holocaust through a resettlement programme to Alaska.[38] Urban borrows Chabon's exuberant style and imbues Wegener with the wise-cracking, *noir* humour of his P. I. Meyer Landsman, thereby suggesting his investigator's 'irreverence toward . . . institutional power' and a 'defiant refusal to be brow-beaten'.[39]

However, Wegener has been left shaken by the disappearance of his former police colleague Josef Früchtl in 2010, and suspects that the *Stasi* abducted or killed him. The older man was Wegener's mentor, and his sardonic wisdom is woven into the narrative in the form of memories and imaginary dialogues:

> A detective is distrustful twenty-four hours a day, Früchtl had said, and a distrustful detective stays until it's all over. A distrustful detective distrusts his colleagues, forensics and the murder victim, because he's distruster number 1. First and foremost, a distrustful detective distrusts himself. The only thing you can trust in is God, Früchtl had said, and you can't even trust him in this country.[40]

A detective working in the GDR has grounds to be distrustful, especially if, like Wegener, he is not a member of the *SED* (the East German Socialist Unity Party) and has received an official warning for covertly investigating Früchtl's disappearance. The *Stasi* was supposedly reined in after 'Revitalisation' in 1990, but Wegener and his fellow citizens know that they are still being monitored: 'Was there anyone in this country who wasn't being watched by anyone else? One thing's for sure, thought Wegener – they know everything about me.'[41] Yet there are still some people whom he trusts, such as his ex-girlfriend Karolina Enders and, to a certain degree, West German detective Richard Brendel.

Like Xavier March in *Fatherland*, Wegener opts to find out hidden truths and pays a high price for the knowledge he gains. In March's case, the murder investigation leads him to the facts of the Holocaust, written out of history after Nazi victory in 1945, and to smuggle classified files from Germany at the likely cost of his life. Wegener's investigation leads him to the *Stasi* file on Karolina, which contains old surveillance photographs of her and Früchtl having sex. He thus discovers that he was betrayed by the two people closest to him, but only after abusing his own professional power to access the file. A little later, he deduces that West German policeman Richard Brendel is a double agent, who has murdered a colleague to protect his cover. As in *Fatherland*, the central protagonist ends up isolated and alone, partly due to his own actions and partly due to the corruption of those around him.

Plan D ends with political documents being smuggled out of East Germany by Albert Hoffmann's daughter Marie, which will trigger a reunification of the two Germanies under the banner of reformed socialism, combining the best of each political system. In contrast to *Fatherland*, in which March arranges the smuggling of Holocaust documentation, a woman is the agent of change in *Plan D*, and she leaves the male detective tied up on the forest floor where the investigation began. Although Wegener had provided Marie with information that allowed the vital documents to be found, he is too much part of the system to be trusted. It remains unclear what awaits this flawed insider-outsider figure: he ends the narrative with little of the professional or personal autonomy that we associate with the wise-cracking, *noir* investigator.

Some of *Plan D*'s reviews have focused on the mischievousness of its comedy, such as the depiction of a senile Margot Honecker (former GDR education minister and wife of former head of state Erich Honecker) singing songs by political dissident Wolf Biermann in an old people's home. As a result, the author feels that the novel's more serious satirical and political dimensions have been overlooked.[42] *Plan D* is extremely ambitious in this respect: not only does it provide a critical reminder of what life was like in the GDR and of the ideological extremes that dominated twentieth-century German history, it also uses its vision of 'what might have been' to reflect on contemporary Germany and the political and social opportunities that were lost in 1990.

Plan D critiques 2011 life in non-reunified East and West Germany by showing discontent on either side of the Berlin Wall: East Germans such as Wegener yearn to leave their repressive state, while West Germans disillusioned by excessive capitalism are applying to live in the GDR. Implicitly, this West German malaise is used to critique present-day Germany and the superficiality of a consumerist lifestyle. The plot's twists and turns are also consciously set against the larger sweep of German history: the depiction of Früchtl, who was both a Nazi and a Communist, draws on Eric Hobsbawm's influential notion of the short twentieth century as an 'age of extremes'.[43] His experiences lead him to reject extreme ideologies, but he is fearful that future generations will not learn the lessons of history. The role played in Hoffmann's murder by two radical factions – the terrorist *Bürger Brigade* (citizens' brigade), intent on destroying East German socialism, and the *Stasi*, keen to preserve a hard-line GDR from Hoffmann's progressive ideas – suggests that Früchtl is right. However, the novel's ending, which sees the murder victim's vision of a socialist democracy on the way to becoming reality, is cautiously optimistic; it is possible that the extremists have been outmanoeuvred after all. This dénouement provides an idealized alternative to the actual events of 1990: left-wing SPD politician Oskar Lafontaine was beaten to the chancellorship by right-wing CDU candidate Helmut Kohl, whose implementation of a fast-track reunification resulted in an 'effective take-over' of East Germany by West Germany.[44] Hoffmann's vision of 'posteritatism' – 'the social justice of communism coupled with the democratic, liberal and rule-of-law qualities of Western market economies' – is a vision of what a slower reunification leading to a merger of both states might have offered.[45]

This chapter's analyses of *Jeder stirbt für sich allein* and *Plan D* illustrate the innovative use that post-1945, German-language, historical crime novels have made of *Detektivroman* and *Kriminalroman* conventions to carry out in-depth explorations of National Socialist and East German society respectively. Their examination of weighty themes, such as the state's capacity for criminality, police corruption and the often elusive nature of justice, shows the ability of the crime genre to engage meaningfully in debates about the legacy of the German past. The texts' frequent focus on difficult or contested aspects of the past, and the political, social and moral questions they pose via their crime narratives, also create opportunities for historical dialogues with a mass readership in the present, harnessing the genre for larger ends.

* * *

Extract from Hans Fallada's *Alone in Berlin*

Petty criminal Enno Kluge has been arrested on suspicion of distributing treasonous postcards. Gestapo Inspector Escherich knows that Kluge cannot be guilty, but tricks the man into a confession to appease his superiors. Deputy Inspector Schröder, who suspects the denunciation of Kluge was false, voices his concerns to Inspector Escherich that they have the wrong man.

'Inspector', said Deputy Inspector Schröder, 'I still can't quite believe that Kluge dropped the card. I watched him when I put the thing in his hand, and it was certainly the first time he'd ever seen it. It was all made up by that hysterical bitch, the doctor's receptionist'.

'But he says in his statement that he dropped it,' objected the inspector, albeit rather mildly. 'Incidentally, if I were you, I would avoid terms like hysterical bitch. No personal prejudices, just objective facts. If you wanted to though, you could question the doctor on the trustworthiness of the receptionist. Ach, no, I wouldn't bother with that either. That would just turn out to be another personal opinion, and we can leave it to the examining magistrate to assess the various witnesses. We work completely objectively here, isn't that right, Schröder, without any prejudice?'

'Of course, Inspector.'

'A witness statement is a statement, and we stick to it. How and why it came about, that doesn't interest us. We're not psychologists, we're detectives. The only thing we're interested in is crime. And if someone confesses to a crime, that's enough for us. At least that would be my way of looking at it, but I don't know, perhaps you have another, Schröder?'

'Of course not, Inspector!' exclaimed Deputy Inspector Schröder. He sounded quite shocked at the idea that his view might differ from his superiors. 'My thoughts exactly! Always opposed to crime in all its forms!'

'I knew it,' said Inspector Escherich drily, and stroked his moustache. 'We old school detectives are always of one mind.' . . . He looked thoughtfully at his junior. 'How long have you been deputy now, Schröder?'

'Three and a half years already, Inspector.'

The eye of the policeman as it rested on the inspector had something rather wistful about it. But the inspector merely said, 'Well, it's about time, then', and he left the station.

Hans Fallada, *Alone in Berlin*, trans. Michael Hofmann (London: Penguin Classics, 2009), pp. 208–10.

Notes

[1] Ray B. Browne, 'Historical Crime and Detection', in Charles J. Rzepka and Lee Horsley (eds), *A Companion to Crime Fiction* (Oxford: Blackwell, 2010), pp. 222–32 (p. 223); Barbara Korte and Sylvia Paletschek, 'Geschichte und Kriminalgeschichte(n): Texte, Kontexte, Zugänge', in Barbara Korte and Sylvia Paletschek (eds), *Geschichte im Krimi: Beitrage aus den Kulturwissenschaften* (Cologne: Böhlau, 2009), pp. 7–28 (p. 15).

[2] *http://www.krimi-couch.de/krimis/es-geschah-in-berlin.html* (accessed 25 August 2015).

[3] Mary Fulbrook, *History of Germany, 1918–2000: The Divided Nation* (London: Blackwell, 2002), p. 281.

[4] See Gary Bruce, 'East Germany', in Lavinia Stan (ed.), *Transitional Justice in Eastern Europe and the Former Soviet Union: Reckoning with the Communist Past* (London: Routledge, 2009), pp. 15–36.

[5] Julian Preece provides a useful survey of post-millennium crime novels engaging with German terrorism. See Julian Preece, 'Terrorism and the German Popular Imaginary: Conspiracies and Counterfactuals', in Julian Preece, *Baader-Meinhof and the Novel: Narratives of the Nation/Fantasies of the Revolution 1970–2010* (New York: Palgrave MacMillan, 2012), pp. 99–119.

[6] I borrow this term from Sascha Gerhards, 'Krimi Quo Vadis: Literary and Televised Trends in the German Crime Genre', in Lynn M. Kutch and Todd Herzog (eds), *Tatort Germany: The Curious Case of German-language Crime Fiction* (New York: Camden House, 2014), pp. 49–50. Gerhards applies the term to crime novels since 1995 that depict German history from Weimar to the immediate post-1945 period, but it can have a much wider application – to earlier twentieth-century crime novels and to other moments of post-war history – as this chapter demonstrates.

[7] See Achim Saupe, 'Der NS-Täter als Psychopath', in Achim Saupe, *Der Historiker als Detektiv – der Detektiv als Historiker. Historik, Kriminalistik und der Nationalsozialismus als Kriminalroman* (Bielefeld: Transcript, 2009), pp. 395–400.

[8] See Katharina Hall, 'The "Nazi Detective" as Provider of Justice in post-1990 British and German Crime Fiction: Philip Kerr's *The Pale Criminal*, Robert Harris's *Fatherland*, and Richard Birkefeld and Göran Hachmeister's *Wer übrig bleibt, hat recht*', *Comparative Literature Studies*, 50/2 (2013), 288–313.

[9] For further analysis of this series see Gerhards, 'Krimi Quo Vadis: Literary and Televised Trends in the German Crime Genre', pp. 52–5.

[10] Korte and Paletschek, 'Geschichte und Kriminalgeschichte(n): Texte, Kontexte, Zugänge', p. 9.

[11] Co-authored by Walter Popp.

[12] See Preece, *Baader-Meinhof and the Novel*, pp. 103 and 115–16.

[13] Anna Richardson, 'In Search of the Final Solution: Crime Narrative as a Paradigm for Exploring Responses to the Holocaust', *European Journal of English Studies*, 14/2 (2010), 159–71 (161).

[14] Named after Dr Eduard Dreher, a former Nazi lawyer working for the West German Ministry of Justice, who put forward the law. Its official title is the 'Einführungsgesetz

zum Ordnungswidrigkeitengesetz' (Introductory Act to the Administrative Offences Law).

[15] Adam Soboczynski and Jens Jessen, 'Das Dreher-Gesetz. Wieso kamen die meisten NS-Verbrecher straffrei davon? Ein Gespräch mit Ferdinand von Schirach', *Die Zeit*, 2 September 2011, *http://www.zeit.de/2011/36/Ferdinand-von-Schirach*. The commission website is *http://www.uwk-bmj.de/amnestie-und-verjaehrung.html* (both accessed 25 August 2015).

[16] Helen Pidd, 'Top German Author Confronts his Grandfather's Nazi Past in New Book', *The Guardian*, 7 September 2011, *http://www.theguardian.com/books/2011/sep/07/german-author-grandfather-nazi-past* (accessed 25 August 2015).

[17] Cited in Achim Saupe, 'Christian von Ditfurth: Die Stachelmann-Romane', *Europolar*, *http://www.europolar.eu/europolarv1/7_dossiers_lecture_ditfurth_de.htm* (accessed 25 August 2015).

[18] Preece, *Baader-Meinhof and the Novel*, p. 103.

[19] Christopher R. Browning, *Ordinary Men: Reserve Police Battalion 101 and the Final Solution in Poland* (New York: Harper Perennial, 1998 [1992]).

[20] Robert Gellately, *Backing Hitler: Consent and Coercion in Nazi Germany* (Oxford: Oxford University Press, 2001).

[21] See Helmut Schmitz (ed.), *A Nation of Victims? Representations of German Wartime Suffering from 1945 to the Present* (New York: Rodopi, 2007) and Katharina Hall, 'The Crime Writer as Historian: Representations of National Socialism and its Post-war Legacy in Joseph Kanon's *The Good German* and Pierre Frei's *Berlin*', *Journal of European Studies*, 42/1 (2012), 50–67.

[22] See Anne Fuchs, Mary Cosgrove and Georg Grote (eds), *German Memory Contests. The Quest for Identity in Literature, Film and Discourse since 1990* (New York: Camden, 2006).

[23] See Katharina Hall, 'The Author, the Novel, the Reader and the Perils of *Neue Lesbarkeit*: A Comparative Analysis of Bernhard Schlink's *Selbs Justiz* and *Der Vorleser*', *German Life and Letters*, 59/3 (2006), 72–88.

[24] Lee Horsley, *Twentieth-century Crime Fiction* (Oxford: Oxford University Press, 2005), p. 159.

[25] Debate about the two versions is ongoing. See Geoffrey Plow, 'Acts of Faith, Faith in Action: What *Alone in Berlin* and the 2011 "ungekürzte Neuausgabe" of *Jeder stirbt für sich allein* tell us about Hans Fallada's View of Anti-Nazi Resistance', *German Life and Letters*, 65/2 (2012), 263–80.

[26] The novel is the first of over 150, post-1945, Nazi-themed crime novels. See Katharina Hall, 'Detecting the Past: Nazi-themed crime fiction database', *https://swansea.academia.edu/KatharinaHall* (accessed 25 August 2015).

[27] Hans Fallada, 'Forward', *Jeder stirbt für sich allein. Ungekürzte Neuausgabe* (Berlin: Aufbau Verlag, 2011 [1947]), p. 5. The Hampels were motivated by the death of Elise's brother (rather than their son) and were denounced (rather than found by the authorities).

[28] Plow, 'Acts of Faith, Faith in Action', pp. 274 and 277.

[29] Wilkes notes that Fallada 'was neither an eager collaborator nor a resistance fighter'. Geoff Wilkes, 'Afterword', *Alone in Berlin* (London: Penguin Classics, 2009), pp. 569–88 (pp. 576–7).

[30] *Alone in Berlin*, p. 166. 'Dinge . . . wie die Unterdrückung aller anderen Parteien, oder die sie nur als zu weitgehend und zu roh durchgeführt verurteilt hatten, wie die Judenverfolgungen.' *Jeder stirbt für sich allein*, p. 214. Anna's membership of the Nazi *Frauenschaft* organization is revealed in chapter 17 of the unabridged edition.

[31] Detlev J. K. Peukert, *Inside Nazi Germany: Conformity, Opposition and Racism in Everyday Life*, trans. Richard Deveson (London: Penguin, 1993 [1982]), pp. 14–15.

[32] In 1936, Heinrich Himmler, the head of the SS, became German chief of police and combined the *Gestapo* and *Kripo* (criminal police) to form the *Sicherheitspolizei* (security police). *Gestapo* and *Kripo* officials were awarded SS ranks. Office of United States Chief of Counsel for Prosecution of Axis Criminality (OUSCCPAC), *Nazi Conspiracy and Aggression: Opinion and Judgement* (Washington, DC: United States Government Printing Office, 1947), p. 92.

[33] See Hall, 'The "Nazi Detective" as Provider of Justice'.

[34] Carsten Würmann, 'Zum Kriminalroman im Nationalsozialismus', in Bruno Franceschini and Carsten Würmann (eds), *Verbrechen als Passion. Neue Untersuchungen zum Kriminalgenre* (Berlin: Weidler, 2004), pp. 143–86 (p. 161).

[35] OUSCCPAC, *Nazi Conspiracy and Aggression*, p. 84; Gellately, *Backing Hitler: Consent and Coercion in Nazi Germany*, pp. 21, 40–3, 50 and 70.

[36] *Alone in Berlin*, p. 418. 'Sie arbeiten für einen Mörder und Sie liefern den Mörder stets neue Beute. Sie tun's für Geld, vielleicht glauben Sie nicht mal an den Mann. Nein, Sie glauben bestimmt nicht an ihn. Bloß für Geld.' *Jeder stirbt für sich allein*, p. 502.

[37] Oskar Lafontaine was West German Social Democratic Party (SPD) candidate for chancellor in the 1990 German elections. His opponent, Christian Democratic Union (CDU) politician Helmut Kohl, became the first chancellor of the reunited Germany. Egon Krenz was the last GDR head of state in 1989.

[38] Michael Chabon, *The Yiddish Policeman's Union* (London: Harper Perennial, 2007).

[39] Ralph Willett, cited in Peter Messent, 'Introduction: From Private Eye to Police Procedural', *Criminal Proceedings: The Contemporary American Crime Novel*, ed. Peter Messent (London: Pluto Press, 1997), pp. 1–21 (p. 4).

[40] Simon Urban, *Plan D* (London: Harvill Secker, 2013), p. 6. 'Der Kommissar ist vierundzwanzig Studen am Tag misstrauisch, hatte Früchtl gesagt, und der misstrausiche Kommissar blieb bis zum Schluss. Der misstrausische Kommissar misstraut den Kollegen, der Spurensicherung und dem Mordopfer, weil er Misstrauer Nr. 1 ist. Der misstrauische Kommissar misstraut an erster Stelle sich selbst. Vertrauen kannst du auf Gott, hatte Früchtl gesagt, und bei uns noch nicht mal auf den.' Simon Urban, *Plan D* (Munich: btb Verlag, 2013 [2011]), p. 12. As a communist state, the GDR discouraged religious beliefs.

[41] Urban, *Plan D* (2013), p. 94. 'Gab es in diesem Land irgendwen, der nicht von jemand anderem beobachtet wurde? Eins ist sicher, dachte Wegener, von mir wissen sie alles.' Urban, *Plan D* (2013 [2011]), p. 107.

[42] Joachim Feldmann, 'Interview mit Simon Urban', *CULTurMAG*, 27 August 2011, *http://culturmag.de/rubriken/buecher/ein-gesprach-mit-dem-schriftsteller-simon-urban/32414* (accessed 25 August 2015).

[43] Eric Hobsbawm, *Age of Extremes. The Short Twentieth Century, 1914–1991* (London: Abacus, 1994).

[44] Reunification took place according to Article 23 of the West German *Grundgesetz* (Basic Law) and saw the creation of an expanded state retaining the West German constitution. The SPD were in favour of the slower reunification suggested by Article 146, which would have seen a new German constitution devised by both governments. See Fulbrook, *History of Germany, 1918–2000*, p. 274.

[45] Urban, *Plan D* (2013), p. 246. 'die soziale Gerechtigkeit des Kommunismus, gepaart mit der demokratischen, freiheitlichen und rechtstaatlichen Qualität westlicher Marktwirtschaften'. Urban, *Plan D* (2013 [2011]), p. 269.

Select bibliography

Bernuth, Christa, *Innere Sicherheit* (Munich: Piper, 2006).
Birkefeld, Richard and Göran Hachmeister, *Wer übrig bleibt, hat recht* (Munich: Deutscher Tachenbuch Verlag, 2002).
von Ditfurth, Christian, *Mann ohne Makel* (Cologne: Kiepenheuer & Witsch, 2002). *A Paragon of Virtue*, trans. Helen Atkins (London: Toby Press, 2008).
Dürrenmatt, Friedrich, *Der Verdacht* (Zurich: Benzinger Verlag, 1953 [1951]). *Suspicion*, trans. Joel Agee (Chicago: University of Chicago Press, 2006).
Fallada, Hans, *Jeder stirbt für sich allein. Ungekürzte Neuausgabe* (Berlin: Aufbau Verlag, 2011 [1947]). *Alone in Berlin*, trans. Michael Hofmann (London: Penguin Classics, 2009).
Frei, Pierre, *Onkel Toms Hütte, Berlin* (Munich: Heyne, 2005 [2003]). *Berlin*, trans. Anthea Bell (London: Atlantic Books, 2005).
Kirst, Hans Hellmut, *Die Nacht der Generale* (Klagenfurt: Eduard Kaiser Verlag, 1962). *The Night of the Generals*, trans. J. Maxwell Brownjohn (London: Cassell, 2002).
Leister, Iris, *Novembertod* (Berlin: Jaron, 2008).
Pittler, Andreas, *Zores* (Vienna: Echomedia, 2012). *Inspector Bronstein and the Anschluss: Tsuris 1938*, trans. Vincent King (Riverside, CA: Ariadne Press, 2013).
Schenkel, Andrea Maria, *Tannöd* (Hamburg: Edition Nautilus, 2006). *The Murder Farm*, trans. Anthea Bell (London: Quercus, 2008).
von Schirach, Ferdinand, *Der Fall Collini* (Munich: Piper, 2010). *The Collini Case*, trans. Anthea Bell (London: Penguin, 2013).
Schlink, Bernhard and Walter Popp, *Selbs Justiz* (Zurich: Diogenes, 1987). *Self's Punishment*, trans. Rebecca Morrison (London: Weidenfeld & Nicholson, 2004).
Urban, Simon, *Plan D* (Munich: btb Verlag, 2013 [2011]). *Plan D*, trans. Katy Derbyshire (London: Harvill Secker, 2013).

Further secondary reading

Fuchs, Anne, Mary Cosgrove and Georg Grote (eds), *German Memory Contests. The Quest for Identity in Literature, Film and Discourse since 1990* (New York: Camden, 2006).
Hall, Katharina, 'The Crime Writer as Historian: Representations of National Socialism and its Post-war Legacy in Joseph Kanon's *The Good German* and Pierre Frei's *Berlin*', *Journal of European Studies*, 42/1 (2012), 50–67.
——, 'The "Nazi Detective" as Provider of Justice in post-1990 British and German Crime Fiction: Philip Kerr's *The Pale Criminal*, Robert Harris's *Fatherland*, and Richard Birkefeld and Göran Hachmeister's *Wer übrig bleibt, hat recht*', *Comparative Literature Studies*, 50/2 (2013), 288–313.
Plow, Geoffrey, 'Acts of Faith, Faith in Action: What *Alone in Berlin* and the 2011 "ungekürzte Neuausgabe" of *Jeder stirbt für sich allein* tell us about Hans Fallada's View of Anti-Nazi Resistance', *German Life and Letters*, 65/2 (2012), 263–80.
Preece, Julian, 'Terrorism and the German Popular Imaginary', in Julian Preece, *Baader-Meinhof and the Novel: Narratives of the Nation/Fantasies of the Revolution 1970–2010* (New York: Palgrave MacMillan, 2012), pp. 99–119.
Saupe, Achim, *Der Historiker als Detektiv – der Detektiv als Historiker. Historik, Kriminalistik und der Nationalsozialismus als Kriminalroman* (Bielefeld: Transcript, 2009).

Richardson, Anna, 'In Search of the Final Solution: Crime Narrative as a Paradigm for Exploring Responses to the Holocaust', *European Journal of English Studies*, 14/2 (2010), 159–71.
Waligórska, Magdalena, '"Darkness at the Beginning": The Holocaust in Contemporary German Crime Fiction', in Lynn M. Kutch and Todd Herzog (eds), *Tatort Germany: The Curious Case of German-language Crime Fiction* (New York: Camden House, 2014), pp. 101–19.

8

Der Fernsehkrimi: an Overview of Television Crime Drama in German

KATHARINA HALL

While the main focus of this volume is crime fiction, the popularity and significance of the German-language *Fernsehkrimi* (television crime drama) must also be acknowledged, both in its own right and as a subgenre that intersects with literary crime fiction in revealing ways. Like crime fiction, the *Fernsehkrimi* can be said to be distinctively German through its celebration of the regional and its focus on issues such as Turkish-German identity and the social implications of re-unification. It also provides an additional basis for measuring the evolution of German-language crime narratives, for example, through the introduction and representation of ethnic minority or female lead investigators. Many *Fernsehkrimis* are extremely long running, with popular investigators and high production values inspiring a loyal following. The television channels ZDF and ARD, both public service broadcasters, each have established crime slots: ARD's flagship crime series *Tatort*, which has run for over forty years, is shown at a quarter past eight on Sunday evenings and has long been a national institution, while ZDF has its 'Freitagabendkrimi' (Friday evening crime).[1]

Early *Fernsehkrimi* production in the late 1950s was shaped to a significant extent by the tensions between East and West Germany, which engendered a political and cultural competitiveness between the two states that was further heightened by the Cold War. The year 1958 saw the appearance of the first major West German television crime series, *Stahlnetz* (Steel Net, 1958–68), which, inspired by the American series *Dragnet* (1951–9), dramatized real cases from around the country using a semi-documentary style. Each episode opened with the depiction of a crime, followed by the statement 'This case is true! It was made using criminal-police documents.'[2] The series title and statement sought to emphasize the steely control of the police over real-life crime (largely robbery or murder), with meticulous police procedure leading to the successful capture of the criminal. For example, the episode 'Die blaue Mütze' (The Blue Hat) shows a robbery being solved thanks to a single lead, the eponymous headwear left at the scene, while 'Das Alibi' (The Alibi) sees the police breaking the apparently perfect alibi of a murdered woman's husband.

East Germany reciprocated in 1959 with its first television crime series, *Blaulicht – Aus der Arbeit unserer Kriminalpolizei* (Blue Light – from the Work of our Criminal

Police, 1959–68), whose cases were also drawn from genuine files. However, the location and the nature of the crimes featured in this series differed to those of *Stahlnetz*. *Blaulicht*'s three policemen, Captain Wenicke, First Lieutenant Thomas and Lieutenant Timm,[3] were shown working in East Berlin and, in common with their counterparts in East German crime fiction, fought crime that originated from the West or was committed by GDR citizens seduced by the promises of capitalism (see also chapter 1). Thus, the episode 'Auftrag Mord' (Mission Murder, 1965) sees a West German black-market dealer being sent to East Germany to repatriate a West German agent using the papers of a murdered man, while 'Antiquitäten' (Antiques, 1961) shows the destruction of a Leipzig smuggling ring that shipped art to West Germany.[4] The series thereby largely sidestepped the problem of depicting crime in a harmonious socialist state with supposedly insignificant levels of criminality, while simultaneously impressing on GDR audiences the continued ideological and criminal threat embodied by the West. Both series ran until 1968 (with *Stahlnetz* briefly revived in 1999), and were succeeded by other influential East and West German crime series in the golden age of 1970s and 1980s television drama.

A number of iconic West German crime series filled the vacuum left by *Stahlnetz*. *Der Kommissar* (The Inspector, 1969–76) showcased the work of Inspector Herbert Keller (played by Erik Ode) and the Munich *Mordkommission* (murder squad) as they solved crimes through a combination of the inspector's superior reasoning skills and the team's outstanding police work. For example, the episode 'Ein rätselhafter Mord' (A Puzzling Murder, 1971) shows Keller expertly weaving his way through the lies and obfuscations of a set of neighbours in order to solve the murder of a young man. The series was one of several that foregrounded the work of talented Munich policemen, such as *Derrick* (1974–88), whose eponymous chief inspector adopted a psychological approach, regularly moving beyond the question 'Wer ist der Täter?' (who is the perpetrator?) to consider 'Wie ist der Täter?' (what is the nature of the perpetrator?).[5] *Der Alte* (The Old Man/The Wise One, 1977–) similarly emphasized the importance of understanding the criminal: psychology was used by wily Chief Inspector Köster (Siegfried Lowitz) to trap culprits or to make them betray themselves. In 'Eine Tote auf Safari' (A Dead Woman on Safari, 1985), Köster uses the prop of an empty coffin and the fear of what lies within to elicit a confession from the murderer.

Tatort (Crime Scene, 1970–), a hugely successful German crime institution that, like *Der Alte*, is still running today, has always had a strongly local character, mirroring the devolved structure of its broadcaster, ARD (a consortium of German public service broadcasters; the equivalent of the BBC in the UK and PBS in the USA). Like *Stahlnetz*, it can be classified as a *Regionalkrimi* (regional crime series), showing police investigators operating in major cities or more rural areas throughout Germany, but also in Austria (in conjunction with broadcaster ORF) and Switzerland (in conjunction with broadcaster SF). Its locations have included Berlin, Bern, Cologne, Frankfurt am Main, Hamburg, Lucerne, Munich, Stuttgart and Vienna, as well as more rural settings in federal states such as

Baden-Württemberg, Schleswig Holstein and the Saarland.[6] With around thirty episodes a year, *Tatort* remains exceedingly popular, due to its quality, its emphasis on character development and the variety provided by its twenty-two sets of investigators and multiple production teams.[7] For example, the Münster episodes are humorous in tone, in contrast to the grittier Hamburg episodes.[8] The series is also strongly topical, highlighting issues such as neo-Nazi violence ('Voll auf Haß'; Full-on Hate, 1987), the impact of seismic historical events such as reunification ('Berlin – Beste Lage'; Berlin – Best Location, 1993) and sex trafficking from the Soviet Union ('Wegwefmadchen'; Disposable Girls, 2012).[9] In this respect, it draws on the socially engaged tradition of the *Soziokrimi* (social crime novel or 'new German crime novel'; see also chapter 1).

In 1971, in response to the success of *Tatort*, East Germany created *Polizeiruf 110* (Police: Dial 110, 1971–). Like *Tatort*, this series moved away from the 'true crime' format of *Stahlnetz* and *Blaulicht* into fictional dramatic territory and, while still engaging with social and political issues deemed important by the state, placed more of an emphasis on entertainment than its heavy-handed, didactic predecessor. In common with its West German equivalent, *Polizeiruf 110* featured investigations in a variety of cities (East Berlin, Rostock, Leipzig, Dresden, Halle) and more rural locations (the Baltic Sea and Harz regions). However, it frequently explored crimes other than murder, with an accent on social problems such as rape ('Blutgruppe AB'; Bloodgroup AB, 1972), youth crime ('Blütenstaub'; Pollen, 1972) and theft ('Der Fall Lisa Murnau'; The Lisa Murnau Case, 1971), and did so from the perspective of the East German citizen. Its popularity was such that it became almost the only GDR television series to survive the fall of the Berlin Wall.[10] While *Tatort* has versions set in Dresden and Leipzig, it has mainly been left to the post-reunification *Polizeiruf 110* to explore modern life in the eastern federal states. As Alan Cornell argues, the latter 'provides the most interesting material on the treatment of the new unified Germany in the *Fernsehkrimi*' via episodes such as 'Gefährliche Küsse' (Dangerous Kisses, 1996), whose police detectives Groth and Hinrichs can be seen as representing the 'Old and New East'.[11]

Arlene Teraoka asserts that 'the phenomenon of the [West] German police inspector has been the most enduring and largest triumph of the German television industry', while the figure of the private investigator has been almost completely absent.[12] She goes on to argue that the dominance of the 'late-middle-aged, lower-middle-class . . . authoritative but benevolent paternal hero' in the *Fernsehkrimi* can be explained by a respect for state authority and concomitant unease produced by the individualist rebellion of the private investigator.[13] Above all, viewers like 'the investigator who restores and guarantees the established social order through knowledge, discipline, and proper procedure'.[14] Arguably, the repeated enactment of this restoration process, episode after episode, provided a means of reassuring early audiences that post-war West German society was fundamentally decent, in contrast to the criminality of the Nazi state, although of course the figure of the respectable police inspector was also used extensively in crime fiction of that era, providing an ironic form of continuity.[15] It is perhaps not a coincidence that the lead investigator in *Der Alte* (The Old Man/The Wise One) was given the same nickname as Konrad Adenauer, West Germany's first chancellor, who took office at the age of seventy-three in 1949 and served until 1963. His prior political experience, which was untainted by National Socialism, allowed him to bring democracy, political stability and economic prosperity to a demoralized, defeated nation. Regarded as the father of modern Germany, and instrumental in the creation of the 1949 *Grundgesetz* (Basic Law/constitution), Adenauer can be viewed as the paternal role model for the early, male, state police inspectors on West German television.

The 1980s saw the beginnings of greater diversity in relation to investigator portrayals, both within and beyond these classic series. In 1981, a new *Tatort* inspector, Horst Schimanski, played by Götz George, burst onto West German television screens and was featured in twenty-nine Duisburg episodes until 1991 (a later spin-off series, *Schimanski*, began in 1997). Schimanski is the antithesis of the staid police inspectors featured in early episodes of *Der Kommissar*, *Der Alte* and *Tatort*. Young and sexually attractive, he comes from a working-class background and, while an employee of the state, is clearly shaped by the 1968 student movement in his anti-authoritarian attitudes and sympathy for social underdogs such as Turkish migrant workers. Respectable grey suits are traded in for a M65 military field jacket or 'Schimanski-Jacke' to signify the new police inspector's street-wise, action-hero status. The latter is accompanied by a dramatic change of pace: the first five minutes of a *Schimanski* episode might see him breaking down a door, chasing a suspect onto a flat roof and trying to stop him from activating a hand grenade ('Schwarzes Wochenende'; Black Weekend, 1986).[16]

Ethnic minority investigators begin to feature in *Fernsehkrimis* in the 1980s and 1990s, but are still under-represented today. There do not appear to have been any Jewish police inspectors or lead investigators. The closest is the figure of Liebling, the lawyer-investigator in *Liebling Kreuzberg* (1986–98), a series conceived and written by Jurek Becker, the highly respected Jewish-German writer who left East Germany in 1977. While Liebling is not identified as Jewish, commentators have observed the presence of a 'dry, alert, never cynical Jewish humour' in the episodes produced by Becker.[17] As Anna-Dorothea Ludewig shows, Jewish topics and themes are sometimes taken up in television crime series such as *Pfarrer Braun* (Father Brown, 2003–), *Schimanski* and *Tatort*, but with varying degrees of success. More nuanced episodes identified are *Pfarrer Braun*'s 'Die Gärten des Rabbiners' (The Rabbi's Gardens, 2008) and the Konstanz *Tatort* episode 'Der Schächter' (The Kosher Butcher, 2003); less successful are the *Schimanski* episode 'Das Geheimnis des Golem' (The Golem's Secret, 2004) and the Munich *Tatort* episode 'Ein ganz normaler Fall' (A Very Ordinary Case, 2011), which are found to be stereotypical and reductive.[18]

In 1986, Inspector Henry Johnson (Charles M. Huber), of African-German heritage, became the first black character in *Fernsehkrimi* history when he joined *Der Alte*'s investigative team under Chief Inspector Leo Kress. However, Alan Cornell places the wider significance of his role in question, as race is seldom addressed in the episodes in which he appears.[19] Johnson was succeeded in 1997 by black police inspector Axel Richter (Pierre Sanoussi-Bliss), who remains part of the current team under Chief Inspector Richard Voss. There has thus been continuous representation of ethnic minorities on the show since 1986, but always in a subordinate role. However, 2008 saw a key development, when well-known actor Mehmet Kurtuluş took the leading role of undercover Turkish-German Chief Inspector Cenk Batu in the Hamburg *Tatort*.

Reactions to the first Batu episode, 'Auf der Sonnenseite' (On the Sunny Side, 2008), were extremely positive. In a *Spiegel* article entitled 'Bye, bye Kebab-Klischee!' (Bye-bye Kebab Cliché), Christian Buß described it as a 'quantum leap' for *Tatort* in terms of its lead character, the writers' avoidance of multicultural stereotypes and the rebooting of a tired crime format.[20] Batu is depicted as intelligent, strong, confident and adept at handling difficult situations. His characterization may have been shaped by a literary forerunner, Jakob Arjouni's private investigator Kemal Kayankaya: like Kayankaya, Batu is a modern, urban male who often identifies more as German than Turkish, but has to deal with racist attitudes and stereotyping in his everyday life (see chapter 1). In a daring move for the franchise, Batu is shown encountering racism from bigoted police colleagues unaware of his undercover role. The Batu episodes have also been viewed as groundbreaking examples of the *Weltkrimi* (global crime narratives), due to their emphasis on globalization rather than regional identities, which are the more usual focus of the series.[21]

Batu occupies an insider-outsider role, operating deep within Hamburg's police structures, but in an isolated position, reporting only to his German handler. He is thus not integrated into a larger police force, has little chance of forging positive professional relationships with colleagues and remains invisible to the public. This portrayal suggests that progress is still required before a Turkish-German character can be depicted as a successful chief inspector leading his or her own *Fernsehkrimi* team. Berna Gueneli also argues that while Batu's depiction moves beyond stereotypical ethnic representations, 'the problem of sexualized or eroticized ethnicization remains', as illustrated by a lingering shot of him showering in 'Auf der Sonnenseite'.[22] These reservations notwithstanding, it is regrettable that Batu's tenure on *Tatort* was so short: he appeared in just six episodes, and was killed off in the 2012 episode 'Die Ballade von Cenk und Valerie' (The Ballad of Cenk and Valerie). Kurtuluş's departure was explained by his desire to pursue a film career, but another factor may have been that ratings for the Batu episodes had dropped.[23]

East Germany led the way in terms of women's representation in *Fernsehkrimis*. From its inception in 1971, *Polizeiruf 110* featured a female police investigator, Lieutenant Vera Arndt, played by Sigrid Göhler – a working mother who was shown contributing to investigations on a par with her male colleagues, although the head of the team was always male. Arndt's presence can be viewed as a reflection of the GDR's more progressive approach to equality, and the acknowledgement, supported by an excellent state childcare system, that working women made a vital contribution both to society and the economy.[24] In West Germany, progress was slower, with women shown only in supporting roles until the 1970s (e.g. secretary Fräulein Rehbein and criminal police assistant Helga Lauer in *Der Kommissar*). The first leading female police investigator appeared on the Mainz *Tatort* in the 1978 episode 'Der Mann auf dem Hochsitz' (The Man in the Hide), with a screenplay by crime writer Richard Hey. Like his literary creation Inspector Katharina Ledermacher (see chapter 1), Chief Inspector Marianne Buchmüller, played by Nicole Heesters, is depicted as intelligent, sexually emancipated, socially progressive and at ease in a man's world. While civilian characters are sometimes surprised to encounter a high-ranking woman in the police force, her male colleagues and superiors are shown accepting her authority and expertise absolutely. This portrayal could be viewed as idealized, but would have helped to normalize the idea of women occupying leadership positions in the police.

While Buchmüller appeared in only three episodes between 1978 and 1980, she led the way for a new generation of female inspectors, both in *Tatort* and other television crime series. In 1981, Hanne Wiegand (Karin Anselm) became the second female *Tatort* chief inspector. She was followed in 1989 by Lena Odenthal (Ulrike Folkerts), 'who revolutionized the role of the female inspector in *Tatort*' through her portrayal of a modern policewoman without clichéd stereotypes (her predecessor Buchmüller may have known how to handle a gun, but was also shown checking her hair in the mirror countless times).[25] Odenthal is still in action in the Ludwigshaven *Tatort* today, and is the series' longest-serving female inspector.[26]

The year 1994 saw a breakthrough, with three new series named for their female protagonists: *Die Kommissarin* (The Female Police Inspector), featuring Frankfurt Chief Inspector Lea Sommer (played by Hannelore Elsner, 1994–2006, ARD); *Bella Block* (based on the 'Bella Block' novels of Doris Gercke; set in Hamburg and played by Hannelore Hoger since 1994, ZDF) and *Rosa Roth* (set in Berlin; played by Iris Berben 1994–2013, ZDF). All are depicted as highly capable professionals, with a strong sense of justice and investigative tenacity. One pleasing aspect of these three series is their longevity, which allows audiences to follow the women through a substantial portion of their careers, and to celebrate the experience and achievements of women in middle age, or even beyond retirement in the case of Block. These older female characters are positively represented as multidimensional characters with full lives, but also reveal the toll that many years of dealing with crime can take. In the episode 'Stich ins Herz' (Stab to the Heart, 2011), we see a world-weary Block climbing out of her car at yet another crime scene, while her voice is heard to say: 'The older I get, the harder I find it to keep my distance from the victims . . . I have become vulnerable.'[27]

The new millennium saw a proliferation of leading women in television crime series. The year 2002 marked the start of *Das Duo* (The Duo, 2002–12, ZDF), which featured a pair of female police inspectors working together for the first time, twenty years after the seminal American series *Cagney and Lacey* (1982–8, CBS). Nine other policewomen were added to existing television crime series such as *Tatort* that year.[28] In 2004, the *Filmmuseum Berlin* exhibition 'Die Kommissarinnen'

(The Female Police Inspectors) honoured the contribution to the genre of the characters and the actresses who have played them. A roll-call of female *Fernsehkrimi* police inspectors covers three densely typed pages of the exhibition's press kit.[29] A quick survey of current *Tatort* inspectors shows that there are sixteen female inspectors out of a total forty-six (around one-third, in line with fairly recent data on female representation within the police).[30] However, *Der Alte* remains out of step, introducing its first woman, pathologist Franziska Sommerfeld, with much fanfare in 2013, a full thirty-six years after the start of the series.[31]

Modern representations of gender and sexuality are found in *SK Kölsch* (1999–2006, Sat. 1), which makes innovative use of the odd couple format by pairing homosexual Chief Inspector Klaus Taube with macho, heterosexual Chief Inspector Jupp Schatz. Similarly, *Mit Herz und Handschellen* (With Heart and Handcuffs, 2002–6, Sat. 1) partners homosexual Chief Inspector Leo Kraft with Chief Inspector Nina Metz. Both series show the professional and personal lives of their gay protagonists, thereby helping to normalize depictions of minority sexuality in mainstream television. More recently, Swiss/Lucerne *Tatort* investigator Liz Ritschard (2012–) is shown to be attracted to women, but her sexuality is not made a key issue in the series. Such depictions remain groundbreaking compared to American and British crime series, which scarcely depict gay investigative characters. A rare exception is the British police series *The Bill*, which explored Sergeant Craig Gilmore and PC Luke Ashton's relationship in 2003.

Since the 1980s, there has been some movement away from the dominant police procedural format, providing viewers with greater varieties of *Fernsehkrimi*. *Ein Fall für Zwei* (A Case for Two, 1981–2013, ZDF) features a lawyer and a policeman-turned-private-detective working together, while *Liebling Kreuzberg* (Liebling/Darling Kreuzberg, 1986–98, SFB and NDR) shows lawyer Robert Liebling solving cases in the Kreuzberg district of Berlin, both before and after the fall of the Berlin Wall. The investigator of *Adelheid und ihre Mörder* (Adelheid and her Murders, 1992–2007, NDR) is a secretary working for the criminal police and *Schwarz, Rot, Gold* (Black, Red, Gold, 1992–6, NDR) shows a customs officer working on criminal cases. *Alles außer Mord* (Anything but Murder, 1993–5, ProSieben) and *Dengler* (based on Wolfgang Schorlau's 'Dengler' series, 2015–, ZDF) feature private detectives, while *Schwarz greift ein* (Black Intervenes, 1994–9, SAT 1.) and *Pfarrer Braun* (Father Brown, based on the stories of G. K. Chesterton, 2003–14, ARD) see priests solving crimes. The star of the long-running Austrian series *Kommissar Rex* (Inspector Rex, 1994–2004, ORF) is an Alsatian police dog solving criminal cases in Vienna (the series was also a popular export to Australia). *Kottan ermittelt* (Kottan Investigates, 1976–84, ORF) was a highly successful Austrian series that parodied police conventions (see also chapter 3); more recently, the German series *Mord mit Aussicht* (Murder with a View, 2007, ARD) and *Heiter bis tödlich* (Sunny with a Chance of Death, 2011–, ARD) satirize provincial life and crime conventions to humorous effect.[32]

Notes

[1] See Alan Cornell, 'The "Fernsehkrimi": Traditions and Developments', *German Life & Letters*, 50/1, 1997, 82–102 (84–9).

[2] 'Dieser Fall ist wahr! Er wurde aufgezeichnet nach Unterlagen der Kriminalpolizei.'

[3] Ranks in the East German police, the *Volkspolizei* (people's police), mirrored those of the army.

[4] A guide to *Blaulicht* epiodes is available in Deutsches Rundfunkarchiv, 'DRA Spezial: *Blaulicht*. Fernseh-Krimireihe des Deutschen Fernsehfunks 1959–1968', nr. 8 (2006), *http://www.dra.de/online/hinweisdienste/spezial/2006/dra-spezial_08-2006_blaulicht.pdf* (accessed 27 August 2015).

[5] Series editor Claus Legal, cited in Cornell, 'The "Fernsehkrimi": Traditions and Developments', 86.

[6] A map showing *Tatort* locations can be seen here: *http://www.daserste.de/unterhaltung/krimi/tatort/kommissare/die-kommissare-wer-ermittelt-wo-100.html* (accessed 27 August 2015).

[7] Current *Tatort* police investigators can be seen here: *http://www.daserste.de/unterhaltung/krimi/tatort/kommissare/tatort-filter-aktuelle-kommissare-100.html* (accessed 27 August 2015).

[8] Michael Kimmelman, 'German Viewers Love their Detectives', *New York Times*, 27 August 2009, *http://www.nytimes.com/2009/08/27/arts/television/27abroad.html?pagewanted=all&_r=0* (accessed 27 August 2015).

[9] A complete *Tatort* episode guide is available here: *http://www.daserste.de/unterhaltung/krimi/tatort/sendung/index.html* (accessed 27 August 2015).

[10] Cornell, 'The "Fernsehkrimi": Traditions and Developments', 89.

[11] Alan Cornell, 'Series, Location, and Change: National Reunification as Reflected in German Television Detective Series', in A. Mullen and E. O'Beirne (eds), *Crime Scenes: Detective Narratives in European Culture since 1945* (Amsterdam and Atlanta: Rodopi, 2000), pp. 3–14 (pp. 6–7).

[12] Arlene Teraoka, 'Detecting Ethnicity: Jakob Arjouni and the Case of the Missing German Detective Novel', *The German Quarterly*, 72/3 (1999), 265–89 (267). However, there are some writers who have made use of private investigator figures, such as Bernhard Schlink ('Gerhard Selb' series) and Wolfgang Schorlau ('Georg Dengler' series).

[13] Teraoka, 'Detecting Ethnicity', 267.

[14] Teraoka, 'Detecting Ethnicity', p. 268.

[15] Some individuals involved in the *Fernsehkrimi* had played a role in the Nazi regime. The star of *Der Kommissar*, Erik Ode, was a successful actor during that period, while scriptwriter Herbert Reinecker was chief editor for the Hitler Youth. See Teraoka, 'Detecting Ethnicity', 268. ZDF announced in 2013 that it would no longer show repeats of *Derrick* after the revelation that its lead, Horst Tappert, had hidden his past in the Waffen SS. 'German TV drops Derrick show over SS actor revelations', *http://www.bbc.co.uk/news/world-europe-22384143* (accessed 27 August 2015).

[16] See also Eike Wenzel, 'Der Star, sein Körper und die Nation. Die Schimanski–TATORTe', in Eike Wenzel (ed.), *Tatort: Recherchen und Verhöre, Protokolle und Beweisfotos* (Berlin: Bertz, 2000), pp. 175–202.

[17] 'trockene, realitätswache, nie zynische jüdische Humor'. 'Mann ist Manne', *Der Spiegel*, 47 (1997), *http://www.spiegel.de/spiegel/print/d-8761460.html* (accessed 27 August 2015).

[18] Anna-Dorothea Ludewig (ed.), *Im Anfang war der Mord: Juden und Judentum im Detektivroman* (Berlin: be.bra Verlag, 2012), pp. 167–76.

[19] Cornell, 'The "Fernsehkrimi": Traditions and Developments', 87.

[20] 'Quantumsprung'. Christian Buß, 'Bye, bye Kebab-Klischee!', *Der Spiegel*, 25 October 2008, *http://www.spiegel.de/kultur/gesellschaft/neuer-hamburg-tatort-bye-bye-kebab-klischee-a-586356.html* (accessed 27 August 2015).

[21] Sascha Gerhards, 'Krimi Quo Vadis: Literary and Televised Trends in the German Crime Genre', in Lynn M. Kutch and Todd Herzog (eds), *Tatort Germany: The Curious Case of German-language Crime Fiction* (New York: Camden House, 2014), pp. 41–60 (pp. 47–9).

[22] Berna Gueneli, 'Mehmet Kurtuluş and Birol Ünel: Sexualised Masculinities, Normalised Ethnicities', in Sabine Hake and Barbara Mennel (eds), *Turkish German Cinema in the New Millennium: Sites, Sounds and Screens* (Oxford: Berghahn Books, 2012), pp. 136–48 (pp. 137 and 147).

[23] Christian Buß, 'Mehmet Kurtuluş verlässt *Tatort*: Abgang eines Alleskönners', *Der Spiegel*, 4 March 2011, *http://www.spiegel.de/kultur/tv/mehmet-kurtulus-verlaesst-tatort-abgang-eines-alleskoenners-a-749152.html* (accessed 27 August 2015).

[24] See Mary Fulbrook, *History of Germany, 1918–2000: The Divided Nation* (Oxford: Blackwell, 2002), pp. 191–6.

[25] '[die] das Rollenbild von der Kommissarin im *Tatort* revolutionierte.' Michaela Krieg and Stefanie Spitzendobler, 'Stereotype Darstellung von Kommissarinnen im *Tatort*. Projektbericht im Rahmen des Masterseminars "Fernsehen in Europa: Strukturen, Programme, Inhalte"', in *kommunikation.medien* (2013), *http://journal.kommunikation-medien.at/2013/05/stereotype-darstellungen-von-kommissarinnen-im-tatort/* (accessed 27 August 2015).

[26] See also Sabine Holtgreve, 'Supergirls – Die Geschichte der TATORT Kommissarinnen', in Wenzel (ed.), *Tatort: Recherchen und Verhöre, Protokolle und Beweisfotos*, pp. 71–82.

[27] 'Je älter ich werde, desto schwerer fällt es mir die Distanz zu den Opfer zu halten . . . Ich bin verwundbar geworden.'

[28] *Filmmuseum Berlin*, 'Die Kommissarinnen' exhibition press pack (2004), p. 14, *https://www.deutsche-kinemathek.de/sites/default/files/public/node-attachments/presse/pressemappen/2004_Pressemappe_Kommissarinnen.pdf* (accessed 27 August 2015).

[29] *https://www.deutsche-kinemathek.de/sites/default/files/public/node-attachments/presse/pressemappen/2004_Pressemappe_Kommissarinnen.pdf* (accessed 27 August 2015), pp. 15–18.

[30] For example, in 2004, the Berlin criminal police was 26 per cent female. Ibid.

[31] *http://deralte.zdf.de/Der-Alte/Der-Alte-5988978.html* (accessed 27 August 2015).

[32] Sabine Tenta, 'Murder on the Box: German TV Crime Series', *http://www.goethe.de/ins/cz/pra/kul/du/lit/kri/en7607608.htm* (accessed 27 August 2015).

Annotated Bibliography of Resources on German-language Crime Narratives

KATHARINA HALL

This bibliography provides selected resources for the study of German-language crime narratives. The aim is to introduce readers to established studies and overviews in both German and English, which give substantial attention to the following: Austrian, German, Swiss and East German authors; crime novels and television dramas; subgenres and writing contexts. The volume's individual chapters provide additional recommended reading.

Archives, bibliographies, encyclopedias

Bochumer Krimi Archiv (BKA). This archive was established in 1984 by author and journalist Reinhard Jahn (also known as H. P. Carr), and has gathered a large collection of secondary materials relating mainly to post-1945 German-language crime fiction. Some BKA materials are available online via the *Lexikon der deutschen Krimi-Autoren*, *http://www.krimilexikon.de/* (accessed 27 August 2015) and in print (see Jockers and Jahn below).

Bonner Krimi Archiv (Sekundärliteratur) (BoKAS). This non-profit archive, established in 1989 by Thomas Przybilka, has amassed a substantial collection of secondary materials relating to German-language and international crime fiction, and provides support to crime researchers. It has close links with the *Bochumer Krimi Archiv* and publishes a bi-annual newsletter that provides an overview of new secondary materials. See *http://www.bokas.de/* (accessed 27 August 2015).

Deutsches Rundfunk Archiv (DRA). The German Radio Archive has a number of useful resources, particularly relating to GDR television crime dramas. Downloadable documents such as *Spezial Nr. 8* on *Blaulicht* and *Spezial Nr. 20* on 'Kriminalfilme in DDR-Fernsehen' provide details of episodes with synopses and analysis. See *http://www.dra.de/online/bestandsinfos/fernsehkrimis/* (accessed 27 August 2015).

Hillich, Reinhard and Wolfgang Mittmann (eds), *Die Kriminalliteratur der DDR, 1949–1990: Bibliographie* (Berlin: Akademie Verlag, 1991). A wide-ranging bibliography of GDR crime writers arranged alphabetically and chronologically. It also includes a useful directory of GDR crime fiction publishers and series.

Jockers, Angelika and Reinhard Jahn (eds), *Lexikon der deutschsprachigen Krimi-Autoren. Unter Mitarbeit der aufgenommenen Autorinnen und Autoren* (2nd edn; Munich: Buch & Media/Verlag der Criminale, 2005). An encyclopedia of over 600 German-language crime authors, co-edited by the founder of the *Bochumer Krimi Archiv*.

Ludewig, Anna-Dorothea (ed.), *Im Anfang war der Mord: Juden und Judentum im Detektivroman* (Berlin: be.bra Verlag, 2012). An encyclopedia of Jewish crime fiction characters created by Jewish and non-Jewish authors from the German- and English-speaking worlds. Contains extensive analysis of representations of Jews and Jewishness in the genre.

Przybilka, Thomas, 'Krimi-Frauen, Frauen-Krimi: eine Auswahlbibliographie der Sekundärliteratur zu weiblichen Autoren und Detektivfiguren der Kriminalliteratur', in Klaus-Peter Walter (ed.), *Lexikon der Kriminalliteratur* (Meitingen: Grundwerk, 1993). A useful bibliography of secondary literature on the works of female crime authors and female detectives.

——, *Krimis im Fadenkreuz. Kriminalromane, Detektivgeschichte, Thriller, Verbrechens- und Spannungsliteratur der Bundesrepublik und der DDR 1949–1990/92. Eine Auswahlbibliographie der deutschsprachigen Sekundärliteratur* (Cologne: Baskerville Bücher, 1998). Bibliography of secondary literature on several subgenres of East and West German crime fiction from 1949 to 1992.

Schädel, Mirko, *Illustrierte Bibliographie der Kriminalliteratur 1796–1945 im deutschen Sprachraum* (Butjadingen: Achilla Presse, 2006), 2 vols. An illustrated bibliography of around 9,000 crime narratives and novels (including translated works) published in the German-speaking world between 1796 and 1945.

Walter, Klaus-Peter (ed.), *Lexikon der Kriminalliteratur* (Meitingen: Grundwerk, 1993 onwards). Wide-ranging encyclopedia of German and international crime fiction examining authors, works and themes, which currently stands at over 13,000 pages.

——, *Reclams Krimi-Lexikon: Autoren und Werke* (Stuttgart: Reclam, 2002). An encyclopedia of German-language and international crime fiction authors and works.

Full-length studies, edited volumes and special journal issues

Alberts, Jürgen and Frank Göhre (eds), *Zehn Krimiautoren sagen aus. Eine Reise durch die Geschichte des deutschsprachigen Kriminalromans* (Hildesheim: Gerstenberg Verlag 1999). A history of German-language crime fiction through the eyes of ten authors, including Irene Rodrian, Ingrid Noll, Michael Molsner and Hansjörg Martin.

Aspetsberger, Friedbert and Daniela Strigl (eds), *Ich kannte den Mörder, wußte nur nicht wer er war. Zum Kriminalroman der Gegenwart* (Innsbruck, Vienna, Munich: StudienVerlag, 2004). An eclectic volume that explores German-language crime fiction and television drama from a variety of perspectives.

Barfoot, Nicola, *Frauenkrimi/polar féminin: Generic Expectations and the Reception of Recent French and German Crime Novels by Women* (Frankfurt a. M.: Peter Lang, 2007). An insightful comparative study that provides a detailed history of the *Frauenkrimi* and its reception with a focus on the work of Pieke Biermann and Maria Gronau.

Birkle, Carmen, Sabina Matter-Seibel and Patricia Plummer (eds), *Frauen auf der Spur: Kriminalautorinnen aus Deutschland, Großbritannien und den USA* (Tübingen: Stauffenburg, 2001). A volume examining the work of female crime writers in Germany, Great Britain and the United States. Contains interviews with Sabine Deitmer, Doris Gercke and Christiane Grän.

Brönnimann, Jürg, *Der Soziokriminalroman: ein neues Genre oder ein soziologisches Experiment? Eine Untersuchung des Soziokriminalromans anhand der Werke des schwedischen Autoren Sjöwall and Wahlöö und des deutschen Autors -ky* (Wupperthal: NordPark, 2004). A groundbreaking comparative study on the Swedish and German social crime novel focusing on work by Sjöwall and Wahlöö and Horst Bosetzky (-ky).

Campbell, Bruce B., Alison Guenther-Pal and Vibeke Rützou Petersen (eds), *Detectives, Dystopias and Poplit: Studies in Modern Genre Fiction* (New York: Camden House, 2014). This volume examines three types of genre fiction: crime fiction, science fiction and poplit. It includes essays on the crime fiction of Hermynia Zur Mühlen, Klüpfel, Kobr and Steinfest, the Jerry Cotton series and the *Krimi* as a site of memory.

Cheesman, Tom, *Novels of Turkish-German Settlement: Cosmopolite Fictions* (New York: Camden House, 2007). This monograph on Turkish-German literature contains extensive analysis of Turkish-German crime fiction.

Claßen, Isabella, *Darstellung von Kriminalität in der deutschen Literatur, Presse und Wissenschaft 1900 bis 1930* (Frankfurt a. M.: Peter Lang, 1988). An exploration of the representation of criminality in the German press and literature from 1900–30.

Ermert, Karl and Wolfgang Gast (eds), *Der neue deutsche Kriminalroman. Beiträge zu Darstellung, Interpretation und Kritik eines populären Genres* (Rehburg-Loccum: Evangelische Akademie Loccum, 1985). A volume of essays exploring the 'new German crime novel' and television crime dramas.

Evans, Richard J., *Tales from the German Underworld: Crime and Punishment in the Nineteenth Century* (London: Yale University Press, 1998). This monograph explores narratives of crime and punishment emerging from four genuine cases (a banknote forger, a female vagrant, a confidence trickster and a prostitute).

Franceschini, Bruno and Carsten Würmann (eds), *Verbrechen als Passion. Neue Untersuchungen zum Kriminalgenre* (Berlin: Weidler, 2004). This volume examines international crime fiction, with chapters on German-language authors and wider areas such as the *Frauenkrimi*, crime fiction under National Socialism and the *Fernsehkrimi*.

Freund, Winfried, *Die deutsche Kriminalnovelle von Schiller bis Hauptmann. Einzelanalysen unter sozialgeschichtlichen und didaktischen Aspekten* (2nd edn; Paderborn: Schöningh, 1980 [1975]). A monograph exploring the German crime novella from Schiller to Hauptmann.

Frizzoni, Brigitte, *Verhandlungen mit Mordsfrauen. Geschlechterpositionierungen im "Frauenkrimi"* (Zurich: Chronos Verlag, 2009). This monograph examines representations of gender in crime fiction by women writers.

Gauß, Karl-Markus and Arno Kleibel (eds), *Österreichischer Krimi*, *Literatur und Kritik*, 417/18 (2007). A special journal issue focusing on the Austrian crime novel.

Germer, Dorothea, *Von Genossen und Gangstern: Zum Gesellschaftsbild in der Kriminaliteratur der DDR und Ostdeutschlands von 1974 bis 1994* (Essen: Verlag Die Blaue Eule, 1998). A wide-ranging monograph exploring the depiction of society in the GDR crime novel and in crime fiction from eastern Germany after 1989.

Götting, Ulrike, *Der deutsche Kriminalroman zwischen 1945 und 1970: Formen und Tendenzen* (Wetzlar: Kletsmeier, 1998). A substantial study that examines over twenty East and West German crime authors and their work.

Hillich, Reinhard (ed.), *Tatbestand. Ansichten zur Kriminalliteratur der DDR 1947–1986* (Berlin: Akademie Verlag, 1989). A volume of essays on East German crime fiction edited by a key theorist in this area.

Hügel, Hans-Otto, *Untersuchungsrichter, Diebsfänger, Detektive: Theorie und Geschichte der deutschen Detektiverzählung im 19. Jahrhundert* (Stuttgart: J. B. Metzler, 1978). A groundbreaking examination of the history of nineteenth-century German-language crime fiction, with an extensive bibliography.

Kehrberg, Brigitte, *Der Kriminalroman der DDR, 1970–1990* (Hamburg: Verlag Dr. Kovač, 1998). Study focusing on East German crime fiction and its ideological functions during the last twenty years of the country's existence. Contains a useful bibliography and publication data.

Kord, Susanne, *Murderesses in German Writing, 1720–1860: Heroines of Horror* (Cambridge: Cambridge University Press, 2009). This monograph explores how the cases of eight famous murderesses in Germany were represented in legal, psychological, philosophical and literary writings.

Korte, Barbara and Sylvia Paletschek (eds), *Geschichte im Krimi: Beiträge aus den Kulturwissenschaften* (Cologne: Böhlau, 2009). A wide-ranging volume on historical crime fiction with an international focus. It includes essays on German crime fiction under National Socialism, East German crime fiction and the *Freud-Krimi* (Freud crime novel).

Krajenbrink, Marieke, *Intertextualität als Konstruktionsprinzip. Transformationen des Kriminalromans und des romantischen Romans bei Peter Handke und Botho Strauß* (Amsterdam and Atlanta, GA: Rodopi, 1996). An exploration of the works of two key writers (one Austrian, one German), which includes substantial analysis of their use of the crime fiction genre.

—— and Kate M. Quinn (eds), *Investigating Identities: Questions of Identity in Contemporary International Crime Fiction* (Amsterdam and New York: Rodopi, 2009). A wide-ranging volume that includes three chapters on German-language crime fiction.

Kutch, Lynn M. and Todd Herzog (eds), *Tatort Germany: The Curious Case of German-language Crime Fiction* (New York: Camden House, 2014). An interesting volume on German-language crime fiction and television drama, which focuses on regional crime, historical crime and crime fiction's treatment of identity.

Marsch, Edgar (ed.), *Im Fadenkreuz: Der neuere Schweizer Kriminalroman* (Zürich: Chronos Verlag, 2007). A useful collection of essays on recent Swiss crime fiction.

Moraldo, Sandro M. (ed.), *Mord als kreativer Prozess: Zum Kriminalroman der Gegenwart in Deutschland, Österreich und der Schweiz* (Heidelberg: Universitätsverlag Winter, 2005). A wide-ranging volume on contemporary Austrian, Swiss and German crime fiction and representations of reunification. Contains analysis of work by Arjouni, Noll, Schlink, Kneifl, Komarek, Haas, Dürrenmatt, Mettler and Schneider.

Nindl, Sigrid, *Wolf Haas und sein kriminalliterarisches Sprachexperiment* (Berlin: Erich Schmidt, 2010). An analysis of Austrian crime writer Wolf Haas's work, focusing in particular on the author's use of language.

Nusser, Peter, *Der Kriminalroman* (3rd edn; Stuttgart: J. B. Metzler, 2003 [1980]). Highly influential study on the history and theory of the *Kriminalroman*, *Detektivroman* and thriller, with an extensive bibliography.

Ott, Paul, *Mord im Alpenglühen: Der Schweizer Kriminalroman – Geschichte und Gegenwart* (Wuppertal: NordPark Verlag, 2005). A comprehensive introduction to Swiss crime fiction that examines the country's major crime writers and includes a full bibliography.

Saupe, Achim, *Der Historiker als Detektiv – der Detektiv als Historiker. Historik, Kriminalistik und der Nationalsozialismus als Kriminalroman* (Bielefeld: Transcript, 2009). An insightful study on German-language and international crime fiction that engages with the National Socialist past. Contains an extensive bibliography.

Scharf, Hannah, *Die Kriminalromane von Wolf Haas. Tradition und Innovation* (Norderstedt: GRIN Verlag, 2010). This doctoral thesis examines Haas's work in the context of classic and hard-boiled crime fiction.

Schilling, Gerhard, *Ostdeutsche Kriminalliteratur nach der Wende: Eine thematische und gattungsgeschichtliche Untersuchung* (Marburg: Tectum Verlag, 2013). A monograph exploring the crime fiction of eastern Germany following the GDR's demise in 1989.

Schmidt, Jochen, *Gangster, Opfer, Detektive: eine Typengeschichte des Kriminalromans* (2nd edn; Hillesheim: KVB Verlag, 2009 [1989]). An extensive study exploring all aspects of the genre in relation to over 1,000 German-language, English-language and European authors. Contains a section on Austrian crime fiction.

Stewart, Faye, *German Feminist Queer Crime Fiction: Politics, Justice and Desire* (Jefferson, NC: McFarland, 2014). A pioneering analysis of German-language queer crime fiction, which uses gender/queer theory to explore texts as allegories of twentieth- and twenty-first-century European upheavals.

Vogt, Jochen (ed.), *Der Kriminalroman. Poetik – Theorie – Geschichte* (2nd edn; Munich: Fink Verlag, 1998). This influential volume brings together essays on crime fiction by German-speaking intellectuals such as Benjamin, Brecht, Bloch and Kracauer, as well as theoretical essays and analyses by German and international critics, with a focus on English-language crime fiction.

Wenzel, Eike (ed.), *Tatort: Recherchen und Verhöre, Protokolle und Beweisfotos* (Berlin: Bertz, 2000). A comprehensive set of essays and interviews on the television crime series *Tatort*, including its Austrian and Swiss productions.

Zwaenepoel, Tom, *Dem guten Wahrheitsfinder auf dem Spur: Das populäre Krimigenre in der Literatur und im ZDF-Fernsehen* (Würzburg: Könighausen und Neumann, 2004). This monograph focuses on television crime dramas produced by ZDF, such as *Derrick*.

Journal articles and book chapters

Augart, Julia, 'Der reisende Detektiv. Ermittler im deutschen Afrikakrimi', *Acta Germanica. German Studies in Africa*, 41 (2013a), 42–55. An exploration of the figure of the German investigator in the *Afrika-Krimi*.

——, '(Inter)cultural Investigation: Kenya in German Crime Fiction', *Journal for Studies in Humanities and Social Sciences*, 2/1 (2013b), 104–16. Journal article exploring German crime fiction set in Kenya since the 1970s, with a focus on cultural encounters.

Beck, Sandra and Katrin Schneider-Özbek (eds), *Gewissheit und Zweifel: Interkulturelle Studien zum kriminalliterarischen Erzählen* (Bielefeld: AISTHESIS VERLAG, 2015). This volume explores intercultural encounters in German-language crime fiction. A number of contributions focus on Turkish-German crime fiction by authors such as Jakob Arjouni and Esmahan Aykol.

Bergfelder, Tim, 'Extraterritorial fantasies: Edgar Wallace and the German crime film', in Tim Bergfelder, Erica Carter and Deniz Göktürk (eds), *The German Cinema Book* (London: BFI, 2002), pp. 39–47. An essay exploring German film adaptations of British crime writer Edgar Wallace's work between 1959 and 1972.

Campbell, Bruce B., 'Justice and Genre: The *Krimi* as a Site of Memory in Contemporary Germany', in Bruce B. Campbell, Alison Guenther-Pal and Vibeke Rützou Petersen (eds), *Detectives, Dystopias and Poplit: Studies in Modern Genre Fiction* (New York: Camden House, 2014), pp. 133–51. This essay explores the way in which German detective fiction is burdened by the memory of German history and functions as a 'site of memory' for German-speaking audiences.

Canoy, Ray, 'The Imaginary FBI: Jerry Cotton, the Nazi Roots of the *Bundeskriminalamt*, and the Cultural Politics of Detective Fiction in West Germany', in Bruce B. Campbell, Alison Guenther-Pal and Vibeke Rützou Petersen (eds), *Detectives, Dystopias and Poplit: Studies in Modern Genre Fiction* (New York: Camden House, 2014), pp. 117–32. An exploration of the pulp detective series 'Jerry Cotton' alongside the history of the Federal Criminal Police Office.

Cornell, Alan, 'The Depiction of Neo-Nazism in Police Series on German Television', *German Politics & Society*, 15/1 (1997), 22–45. An essay focusing on the engagement of German TV crime series with the issue of far-right politics.

——, 'The "Fernsehkrimi": Traditions and Developments', *German Life & Letters*, 50/1 (1997), 82–102. This essay provides a very good overview of the pre-millennium *Fernsehkrimi*.

——, 'Series, Location, and Change: National Reunification as Reflected in German Television Detective Series', in A. Mullen and E. O'Beirne (eds), *Crime Scenes: Detective Narratives in European Culture since 1945* (Amsterdam and Atlanta: Rodopi, 2000), pp. 3–14. A useful essay on representations of reunification in the *Fernsehkrimi*.

Costabile-Heming, Carol Anne, '"Der Fall Loest": A Case Study of Crime Stories and the Public Sphere in the GDR', in Lynn M. Kutch and Todd Herzog (eds), *Tatort Germany: The Curious Case of German-language Crime Fiction* (New York: Camden House, 2014), pp. 139–54. This essay explores author Erich Loest's relationship with the East German authorities and how it shaped his career as a crime writer.

Drexler, Peter, 'The German Courtroom Film during the Nazi Period: Ideology, Aesthetics, Historical Context', *Journal of Law and Society*, 28/1 (2001), 64–78. An article exploring how the films of the Weimar and Nazi periods addressed questions of justice and the administration of the law.

Forshaw, Barry, 'Germany, Austria and Switzerland', in Barry Forshaw, *Euro Noir: The Pocket Essential Guide to European Crime Fiction, Film and TV* (Harpenden: Pocket Essentials, 2014), pp. 83–101. A lively overview of German-language crime narratives, with case studies and commentary from German publishers.

Gerhards, Sascha, 'Ironizing Identity: The German Crime Genre and the Edgar Wallace Production Trend in the 1960s', in Jaimey Fisher (ed.), *Generic Histories of German Cinema: Genre and its Deviations* (New York: Camden House, 2013), pp. 133–55. An essay exploring the influence of British crime writer Edgar Wallace in the context of 1960s film adaptations of his works and questions of national identity.

——, 'Krimi Quo Vadis: Literary and Televised Trends in the German Crime Genre', in Lynn M. Kutch and Todd Herzog (eds), *Tatort Germany: The Curious Case of German-language Crime Fiction* (New York: Camden House, 2014), pp. 41–60. An exploration of German regional crime fiction and recent trends such as the *Weltkrimi* (global crime narrative) and the *Verarbeitungskrimi* (crime novel engaging with historical legacies).

Götz von Olenhusen, Irmtraud, 'Mord Verjährt nicht. Krimis als historische Quelle (1900–1945)', in Barbara Korte and Sylvia Paletschek (eds), *Geschichte im Krimi: Beiträge aus den Kulturwissenschaften* (Cologne: Böhlau, 2009), pp. 105–26. A useful essay on the under-researched area of crime fiction produced under National Socialism.

Guenther-Pal, Alison and Arlene A. Teraoka, '"God, How Idyllic": The German Countryside and the Abject of Enlightenment in Doris Gercke's *Weinschröter, du mußt hängen* (1987)', *Women in German Yearbook*, 27 (2011), 150–75. An exploration of the relationship between depictions of the countryside and social critique in Gercke's text.

Hall, Katharina, 'The Author, the Novel, the Reader and the Perils of *Neue Lesbarkeit*: A Comparative Analysis of Bernhard Schlink's *Selbs Justiz* and *Der Vorleser*', *German Life and Letters*, 59/3 (2006), 72–88. This article explores the use of popular literary codes in Schlink's first crime novel and *The Reader*.

——, 'The Crime Writer as Historian: Representations of National Socialism and its Post-war Legacy in Joseph Kanon's *The Good German* and Pierre Frei's *Berlin*', *Journal of European Studies*, 42/1 (2012), 50–67. This essay examines the links between crime fiction and the historiography of National Socialism, with a focus on the 'history of everyday life' and debates on German wartime suffering.

——, 'The "Nazi Detective" as Provider of Justice in post-1990 British and German Crime Fiction: Philip Kerr's *The Pale Criminal*, Robert Harris's *Fatherland*, and Richard Birkefeld and Göran Hachmeister's *Wer übrig bleibt, hat recht*', *Comparative Literature Studies*, 50/2 (2013), 288–313. An exploration of the possibilities and limitations of crime fiction investigators who are positioned as employees of the Nazi regime.

Herzog, Todd, 'Crime Stories: Criminal, Society, and the Modernist Case Study', *Representations*, 80 (2002), 34–61. An article examining the overlooked 1920s Berlin crime series 'Outsiders of Society: The Crimes of Today'.

Hillich, Reinhard, 'Spielmaterial. Zur Darstellung des Ministeriums für Staatssicherheit in der Kriminalliteratur der DDR', *Horch und Guck: Zeitschrift zur kritischen Aufarbeitung der SED-Diktatur*, 2 (1993), 1–10. An article exploring the representation of the Ministry of State Security in GDR crime fiction.

Holtgreve, Sabine, 'Supergirls – Die Geschichte der TATORT Kommissarinnen', in Eike Wenzel (ed.), *Tatort: Recherchen und Verhöre, Protokolle und Beweisfotos* (Berlin: Bertz, 2000), pp. 71–82. An overview of the history of female police detectives in the TV crime series *Tatort*.

Huck, Christian, 'Travelling Detectives: Twofold Mobility in the Appropriation of German Crime Fiction in the Interwar Period', *Transfers*, 2/3 (2012), 120–43. This article examines German interwar crime 'dime novels' in relation to their American predecessors and the theme of travel.

Jones, Christopher, 'Images of Switzerland in Swiss Crime Fiction', in Arthur Williams, Stuart Parkes and Julian Preece (eds), *German-language Literature Today: International and Popular?* (Bern and Oxford: Peter Lang, 2000), pp. 85–98. This essay provides an analysis of four 1990s texts by Heimann, Knellwolf, Bär and Graf.

——, '"Bestialisch dahingeschlachtet": Extreme Violence in German Crime Fiction', in Helen Chambers (ed.), *Violence, Culture and Identity: Essays on German and Austrian Literature, Politics and Society* (Bern: Peter Lang, 2006), pp. 401–15. This essay explores the representation of serial killers in German crime fiction, with a particular focus on the work of Thea Dorn and Sabine Deitmer.

Jordan, Jim, 'Of Fables and Multiculturalism: The Felidae novels of Akif Pirinçci', in Arthur Williams, Stuart Parkes and Julian Preece (eds), *German-language Literature Today: International and Popular?* (Bern and Oxford: Peter Lang, 2000), pp. 255–68. A perceptive article on the crime fiction of this important Turkish-German writer.

Kemmerzell, Anja, 'Was ist ein Frauenkrimi?', *Ariadne Forum*, 4 (1996), 5–6. A short essay that seeks to define the *Frauenkrimi*.

Knittel, Susanne C., 'Case Histories: The Legacy of Nazi Euthanasia in Recent German *Heimatkrimis*', in Lynn M. Kutch and Todd Herzog (eds), *Tatort Germany: The Curious Case of German-language Crime Fiction* (New York: Camden House, 2014), pp. 120–38.

This essay explores the treatment of the Nazi past in two regional crime novels by Rainer Gross.

Krajenbrink, Marieke, 'Unresolved Identities in Roth and Rabinovici: Reworking the Crime Genre in Austrian Literature', in Marieke Krajenbrink and Kate M. Quinn (eds), *Investigating Identities: Questions of Identity in Contemporary International Crime Fiction* (Amsterdam and New York: Rodopi, 2009), pp. 243–60. This essay explores the innovative contributions of two Austrian (crime) writers to the genre.

Lange, Horst, 'Nazis vs. the Rule of Law: Allegory and Narrative Structure in Fritz Lang's *M*', *Monatshefte*, 101/2 (2009), 170–85. This article examines conceptualizations of policing, punishment and justice in Lang's Expressionist film.

Linder, Joachim, 'Feinde im Inneren. Mehrfachtäter in deutschen Kriminalromanen der Jahre 1943/44 und der "Mythos Serienkiller"', *Internationales Archiv für Sozialgeschichte der deutschen Literatur*, 28/2 (2003), 190–227. An article exploring the representation of serial killers in German crime novels of the 1940s.

——, 'Polizei und Strafverfolgung in deutschen Kriminalromanen der dreißiger und vierziger Jahre', in Michael Walter, Harald Kania and Hans-Jörg Albrecht (eds), *Alltagsvorstellungen zur Kriminalität. Individuelle und gesellschaftliche Bedeutung von Kriminalitätsbildern für die Lebensgestaltung* (Münster: LIT Verlag 2004), pp. 87–115. An essay exploring the representation of policing in German crime novels of the 1930s and 1940s.

Lindner, Martin, 'Der Mythos "Lustmord". Serienmörder in der deutschen Literatur, dem Film und der bildenden Kunst zwischen 1892 und 1932', in Joachim Linder and Claus-Michael Ort (eds), *Verbrechen – Justiz – Medien. Konstellationen in Deutschland von 1900 bis zur Gegenwart* (Tübingen: Niemeyer Verlag, 1999), pp. 273–305. This essay explores the representation of the serial killer in German art, literature and film between 1892 and 1932.

McChesney, Anita, 'The Female Poetics of Crime in E. T. A. Hoffmann's "Mademoiselle Scudéri"', *Women in German Yearbook*, 24 (2008), 1–25. An article examining the role of the female detective in the famous 1819 novella and crime narrative.

Mattson, Michelle, '*Tatort*: The Generation of Public Identity in a German Crime Series', *New German Critique*, 78 (1999), 161–81. This article explores the representation of 'the foreigner' from the early 1980s to the mid-1990s in the TV crime series *Tatort*.

Meyer, Friederike, 'Zur Relation juristischer und moralischer Deutungsmuster von Kriminalität in den Kriminalgeschichten der "Gartenlaube", 1855–1870', *Internationales Archiv für Sozialgeschichte der Literatur*, 12 (1987), 156–89. A journal article examining representations of criminality in crime stories published by the literary newspaper *Die Gartenlaube*.

Neuhaus, Volker, '"Zu alt, um nur zu spielen": Die Schwierigkeiten der Deutschen mit dem Kriminalroman', in Sandro M. Moraldo (ed.), *Mord als kreativer Prozess: Zum Kriminalroman der Gegenwart in Deutschland, Österreich und der Schweiz* (Heidelberg: Universitätsverlag Winter, 2005), pp. 9–19. An article exploring German academia's difficulties in engaging with crime fiction from the German-speaking world.

O'Brien, Traci S., 'What's in Your Bag? "Freudian Crimes" and Austria's Nazi Past in Eva Rossmann's *Freudsche Verbrechen*', in Lynn M. Kutch and Todd Herzog (eds), *Tatort Germany: The Curious Case of German-language Crime Fiction* (New York: Camden House, 2014), pp. 155–74. This essay examines the use of Freudian notions in an Austrian crime novel to explore the post-war repression of the Nazi past.

Pailer, Gaby, '"Weibliche" Körper im "männlichen" Raum. Zur Interdependenz von Gender und Genre im deutschsprachigen Kriminalroman von Autorinnen', *Weimarer Beiträge*,

46 (2000), 561–81. A journal article examining issues of gender and genre in the context of German-language crime writing by women.

Preece, Julian, 'Terrorism and the German Popular Imaginary: Conspiracies and Counterfactuals', in Julian Preece, *Baader-Meinhof and the Novel: Narratives of the Nation/ Fantasies of the Revolution 1970–2010* (New York: Palgrave MacMillan, 2012), pp. 99–119. This chapter contains extensive analysis of German-language detective novels and thrillers featuring Baader-Meinhof terrorists.

Przybilka, Thomas, 'Krimiszene Deutschland. Zeitschriften, Magazine, Preise, Verbände, Gesellschaften und Archive – Übersicht und Rückblick', *Jahrbuch der deutsch-finnischen Literaturbeziehungen* (1996), 80–8. An overview of Germany's crime-writing scene in 1996, including information about prizes, associations and archive resources.

Richardson, Anna, 'In Search of the Final Solution: Crime Narrative as a Paradigm for Exploring Responses to the Holocaust', *European Journal of English Studies*, 14/2 (2010), 159–71. This article explores crime fiction's capacity for engaging with the Holocaust, with particular reference to the work of Jewish-American author Michael Chabon.

Riegel, Dieter, 'Africa in West German Crime Fiction', in Eugene Schleh (ed.), *Mysteries of Africa* (Bowling Green: Bowling Green State University Popular Press, 1991), pp. 50–64. This chapter examines representations of Africa in West German crime fiction of the 1980s.

Rothemund, Kathrin, 'Facing Complex Crime: Investigating Contemporary German Crime Fiction on Television', *Northern Lights. Film and Media Studies Yearbook*, 9/1 (2011), 127–42. This article explores recent German television crime series *KDD – Kriminaldauerdienst* (KDD – Berlin Crime Squad) and *Im Angesicht des Verbrechens* (In the Face of Crime).

Schmiedt, Helmut, 'Gesellschaftskritische Mordfälle. Themen und Techniken des neuen deutschen Kriminalromans am Beispiel -kys und Richard Heys', *Die Horen*, 31/4 (1986), 51–62. An article exploring the German social crime novel, with a focus on the work of -ky and Hey.

Schönert, Jörg, 'Kriminalgeschichten in der deutschen Literatur zwischen 1770 und 1890. Zur Entwicklung des Genres in sozialgeschichtlicher Perspektive', *Geschichte und Gesellschaft*, 9/1 (1983), 49–68. Article exploring crime narratives between 1770 and 1890 from a socio-historical perspective.

Sieg, Katrin, 'Post-colonial Berlin? Pieke Biermann's Crime Novels as Globalization Critique', *Studies in 20th & 21st Century Literature*, 28/1 (2004), 152–82. An exploration of Biermann's work in relation to the issue of globalization.

Stewart, Faye, 'Dialogues with Tradition: Feminist-queer Encounters in German Crime Stories at the Turn of the Twenty-first Century', *Studies in 20th & 21st Century Literature*, 35/1 (2011), 114–35. A comparative analysis of two short story collections edited by Pieke Biermann and Lisa Kuppler, which investigates how each negotiates the gendered conventions of crime fiction, and of feminist and queer crime.

Sutherland, Margaret, 'Images of Turks in Recent German Crime Fiction: A Comparative Case Study in Xenophobia', in Jean Anderson, Carolina Miranda and Barbara Pezzotti (eds), *The Foreign in International Crime Fiction* (London: Continuum, 2012), pp. 188–99. This chapter provides a comparative analysis of representations of Turkish characters and culture in a controversial 2007 *Tatort* episode and in a 2009 crime novel by Gabriele Brinkmann.

Teraoka, Arlene, 'Detecting Ethnicity: Jakob Arjouni and the Case of the Missing German Detective Novel', *The German Quarterly*, 72/3 (1999), 265–89. An influential article that explores the lack of private investigator narratives in German-language crime fiction prior to Jakob Arjouni's works.

Vogel, Marianne, 'Ein Unbehagen in der Kultur: Zur Kriminalliteratur deutschsprachiger Schriftstellerinnen in den 90er Jahren', in Ilse Nagelschmidt, Alexandra Hanke, Lea Müller-Dannhausen and Melani Schröter (eds), *Zwischen Trivialität und Postmoderne: Literatur von Frauen in den 90er Jahren* (Frankfurt a. M.: Peter Lang, 2002), pp. 49–67. An essay exploring the works of female, German-language crime authors of the 1990s.

Vogt, Jochen, '*Tatort* – der wahre deutsche Gesellschaftsroman. Eine Projektskizze', in Jochen Vogt (ed.), *Medien-Morde: Krimis intermedial* (Munich: Fink, 2005). An exploration of the *Tatort* TV series as a contemporary example of the social novel.

Waligórska, Magdalena, '"Darkness at the Beginning": The Holocaust in Contemporary German Crime Fiction', in Lynn M. Kutch and Todd Herzog (eds), *Tatort Germany: The Curious Case of German-language Crime Fiction* (New York: Camden House, 2014), pp. 101–19. An essay exploring the possibilities and limitations of representing the Holocaust in crime fiction.

Wallace, Ailsa, 'Murder in the Weimar Republic: Prejudice, Politics and the Popular in the Socialist Crime Fiction of Hermynia Zur Mühlen', in Bruce B. Campbell, Alison Guenther-Pal and Vibeke Rützou Petersen (eds), *Detectives, Dystopias and Poplit: Studies in Modern Genre Fiction* (New York: Camden House, 2014), pp. 91–116. An essay exploring the 1920s crime fiction of this important woman writer.

Wigbers, Melanie, 'Von Paris über "Bramme" in die Eifel. Orte und Schauplätze in kriminalliterarischen Texten von der Romantik bis in die Gegenwart', *Wirkendes Wort*, 52/3 (2002), 1–16. Journal article exploring the use of setting in crime narratives from Romanticism to the present.

Wilke, Sabine, 'Wilde Weiber und dominante Damen: Der Frauenkrimi als Verhandlungsort von Weiblichkeitsmythen', in Carmen Birkle, Sabina Matter-Seibel and Patricia Plummer (eds), *Frauen auf der Spur: Kriminalautorinnen aus Deutschland, Großbritannien, und den USA* (Tübingen: Stauffenburg, 2001), pp. 255–71. An essay exploring the *Frauenkrimi* as a site of myths of femininity.

Würmann, Carsten, 'Zum Kriminalroman im Nationalsozialismus', in Bruno Franceschini and Carsten Würmann (eds), *Verbrechen als Passion. Neue Untersuchungen zum Kriminalgenre* (Berlin: Weidler, 2004), pp. 143–86. An essay on crime fiction under National Socialism by a key researcher in this until recently under-explored field.

Websites and web resources

'50 Jahre Deutscher Fernsehkrimi, Ein Project des Instituts für Medien, Kommunikation und Sport, Universität Halle', *http://server4.medienkomm.uni-halle.de/krimi/default.shtml* (accessed 27 August 2015). A comprehensive database of German television crime series, which allows data to be viewed alphabetically, chronologically and by region. Contains a useful bibliography of secondary criticism.

AIEP Austria, *www.krimiautoren.at* (accessed 10 August 2015). The website of the Austrian Crime Writers' Association, with information about authors, works and events.

Blaulicht, *http://sbwd.de/seiten/rahmen.php?nav=blaulicht* (accessed 27 August 2015). A complete list of the dime novels published in the East German 'Blaulicht' series from 1958 to 1990.

Deutscher Krimi Preis (German Crime Fiction Prize), *http://www.krimilexikon.de/dkp/index.html* (accessed 27 August 2015). Details of all the authors and works that have been shortlisted for or won this key prize, which was established in 1985 by the *Bochumer Krimi Archiv* (BKA).

Filmmuseum Berlin, 'Die Kommissarinnen' exhibition press pack (2004), *https://www.deutsche-kinemathek.de/sites/default/files/public/node-attachments/presse/pressemappen/2004_Pressemappe_Kommissarinnen.pdf* (accessed 27 August 2015). Contains comprehensive information about female police investigators featured in television crime series, and celebrates their contribution to the genre.

kaliber.38, *http://www.kaliber38.de/neu.htm* (accessed 27 August 2015). A comprehensive crime fiction site that provides information on authors, publishers and prizes, as well as reviews of German-language and international crime fiction.

Krimi-Couch.de, *http://www.krimi-couch.de/* (accessed 27 August 2015). Germany's premiere crime fiction website has been running since 2002 and is an outstanding resource, providing reviews, overviews of individual authors and their works, and publishing information. Covers both German-language and international crime.

KrimiZEIT-Bestenliste, *http://www.zeit.de/serie/krimizeit-bestenliste* (accessed 27 August 2015). A monthly list of top crime fiction compiled by journalist and critic Tobias Gohlis and his team.

Lexikon der deutschen Krimi-Autoren, *http://www.krimilexikon.de/* (accessed 27 August 2015). Extensive database of German crime authors, established in 1986, which is affiliated to the *Bochumer Krimi Archiv* (BKA).

Mörderische Schwestern, *http://www.moerderische-schwestern.eu/* (accessed 27 August 2015). The website of the Association of German-language Women Crime Authors.

Mrs. Peabody Investigates, *http://mrspeabodyinvestigates.wordpress.com/* (accessed 27 August 2015). International crime fiction blog run by Katharina Hall, which regularly examines crime fiction from and about the German-speaking world.

New Books in German, *http://www.new-books-in-german.com/english/home/-/273,273,129002,liste9.html* (accessed 27 August 2015). This website promotes German-language literature to publishers and readers in the English-speaking world and frequently showcases crime fiction from Austria, Germany and Switzerland.

Ott, Paul, 'Crime Scene: Switzerland. A Practical Guide', *http://www.crimetime.co.uk/crimescene/crimescene_switzerland.pdf* (accessed 27 August 2015). A useful English-language summary of the history of Swiss crime writing, its key authors and trends.

Das Syndikat. Autorengruppe deutschsprachige Kriminalliteratur, *http://www.das-syndikat.com/* (accessed 27 August 2015). Website of the German-language Crime Fiction Authors' Association.

Tatort, *http://www.daserste.de/unterhaltung/krimi/tatort/index.html* (accessed 27 August 2015). This official website is a rich source of information about Germany's most well-known television crime series.

Tenta, Sabine, 'Murder on the Box: German TV Crime Series', *http://www.goethe.de/ins/cz/pra/kul/duc/lit/kri/en7607608.htm* (accessed 27 August 2015). An overview of the *Fernsehkrimi*.

togohlis.de, *http://www.togohlis.de/index.htm* (accessed 27 August 2015). Tobias Gohlis, the crime fiction reviewer for the broadsheet *Die Zeit*, has done much to showcase the genre and bring it into mainstream literary discussion in Germany. This site features his reviews of German-language and international crime fiction.

Index